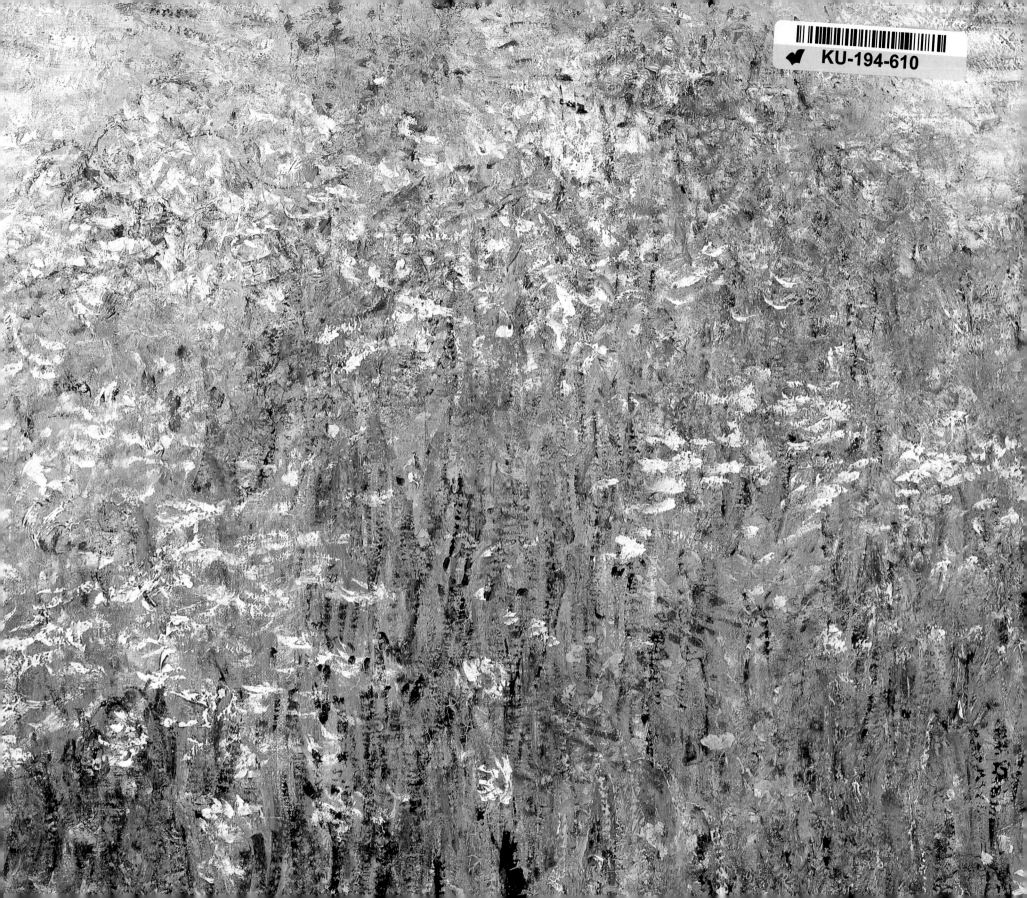

River of Light

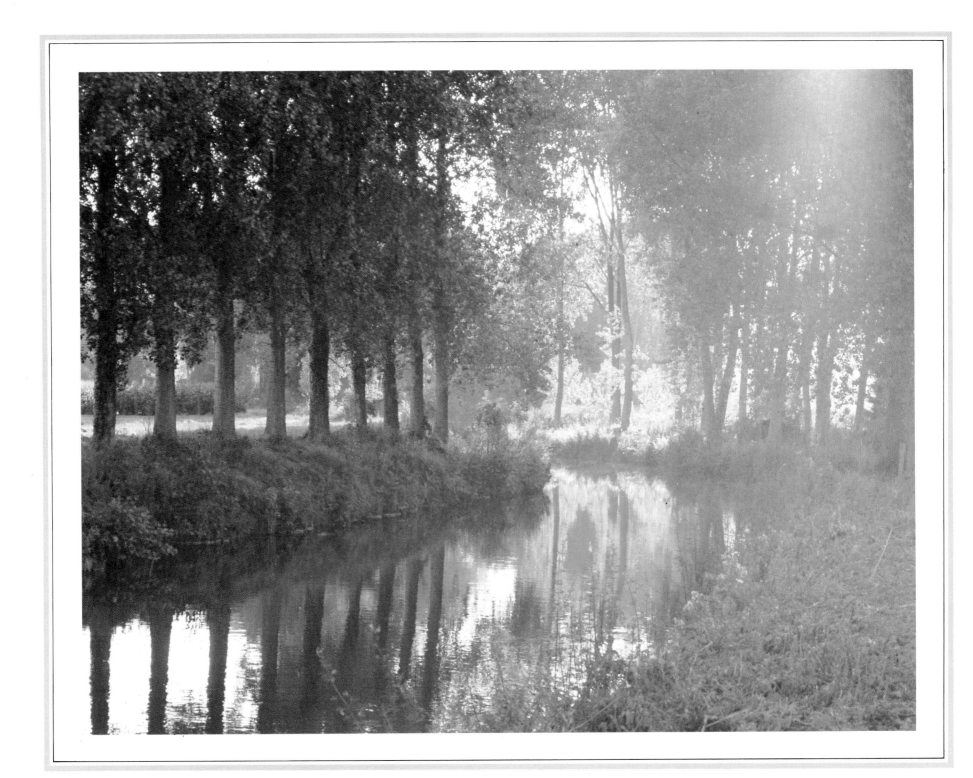

River of Light

Monet's Impressions of the Seine

DOUGLAS SKEGGS

London
VICTOR GOLLANCZ LTD
1987

Designed and produced by
Breslich & Foss
Golden House
28-31 Great Pulteney Street
London W1R 3DD

Editor: Judy Martin
Picture Research: Jim Abram
Designer: Roger Daniels
Map Illustrations: Kate Rogers

First published in Great Britain 1987 by
Victor Gollancz Ltd,
14 Henrietta Street, London WC2E 8QJ

British Library Cataloguing in Publication Data

Skeggs, Douglas
    River of light: Monet's impressions of
    the Seine.
    1. Monet, Claude – Criticism and
    interpretation   2. Seine River Region
    (France) in art
    I. Title
    759.4   ND553.M7

ISBN 0-575-03903-5

Photoset in Great Britain by Lineage Ltd, Watford.
Originated in Hong Kong by Fotographics Ltd, London-Hong Kong.
Printed and bound in Italy by Arnoldo Mondadori Editore.

The author would like to thank Nick Robinson, who first
suggested the idea for this book, and Simon Taylor and Caroline
Laing at Sotheby's, London.
Breslich & Foss would like to thank Marie-Hélène About for her
assistance in research and Michael McGuinness for his contribution
to the design of this book.

CONTENTS

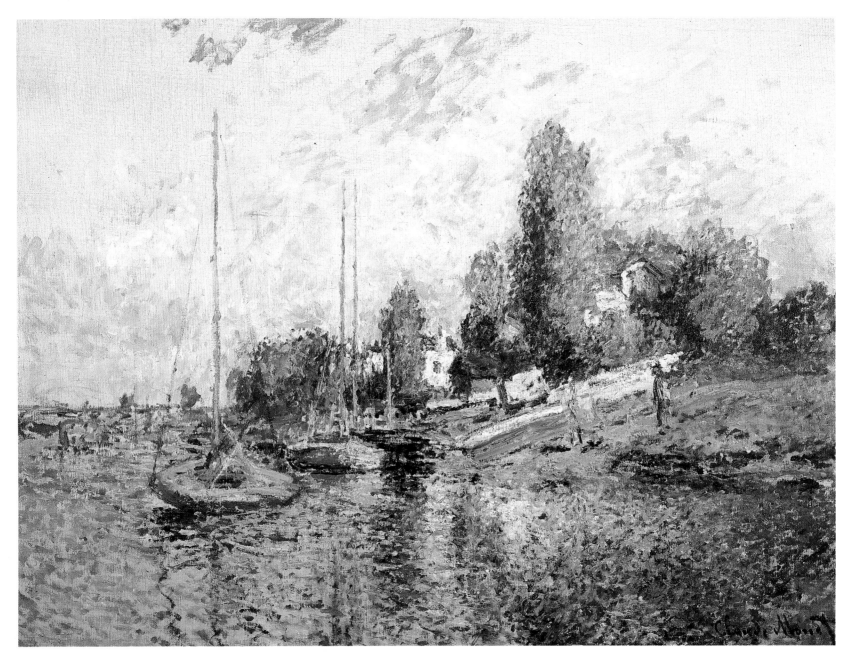

BOATS ON THE BANKS OF THE SEINE AT GENNEVILLIERS

1875

The river Seine was Monet's landscape, his subject and his home. The lessons that he learned from painting its water inadvertently altered the course of the arts. The vision that he imposed on it is still with us today.

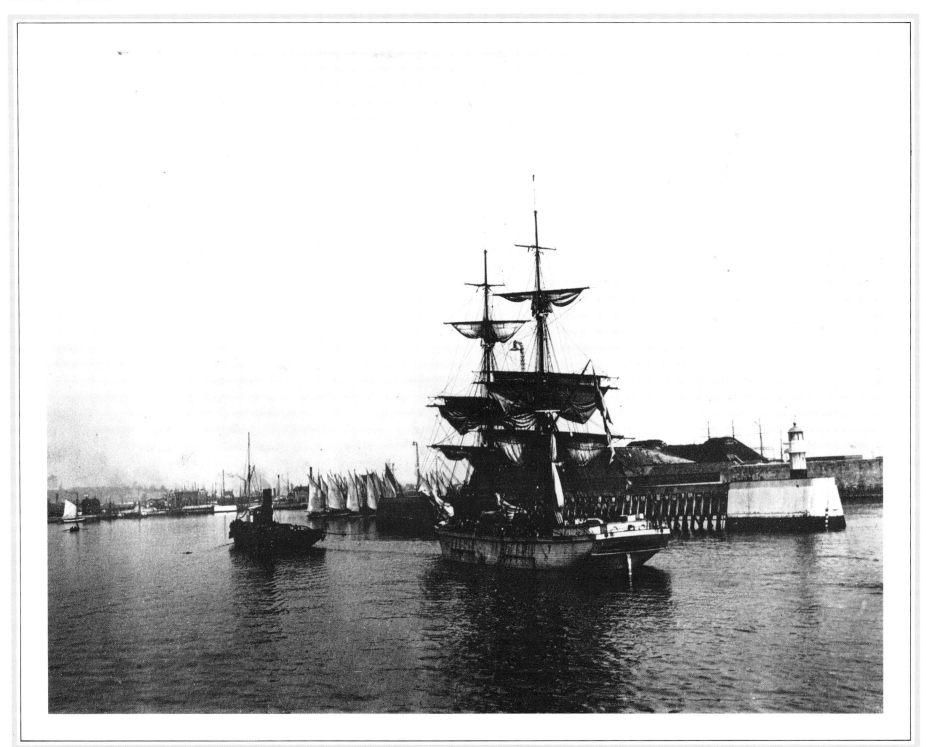

The Seine Estuary

LE HAVRE

1845–1859

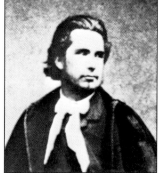

CLAUDE MONET, c.1858

Founded in the seventeenth century after the old port of Harfleur had silted up and become useless to shipping, Le Havre was built on a salt marsh in the mouth of the Seine. This site quickly proved impractical as the ground was too soft for the foundations and the sea-walls collapsed on several occasions. The harbour was eventually restructured by an Italian engineer who had encountered similar problems in Venice; thereafter the city was watertight and began to prosper. By the time the Monets arrived in 1845, Le Havre had become the largest port on the northern coast of France and the direct link between Paris and the New World. The nineteenth-century poet Casimir Delavigne claimed that Le Havre was one of the greatest cities in the world, second only to Constantinople in beauty.

Le Havre stands at the head of the Seine, where the river slides out to meet the sea. In the mid-nineteenth century it was the largest and most thriving port on the northern coast of France; a maze of docks and waterways linked together by the centipede legs of wooden quays. At high tide each day the sea-gates were opened; steam tug boats busied themselves around the harbour, liners and packet boats manœuvered through the entrance and fishing smacks with sails as brown as moth-wings glided out to sea. The main commercial harbour was 'full of shipping which overflowed into other basins, in which huge hulls, belly to belly, were touching each other four or five deep. All the numberless masts along several kilometres of quays, with their yards, mastheads and cordage, made this open space in the middle of the town look like a great dead forest.'

It was a town of easy money and instant millionaires, a hive of investment and speculation: fortunes were made and lost overnight and the town hummed with rumours. One told of the son of a cook-maid who had inherited a few coins when his mother died; with these he bought some salted-fish, sold it by the end of the same day and went on to build himself a financial empire on that first slender profit. It was not all rags to riches by any means; there were also stories of financial disaster, and in the 1840s the most recent incident of foul play on the cotton exchange had put one or two of these self-made men back where they'd begun. Another story described a cobbler who struck lucky on the stock exchange, but kept his awl and tools with him throughout his life in case fortune should turn against him.

What had given Le Havre the advantage over other French ports was that it faced north-west, towards the Atlantic, at a time when trade with America was beginning to boom. The port was the direct link between Paris and the New World and all the cotton, coffee, sugar and tobacco that reached the shops in the capital had at some time passed through the docks of Le Havre. The town supported twenty thousand workers in its industries: it had its own tanneries and fur-houses; factories refined raw cane into sugar; bales of cotton were lifted from the ships and sent to local mills to be woven into cloth or fashioned into lace, which were then shipped on to Paris.

One of the many businessmen who made a living from the ceaseless activity of the Le Havre docks was Jacques Lecadre, a wholesale grocer, '*épicier en gros, approvisionneur de navires*'. His offices were on the Rue Fontenelle, alongside the Commercial Dock where he struck his deals, and he owned a spacious town-house next door. In addition to this he had a holiday villa in Sainte-Adresse, the seaside resort on the outskirts of town.

Encouraged by these evident signs of prosperity Lecadre's brother-in-law, Adolphe Monet, moved up from Paris to Le Havre and joined the firm. Business had been poor in his own small grocer's shop in the capital, and he was finally forced to sell up and leave. He arrived in Le Havre in 1845, with his wife and two sons, Léon and Oscar Claude.

The timing couldn't have been better, as the grocery trade was a rapidly expanding market in Le Havre. Emigration was getting under way; passenger liners were beginning to make the Atlantic crossing and a steady stream of traffic was passing through the port on its way to the United States. In 1850, five years after the Monets settled in the town, the steamship 'Franklin' left harbour and thrashed its way across to New York, with the assistance of both sail and paddle-wheels, to arrive in the record time of fourteen days. Ten years later such voyages were commonplace and the crossing had become a regular service. To a grocer this human cargo meant profit. Whether heading for the New World or just ferrying tourists over to Trouville, every ship that left port needed supplies, and in a matter of years the Monets' fortunes had changed for the better. Commercial success brought them a higher standard of living and the inevitable desire for respectability. With their new-found wealth the Monets were able to move away from the town centre and buy a house in the Rue d'Epremenil, in a fashionable district of Le Havre known as Ingouville that stood on a hillside to the north of the docks.

'The finest view of the town is from the upper town, called Ingouville,' wrote one traveller at this time, 'an immense number of suburban villas rising from the base, in irregular order, to the summit of a commanding hill. Here are terraces, gardens and pleasure grounds, of the most handsome and tasteful kind; beneath lies the city, with its docks and forest of masts, and the broad Seine and the broader sea beyond; Honfleur and Harfleur to the left. The town is free from smoke, and very quiet – there is not even the rolling of an omnibus to disturb the calm.'

The place was not as bland or as primly ornamental as this may sound and still retained something of its provincial character, as the same writer went on to explain: 'Those who study the habits and manners of a people, will find matter of amusing contemplation in the guinguettes in Ingouville, where the lower orders spend their Sunday and Thursday evenings in summer. Nothing can exceed the animation of these *fêtes champêtres*, at which feasting and dancing, singing, music, domino and card playing, are enjoyed; and yet, though wine and cider are freely drunk, there is no rioting, nor an impropriety of behaviour – thanks, perhaps, sometimes to the police, who never permit serious disputation, though they do not check the flow of mirth, however noisy. All the dancing, capering,

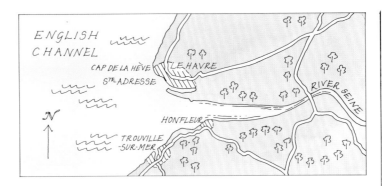

squeezing, eating, drinking, imaginable in a great crowd, are performed at some of the guinguettes, on about an acre of land, three-fourths of which are covered in tables, benches and arbours.'

AT INGOUVILLE the Monets established themselves as stolid and influential members of the community, and it was in an atmosphere of polite middle-class respectability, in which everything from drinking coffee to taking a walk had its allocated time and place, that Oscar Claude Monet was brought up. Born in Paris in 1840, the younger of the brothers, he was five when the family arrived in Le Havre.

His schooling was minimal, he looked upon the place as a prison and went out of his way to play truant. 'I could never resign myself to staying there even for four hours a day,' he said later, 'when the sun was inviting, the sea so calm, and when it was so pleasant to run along the cliffs or splash in the water. To my parents despair I passed this irregular but healthy existence until I was fourteen or fifteen. In the meantime I managed to pick up the essentials of education, including a bit of spelling.'

Whether this account is strictly true, it is hard to say. In later life Monet often spoke of his childhood but his descriptions are not always reliable; he was inclined to improve on the story, editing the facts where it suited him and more concerned with the legend than the exact detail. One thing we can be sure he did gain from these years was a love and understanding of boats; much of his spare time was spent hanging around the dockside, or paddling himself about the beaches near his aunt's home in Sainte-Adresse. This interest in boating, coupled with his affinity for the estuary of the river Seine, came at a formative stage of Monet's childhood.

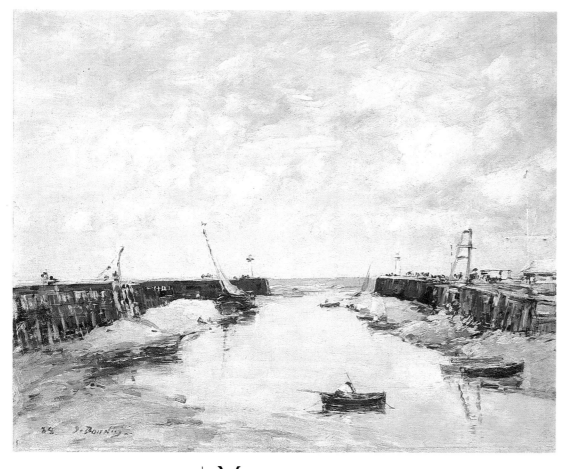

EUGÈNE BOUDIN: THE ENTRANCE
TO TROUVILLE HARBOUR

In rapid, sketch-like paintings
such as this, Boudin explored
the atmospheric effects of the
Seine estuary. Working in the
open air with his easel set up
before the subject, he noted
down the formation of the
clouds and the restless
sequences of light reflected on
the water with quick, darting
brushstrokes of fresh colour.
It was this direct and
spontaneous approach to
landscape painting that had a
profound effect on the young
Monet.

MONET'S CAREER as an artist started while he was still at school. During lessons he had begun to make sketches of his masters in the margins of his notebooks, exaggerating their features, giving them huge heads and tiny bodies that tapered away beneath, a style he had adapted from illustrations in the newspapers and pictorial magazines of the day. One of these caricatures shows his drawing master, M. Ochard, gazing out through the single lens of his monocle, his moustaches drooping and the scrag end of his side whiskers sticking out in tufts on either side. The drawings were an instant success and Monet quickly extended his range of victims to include every celebrity and civic dignitary in the town. His ability, for a sixteen-year-old, was astonishing. The pencil line in each drawing is clear and incisive, the figures are described with a facility that many more experienced caricaturists would have displayed with pride. When a frame-maker called Gravier offered to

exhibit them in his shop window, Monet accepted at once and it was only a matter of time before he reckoned himself quite 'an important personage' around Le Havre. To the embarrassment of his parents, who felt that money should be made but never mentioned in public, Monet pushed his prices up to 20 francs apiece and was able to boast that the caricatures still sold as fast as he could draw them. This new-found fame went straight to his head; he began to loiter around in front of the shop eavesdropping on the admiring comments until, as he confessed later, he was 'nearly choked with vanity and self-satisfaction'.

The only thing that broke the mirror of Monet's complacency at this stage of his career was that his pictures were not exhibited alone in the shop window. Often hanging next to them were pastels and watercolours by the local painter Eugène Boudin; small scenes of the Seine estuary floated together in luminous colours and uncluttered by detail. Monet was not impressed by them: they were competition for his caricatures and in addition to this seemed too sketchy, too lazily painted to be taken seriously, 'used as I was to the false and arbitrary colour and fantastical arrangements of the painters then in vogue'. This aversion to the paintings was extended to Boudin himself; although they'd never met, Monet decided he didn't like the man and refused to be introduced. It was only chance, therefore, that brought them together; Monet came into the shop one day without noticing that his *bête noire* was there. Seeing the two artists together, Gravier seized his chance to make the introductions.

The meeting was not in the least as Monet had expected: 'Boudin, without hesitation, came up to me, complimented me in his gentle voice and said: "I always look at your sketches with pleasure; they are amusing, clever, bright. You are gifted; one can see that at a glance. But I hope you are not going to stop there. It is all very well for a beginning, yet soon you will have had enough of caricaturing".'

Boudin was a painter born with the sea in his blood. Brought up in Honfleur, on the far shore of the estuary, he came from a long line of sailors. His father had served as a gunner in the Napoleonic wars and had gone on to become the captain of a steam ship nicknamed *'La Polichelle'*. Wallowing and rolling in the water, this old steam kettle of a ship had nudged its way from Le Havre to Rouen each week carrying barrels of cider and as many passengers as it could pick up from the riverports along the way. Boudin passed his childhood on board serving as a cabin boy and it has been said that his first drawings were made with the black tar intended for caulking the hull; if this is so then none have survived to prove the story. He never attempted to go to sea after this but moved instead to Le Havre where he worked in a stationer's shop. It was here that he was given his first paintbox and began his career as an artist. A few years later, in partnership with a friend, he was able to open his own shop. He extended the business to frame-making and it was through this that he began to meet other artists, such as the landscape painter Troyon, Isabey and Millet. Since painting eventually occupied Boudin's whole attention, he left the shop in the hands of an assistant, Gravier, the same man who later discovered the drawings of Monet.

At that first meeting, when Boudin advised Monet to give up his caricatures, he also suggested that Monet concentrate his efforts on landscape painting instead. 'Study, learn to see and to paint,' he told him, 'draw, make landscapes.

Monet didn't want to take up painting, pleased enough with the success of his little figures. Boudin persisted and offered to take him out painting one day to demonstrate his own working methods. Monet refused; he was puzzled by Boudin. Despite his earlier reservations he had taken a liking to the artist, but he still couldn't digest the paintings. It was not until the summer holidays came and he could think of no further excuse that he accepted the invitation: 'I gave in at last, and Boudin with untiring kindness undertook my education'.

They went to the village of Rouelle and here Boudin set up his easel. Monet stood behind him and watched as the artist set to work building up his picture stroke by stroke. Monet said that as he looked on and saw the picture coming to life it was as if a veil was being torn from his eyes and he saw nature for the first time.

Boudin's secret, revealed to Monet that day, was that he painted only what he could see. His pictures were begun and finished in front of the subject, a far cry from the studio-based contrivances of academic painting traditions. 'Everything that is painted on the spot,' Boudin explained, 'has always a strength, a power, a vividness of touch that one doesn't find again in the studio.'

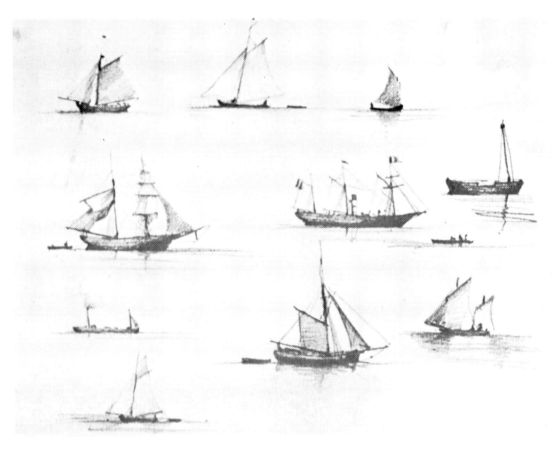

Boudin treated nature as a whole rather than as an inventory of separate objects. He began his picture not by defining the outline of each form but by noting down arrangements of colour that corresponded in general to what he could see in front of him. The paint was laid on the canvas in direct response to what his eyes were telling him. 'It's not a single part that should strike one in a picture,' he would say, 'but the whole.' Gradually as the picture progressed, he made the forms more explicit, clarifying the individual parts and at the last minute adding in the tiny details with a fine brush. The picture must have literally drifted into focus as he worked, the landscape emerging miraculously from an initial blush of atmosphere.

Above all Boudin was a master at painting skies; Corot had called him the 'King of the heavens'. Often he gives over two-thirds of his picture to the empty expanse of the sky, working fine veils of colour over each other, feathering the pigeon-grey tones together and streaking them with

Pages from Monet's Sketchbook, 1857

These meticulous drawings, studiously arranged on the pages of a sketchbook, were made when Monet was seventeen. They reflect Boudin's advice that he should abandon caricaturing and turn his attention to the landscape. As a young man, Monet's ambition was to establish a reputation for himself as a marine artist; he was fascinated by ships and constructed many of his early paintings around them. His love of the sea was the legacy of his childhood on the Seine estuary, and the origin

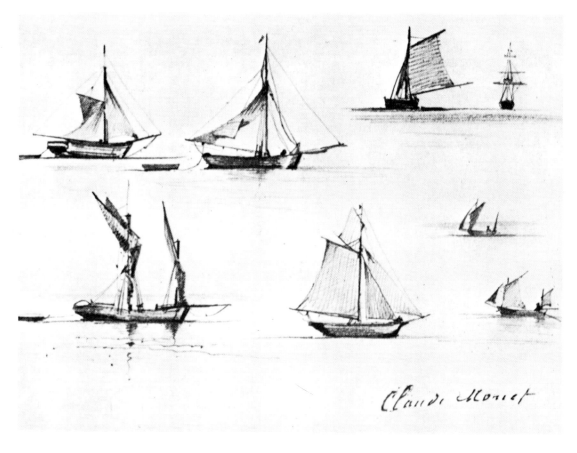

Claude Monet

of his much-quoted remark: 'I want to live always on it, or beside it, and when I die to be buried in a buoy.'

touches of white where the light breaks through.

Boudin's pictures are about climate as much as landscape. The weather in the Seine estuary is moody and changeable, sudden squalls blow up darkening the water, chopping the surface and sending high cloud scurrying overhead. Long days of unbroken sun and calm seas with puffs of cumulus ranged out along the horizon can give way to silent drizzle that drifts in from the Channel, blotting the colour from the view. It was the presence of this restless atmosphere that Boudin sought in his paintings:

> I still feel this abundancy, a shining light that transforms everything before my eyes. I simply cannot put that across with my grubby palette. It must be twenty times now that I have started all over again to try to capture that delightful quality of light which plays over everything around. What freshness there is about it, at once fugitive, a shade pink. Objects become dissolved, so that there are only variations in density everywhere.

Monet's vocation as a landscape painter began that day as he stood in the meadows behind Le Havre and watched Boudin at work. He said that at that moment his eyes were finally opened, he understood nature and in understanding it came also to love it.

Few landscapes have survived from Monet's first years as an artist. It may be that some of his paintings have been lost, others were victims of the Franco-Prussian War, but it was Monet himself who was responsible for destroying the rest. All his life he was doggedly self-critical; he refused to keep anything that didn't measure up to his expectations and as a result many of his early canvases were burned or had the paint scraped off and were used again. Added to this, when he ran out of money, Monet was known to have slashed some of his pictures rather than allow them to fall into the hands of his creditors. There are some sketchbooks, however, that date from these first years. In one of them he has filled the pages with pencil studies of ships lying out in the estuary, carefully recording their profiles on the water, the arrangements of the masts and the set of the sails. He makes no attempt to describe the seascape around them but simply lists them on the page: a catalogue of fishing boats, brigs and paddle steamers.

WHEN MONET WAS SEVENTEEN, the steady current of his childhood was disrupted by the unexpected death of his mother. All his life he was strangely silent about the women close to him and he rarely mentioned his mother's name after the funeral, remembering her only for her beautiful singing voice. Seven months later Jacques Lecadre died, and this led to a complete reversal of family politics. Adolphe Monet now became the head of the family; the wheel had swung full circle and the failed grocer who had arrived in Le Havre looking for charity found himself the owner of a successful wholesaling company. He took command of the business premises alongside the dockyards and, claiming his full rights of possession, sold his property in Ingouville and moved into the dead man's house. His half-sister, Monet's aunt, was deposed and given a small apartment of her own to live in elsewhere.

Following the death of his mother, Monet became unmanageable. Unlike his brother Léon, he had no interest in going into business and wanted only to leave school and become an artist. His father refused to allow it but his aunt was more understanding and encouraged him to push ahead with his career. Tante Lecadre was an amateur painter herself and could claim among her friends a number of well-known Parisian artists. Her views on art were to prove unimaginative, but the fact that she had formed opinions at all was possibly remarkable at this time, as society ladies in Normandy were not renowned for the sharp cutting edge of their wits: 'The French ladies are certainly very artificial in all their movements,' one visitor to the district complained. 'owing to the training which they undergo from infancy. Everything is done for effect, attitude and appearance are continually studied. Their education is extremely artificial.'

Tante Lecadre was evidently an exception to this rule. Since she appeared to be sympathetic towards her unruly nephew, and not having anyone to direct the domestic affairs of the house, Adolphe Monet invited her to return to the family home to act as hostess and surrogate mother. Some time before, she had converted an attic into a studio, which she now invited Monet to use as his own. Rummaging around among the paintings up there one day, he came across a small landscape by Daubigny. He took such a liking to this little picture that she allowed him to have it and he kept it with him for the rest of his life.

A photograph of Monet taken at about this time shows him to be short and stocky, with a mane of dark hair, an *impériale* beard on the point of his chin and his upper lip shaded by a fine moustache, the best that his nineteen years can manage. In later years many of his friends and biographers were to comment on his powerful build, the exceptional intensity of his blue eyes and the low flashpoint of his temper. He was stubborn, headstrong and, by all accounts, a compelling personality.

Monet's one ambition at this stage of his career was to get out of 'that cotton-town Le Havre', as he called it, and go up to Paris to study. It was probably Boudin who had put the idea into his head. 'One does not invent an art all by oneself,' Boudin had told him, 'in an out of the way spot, without criticism, without means of comparison.'

Money was the only stumbling block as his father either could not, or would not, fund the venture. Boudin suggested that Monet should apply to the Municipal Council of Le Havre for a grant, as he himself had done fourteen

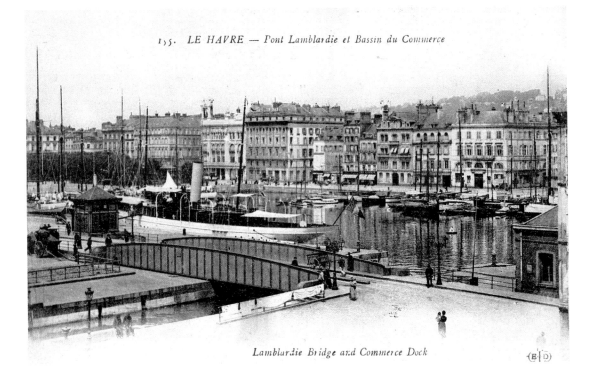

155. LE HAVRE — *Pont Lamblardie et Bassin du Commerce*

Lamblardie Bridge and Commerce Dock

years before. In March 1859 a still life was presented to the Council as an example of Monet's work, accompanied by a formal letter of introduction from his father:

> I have the honour to state to you that my son Oscar Monet, aged eighteen years, having worked with M.M.Ochard, Vasseur, and Boudin, wishes to become a candidate for the title of Pensioner of Fine Arts of the city of Le Havre. His natural inclinations and his taste, which he definitely fixed upon painting, oblige me not to turn him away from his vocation, but since I have not the necessary means to send him to Paris to attend the courses of the important masters, I hereby beg you to be so kind as to accept favourably my son's candidacy.

The Council debated the request for two months and then rejected it. They felt that Monet's natural talents as a caricaturist might interfere with his more serious studies as a painter and, since they themselves had probably been the butt of his wit on occasion, they politely declined the chance of furthering his career. As it happened this made little difference, for by the time the rejection arrived, Monet was already in Paris. His father had allowed him to

THE COMMERCIAL DOCK AT LE HAVRE

This was the largest of the thirteen docks of Le Havre harbour, and the financial nerve-centre of the town. Monet's father, a wholesale grocer to the shipping trade, had his offices alongside these docks and eventually moved the family into a house nearby. Before this they had lived in the fashionable suburb of Ingouville, which can just be seen on the hillside to the right of the picture.

CARICATURE OF MARIO OCHARD

At the age of sixteen, Monet began to make a name for himself in Le Havre as a caricaturist, with drawings which displayed a remarkable command of technique. Ochard, the victim of this particular caricature, was Monet's drawing master at college and responsible for the artist's first formal lessons in perspective and composition.

go to the capital for a few weeks to visit the Salon, the Second Empire's great annual exhibition of paintings.

THE PARIS SALON was more than just a marketplace for paintings and sculpture, it was a spectacle, a major event in the social life of the city, a place to see and be seen. In addition to this, it was the testing ground for young and aspiring artists where reputations could be made or broken overnight. It was staged each spring in the Salon d'Industrie, the huge architectural shell of glass and cast-iron that had been built on the banks of the Seine to house the Universal Exhibition of 1855. Here, in the rabbit warren of its thirty-five separate galleries, were canvases that told tales from the bible or patriotic stories of military glory; there were mythologies with their cast of nubile figures, together with landscapes, portraits and still lifes. 'Gilt frames full of shadows,' Emile Zola called them, 'black pretentious things, nude figures showing yellowish in a cellar-like light, the frippery of so-called classical art, historical, genre and landscape painting, all showing the same conventional black grease.'

Monet studied the landscape painters in the Salon and then dutifully reported back to Boudin: 'I haven't been able to go more than once to the Salon.' he told him. 'The Troyons are superb, the Daubignys are for me something truly beautiful. There are some nice Corots.'

It was the caricatures that had made this stay in Paris possible; over the years Tante Lecadre had been saving his earnings, giving him only as much as he needed for pocket money in the meantime, and it was with this massed fortune in his pocket that Monet had arrived in Paris. She had also arranged for him to pay a visit to her artist friend Armand Gautier. Through him in turn, Monet was introduced to the landscape painter Troyon, who conveniently advised him to stay on in Paris and study there. He urged Monet to concentrate on his drawing. 'In this way' he told him, 'you'll acquire proficiency, you'll go to Le Havre and you'll be able to do good sketches in the country, and in the winter you'll come back to settle here definitely.'

Monet had been given permission to stay in Paris for two months but the time soon became elastic and stretched to cover all that summer. His father didn't try to force him to return home; Adolphe Monet was prepared to let his son remain in the city provided he was studying hard. However, when he heard that Monet had refused to enrol in an accredited art-school and was attending classes at the Académie Suisse, a bohemian life-class held in a studio at the end of the Pont Saint-Michel, he decided it was time to bring him to heel and promptly cut off his allowance. This had no immediate effect on Monet, who was still receiving monthly instalments of his own money from Tante Lecadre. A few weeks later, however, he drew an unlucky number in the lottery for National Service and his father took revenge. He refused to buy him out and Monet was drafted into the French army for a seven year term.

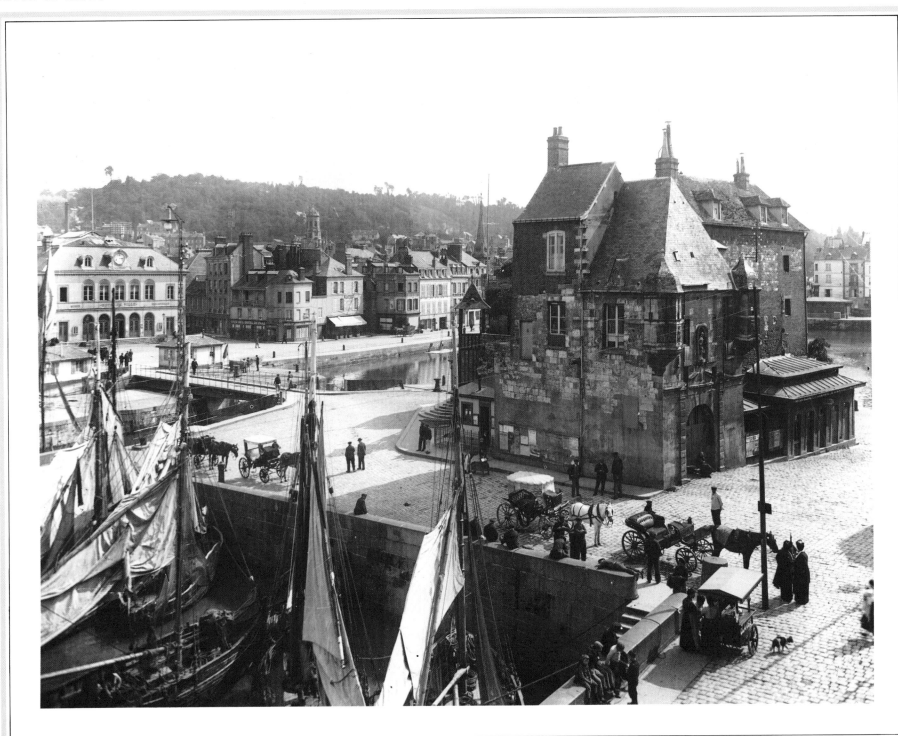

The Seine Estuary
HONFLEUR
1862–1866

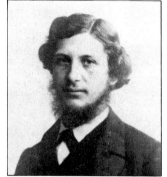

FRÉDÉRIC BAZILLE

THE PORT OF HONFLEUR

The ramshackle building in the centre of this photograph, which also appears in Monet's painting of 1864, was known as the 'Lieutenance'. It was the official customs house of of the port, and the last remaining fragment of the medieval walls of the town. Beyond it is the *Vieux Bassin*, the original harbour around which the town was built.

This picture was taken from an upper window of the Hôtel Cheval Blanc, where Monet stayed in 1866 while working on 'Fishing Boats in Honfleur', the setting for this later painting being the quayside in the extreme foreground of the picture.

Two years after being signed into the army, Monet was back on the Seine estuary, convalescing from a tropical disease he had contracted while on service in Africa. He at once renewed his friendship with Boudin and throughout the summer of 1862 they worked together in and around the old harbour of Honfleur that lies on the southern shore of the river mouth.

Honfleur was peaceful place, a fishing port directly descended from a walled town, all medieval brown and grey. There had been a colony of artists working there long before Monet discovered it; the picturesque harbour with its muddled streets and slate-hung buildings had attracted painters for many years. They came each summer with their sketching easels, their clay pipes and straw hats, drawn from the stillness of their Paris studios like bees to a bunch of flowers.

The unofficial headquarters for these artists was the Ferme Saint-Siméon, a country inn that stood on the hillside above Honfleur. Set in an orchard of apple trees, the farm was a simple place on the outskirts of the town. A painting by Corot, made in the 1840s, shows it with humped walls and a thatched roof that wraps over the stonework like the layer of fat on a bacon joint. Trestle tables were arranged outside under the trees and here the painters met to talk and drink, whiling away their time in the shade or playing games of dominos and skittles in the afternoon sunlight. Below them stretched the great expanse of the estuary, almost nine miles wide at this undefined point where the river merges with the sea. From morning to nightfall the wind-ruffled water was flecked with fishing boats, the bright colours of their patched sails giving it 'the appearance of a flower-bespangled meadow'.

The inn was run by the farmer's wife, Mère Toutain, who served at table with her servant girl Rosie and her daughter, 'la belle Marie'. Corot had stayed at the farm as had Cals, Isabey, Millet, Diaz and many more. Boudin had taken Courbet up there to drink but the realist painter had complained that the cider was good for nothing but washing his hands in, although this criticism hadn't prevented him from putting away a fair measure and then sleeping off its after-effect under a tree. The Ferme Saint-Siméon had its own cider-press and also a still to concentrate the fermenting juice of the apples into Calvados, the tart spirit whose name derives from this district of the Normandy coast. The results of this primitive device are hard to imagine but apparently proved lethal to Mère Toutain's son, who one day suffered a terrible attack of delirium tremens. Carried inside the farmhouse, he was laid out in a room whose walls had been painted by two of the visiting artists with vivid scenes of the Last Judgement. It was known as 'the Chamber of Hell' and it was here that the poor fellow died, scared out of his wits 'by the twitching burning men'.

'Oh the Ferme Saint-Siméon,' said Boudin as an old man, thinking back on the days he had spent there, 'what a wonderful legend could be written about that inn.'

Boudin's work had developed considerably in the two years since Monet had last seen him. Courbet had encouraged him to be more bold in his handling of the paint and Boudin had dutifully noted down this advice in the margin of his sketchbook. Through Courbet he had been introduced to the poet Baudelaire who, though indifferent to Boudin's formal compositions, had nothing but praise for his pastel studies of the sky. 'Cover the inscription with your hand,' the poet announced after looking at these drawings, 'and you could guess the season, the time and the wind. I am not exaggerating. I have seen it. In the end all these clouds with their fantastic and luminous forms; these ferments of gloom; these immensities of green and pink suspended and added upon each other; these gaping furnaces; these firmaments of black or purple satin, crumpled, rolled or torn; these horizons in mourning, or streaming with molten metal – in short, all these depths and all these splendours rose to my brain like a heady drink or like the eloquence of opium.'

Baudelaire was often around Honfleur at this time as his mother, Madame Aupick, lived in a little 'toy house' there. He had just published the second edition of his poems *Les Fleurs du Mal*, a book that his publisher had warned was going to cast 'a stain on your whole life'. Baudelaire was little concerned with what the public would make of his poetry: 'being as chaste as paper, as sober as water, as devout as a woman at communion, as harmless as a sacrificial lamb, it would not displease me to be taken for a debauchee, a drunkard, an infidel, a murderer'.

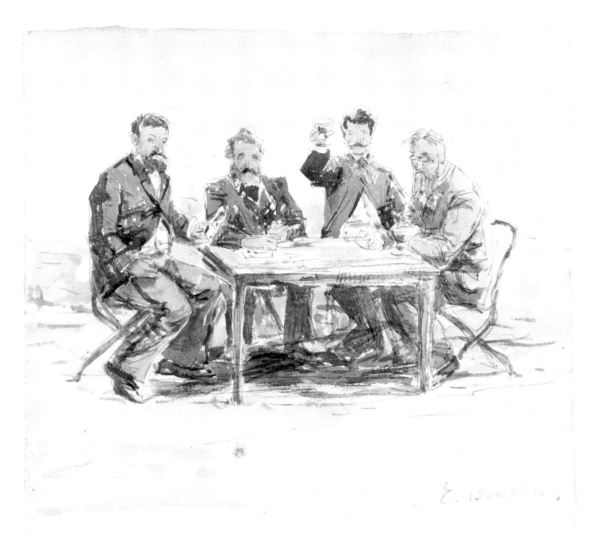

Later that autumn, while Monet was working in Honfleur, he was fortunate enough to meet the painter Johan Barthold Jongkind. The introduction was brought about by an Englishman who had obligingly held onto a cow that had been refusing to stand still while Monet painted it. The following Sunday this man arranged for Monet and Jongkind to lunch with him: 'What a good time we had,' Monet recalled afterwards, 'out of doors, under the trees, in the garden of a rustic inn, with good country cooking. With a full glass in front of him, sitting between two admirers whose sincerity could not be questioned, Jongkind was beside himself with joy. It was an unexpected treat and put him in the best of humour.'

Monet had first seen Jongkind's paintings at the 1859

Salon and was unimpressed; his diagnosis at the time was that Jongkind was 'dead to art', but now, after meeting the man, he revised this opinion completely. As with Boudin before, Monet seemed to appreciate the art only when he'd first come to terms with the artist.

Jongkind's method of painting was personal and highly distinctive. His pictures are built from short, stabbing strokes of the brush that seem to quiver on the canvas, defining a quality of light as much as the details of the landscape. They were not necessarily painted in the open air, however. Jongkind was less concerned with the spontaneity of his vision than Boudin and preferred to work in the silence of his studio, piecing his subjects together from notes and watercolour sketches made on the spot.

EUGÈNE BOUDIN:
AT THE FERME SAINT-SIMÉON

This watercolour by Boudin shows a group of his friends at the Ferme Saint-Siméon in the autumn of 1862. The Dutch painter Jongkind is the figure on the left, and beside him is Emile Van Marcke. Monet, who was on leave from national service at the time, raises his glass towards the artist, while to the right sits Jean Achard.

Jongkind's shrewd and unpretentious observation of nature had an immediate effect on Monet, who later claimed that it was to this painter that he owed the definitive education of his eye: 'complementing the teaching that I received from Boudin, Jongkind was from that moment my true master.'

An important characteristic of Jongkind's painting was that he explored the atmospheric changes of a landscape. He often made two versions of the same picture, recording the scene at different times of the year from the same spot. This was an idea that Monet quickly adapted and was to develop during the course of his life until, in his late 'series' paintings, it became the dominant technique of his work, a controlled system that enabled him to analyze every variation of light that he found in nature.

There is a watercolour by Boudin, painted that autumn with the simple intention of a snapshot, that shows the painters together at the Ferme Saint-Siméon: Jongkind sitting slumped at the table, on the lefthand side, while Monet, still sporting his military-style waxed moustaches, raises his glass towards the artist as he works. Jongkind was in his forties at the time of this picture. He was a man of melancholy personality, troubled by a persecution complex that had gnawed at his mind and finally driven him into the sanctuary of drink. He spoke in a heavy Dutch accent, with total disregard for grammar and syntax, and only appeared to relax when he was talking on the subject of painting. When Monet met him that autumn he was in better health than he had been for some time, however, and was drinking with less determination.

Tante Lecadre didn't approve of Monet's behaviour at the Ferme Saint-Siméon; she looked upon both Jongkind and Boudin as reprobate artists and bad influences on her nephew. As far as she could see they were leading him astray, filling his head with nonsense about landscape painting in the open air. She aired these grievances in a letter to her painter friend Armand Gautier:

> His sketches are always rough drafts, like those you have seen; but when he wants to complete something, to produce a picture, they turn into appalling daubs before which he preens himself and finds idiots to congratulate him.

Tante Lecadre was clearly put out by this haphazard approach to painting, but what really cut her to the quick was that Monet appeared to be quite unmoved by her opinion: 'He pays no attention to my remarks.' she complained. 'I am not up to his level, so now I keep the most profound silence.'

Despite this familial disapproval, Monet was allowed to take up his career as a painter once more. At the end of that summer he was due to return to the army but his family finally relented and allowed him to resign. It was his aunt who paid the necessary fee for his release, but she only did so on the condition that Monet return to Paris and enrol himself in a proper academy. Before Monet left for the capital, his father clarified these terms: 'It is well understood that this time you are going to work in dead earnest,' he informed Monet. 'I wish to see you in a studio under the discipline of a well-known master. If you resume your independence, I will stop your allowance without further ado.'

The painter Auguste Toulmouche had recently married one of Monet's cousins and was now appointed as Monet's guardian in Paris, with instructions to supervise his career and to make certain Monet kept his nose to the grindstone while he was there. Toulmouche was a successful painter of conversation pieces, pale pictures of sickly sentiment that earned him a good income and for which he had just been awarded a gold medal. Monet reported to him on his arrival in Paris. He showed him a still life which Toulmouche felt was promising, but which he described as being too 'tricky' in its handling. After some discussion, he recommended that Monet should be sent to study in the studio of Charles Gleyre, an academic painter who had turned his attentions to teaching. It is interesting to note that when Monet arrived as a student in Gleyre's studio at the age of twenty-two, the formative lessons of his life had been learned. His family might look upon his friendship with Boudin and Jongkind as a symptom of his rebellious nature, but it was also a measure of Monet's single-minded determination as an artist, for in these two painters he had instinctively discovered his own teachers. It was from them that he inherited the direct observation of nature, the open-air technique and the study of atmospheric change that were to become the hallmarks of his painting.

When Monet returned to Honfleur in the spring of 1864 he brought with him his new friend Frédéric Bazille.

They had met at Gleyre's studio eighteen months before and had since then become inseparable companions. Bazille was a tall, willowy figure, good natured and generous. 'A little in the style of Jesus, but virile' was Emile Zola's description of him, 'A very handsome fellow.' Bazille had originally come to Paris to study medicine, but after seeing Corot's painting in the Salon he had decided to become a painter instead and joined the classes at Gleyre's studio, dividing his time evenly between the two professions. He had taken his medical exams that year and was waiting for the results to come through when Monet persuaded him to join him in Honfleur.

'I'll have to be back in Paris soon, to that horrible medicine, which I more and more detest,' Bazille wrote to his parents on arrival on the coast.

They rented rooms above a baker's shop in town and at once set to work painting in the open air around the Ferme Saint-Siméon. 'As soon as we arrived in Honfleur, we looked for landscape motifs,' wrote Bazille. 'They were easy to find because the country is heaven. One could not see richer meadows and more beautiful trees; everywhere there are cows and horses at pasture.'

Their working day started at five in the morning and continued until the light faded. Bazille had been impressed by Monet's ideas from the time of their first meeting and, despite their close friendship, was inclined to treat him more as a teacher than as a fellow student. While they were in Honfleur together he did his best to adopt Monet's working methods and to paint directly from what he saw, although the results were not always successful, as he warned his parents: 'You mustn't expect me to bring back good landscapes; I'm making progress and that's all – it's all that I want. I hope to be satisfied with myself after three or four years of painting.'

The evenings were spent at the tables around the farm where they ate and drank and discussed the day's achievements as the sun sank over the estuary. Normandy, with its conjunction of sea, orchards and rich pasture-land, was famous for its cuisine. When André Gill came to paint a sign for the inn he included rabbits, salmon, eggs, cider, swan, duck and pork chops, all queuing up for the cooking pot. Meals were taken very seriously and appetites in those days were undoubtedly healthy.

Both Monet and Bazille enjoyed the relaxed lifestyle of the Ferme Saint-Siméon, although neither of them was rustic by inclination or upbringing. Bazille came from an influential family in the south of France who lived in the little town of Montpellier. He was well connected and, having a respectable private income, was able to live comfortably in Paris.

Monet was to make frequent attempts to share in his friend's allowance whenever his own was under threat since, even as a student, he was incapable of living within his income. He was fastidious in his dress and had been nicknamed 'the dandy' at Gleyre's studio. His suits were cut by the most expensive tailor in Paris whom he couldn't possibly afford and whose bills he never paid, threatening to take his custom elsewhere whenever the man lodged a complaint. As a result of extravagant behaviour such as this, Monet spent the first fifty years of his life in debt and frequently found it necessary to move house to avoid his creditors. He did, however, make valiant attempts to pay his bills at the Ferme Saint-Siméon: 'Madame Toutain is so good' he told Bazille later that summer, 'that I would not like to make her lose a sou.'

Down in the old port of Honfleur, where the slate-faced buildings glisten with the metallic grey-blue of flint, Monet worked that year on a little canvas showing the 'Lieutenance' (opposite). This was the official customs building for the town, an incoherent jumble of ancient masonry, hipped roofs, chimneys and dormer-windows. Ungoverned by any overall intention, it had grown with the years; parts had been added, others amputated until it reached its present form more by default than by design. The stonework was soft and brown, eroded by the beating of the Channel rain, and plants grew from its crevices as if it were a rock garden. In medieval times Honfleur had been a fortified town, dominating the mouth of the Seine, and during the Hundred Years' War its ownership had shuttled backwards and forwards between the French and the English. The Lieutenance had been built on the walls of the old town but these had long since been knocked away, leaving it standing on the quayside like the last remaining fragment of a sandcastle washed over by the tide. Beside it, and just visible on the righthand side of the painting, are the lock-gates that control the level of water in the basin, acting as a stopper to the shifting level of the tide.

Monet's colour in this painting is subdued and almost

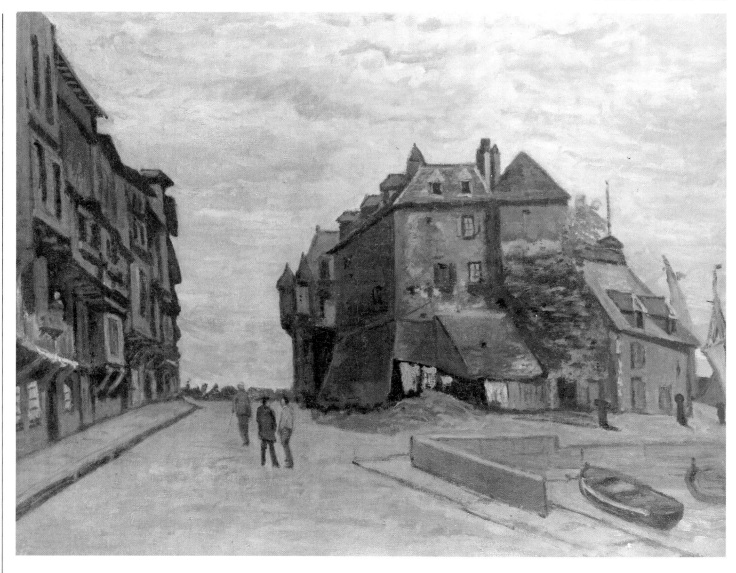

THE LIEUTENANCE;
THE HOUSE OF THE
HARBOURMASTER AT HONFLEUR

1864

melancholy. The only light is in the sky, where rippling strokes of cobalt and white stand out in stark contrast to the shadowed buildings below. It appears that Monet has actually darkened the rest of the picture to emphasize this one effect, making the division between light and shade as brutal as possible. Even at this early stage of his career, the true subject of his painting is the impact of light and he has ruthlessly pulled down the tones of the foreground to boost the luminosity of the sky above. Later Monet learned to create daylight from the interplay of colour; here he is already pursuing this ambition, but attempting to do it in terms of contrasting tone. This is hardly surprising, as in the mid-nineteenth century colour was treated with the greatest suspicion. Gleyre would no doubt have taught his students that colour should be controlled; it was the 'animal part of painting', sensuous and dangerous, and they were advised to keep it on a leash. In its place, teachers would recommend firm drawing and a careful analysis of tone. There was a saying around the academies that tone was more important than colour; that if an artist placed his tones correctly on the canvas the colours would take care of themselves.

AT THE END OF JUNE, Bazille returned to Paris to discover he'd failed his exams. Faced with the thought of retaking them once more, he returned home and persuaded his parents to let him abandon the medical profession altogether and turn his attention to painting. Monet wrote to him frequently that summer, keeping him abreast of the news in Honfleur and describing his own ambitions:

> Every day I discover more and more beautiful things; it's enough to drive one mad; I have such a desire to do everything my head is bursting with it ... I'm fairly well satisfied with my stay here, although my sketches are far from what I would like; it is indeed frightfully difficult to make a thing complete in all aspects ... Well my good friend, I intend to struggle, scrape off, begin again, because one can produce what one sees and what one understands ... it is on the strength of observation and reflection that one finds it.

During the course of this letter a note of authority begins to slip into Monet's voice, as if he too sees himself as Bazille's self-appointed master and feels obliged to keep him up to the mark: 'What I'm certain of is that you don't work enough, and not in the right way. It's not with playboys, like your Villa and others, that you can work. It would be better to be alone, and yet, all alone there are some things that one cannot fathom; well all that is terrific and it's a stiff job. I have in mind splendid projects for the time I shall be in Sainte-Adresse and in Paris during the winter. Things are fine at Saint-Siméon – they often talk about M. Bazille.'

The 'projects' that Monet refers to in this letter were a series of paintings that he was making of the Seine estuary. These were his most ambitious pictures to date and occupied him throughout the rest of that year. It is possible that he'd had them in mind for some time for, on his first visit to the Salon in 1859, he had written to Boudin commenting that there were no marine paintings worth mentioning on show: 'Marines are completely missing,' he had assured him, and went on to point out that they might well be 'a road that would take you far'. Now, almost five years later, Monet himself began to test just how far this might be.

The first studies for these paintings of the river mouth were made from the tip of the harbour walls. A long pier had been built in Honfleur to preserve the approach

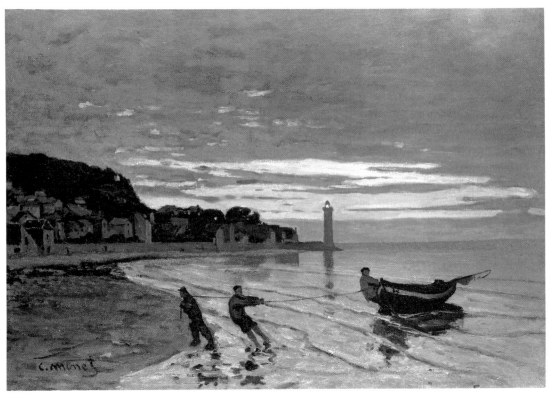

HAULING A BOAT, HONFLEUR

1864

channel and prevent it from silting up. It jutted out into the estuary, giving a clear view across the bay towards the Hospice lighthouse, and it was from this promontory that Monet worked. In 'Hauling a Boat' (above) the tide is out and the long curve of the beach snakes away into the middle distance. The sky is breaking across the horizon and the last rays of the sun glow through the tatters of the evening cloud. The headland stands out hard and dark while the stump of the lighthouse and the outlying buildings beside it are reflected in the water. The bay is scored with ripples that develop the rhythm of the shoreline, fanning out towards the viewer and then streaming away into the lower right corner of the canvas. In the foreground Monet has added the silhouettes of three figures who haul their boat onto the shore and pull the composition back into balance as they do so, reversing the righthand thrust of the rippling sea and linking it with the beach once more.

The whole picture has been beautifully thought out in terms of pattern and design. Monet has controlled the contrast of tones in every part of the canvas, constantly offsetting dark against light, detail against open space: the shadowed forms of the fishermen against the silver traces of the water, for example, or the dull masses of land against the sharp rent of the evening sky.

A second version of this scene (below) is taken from exactly the same spot on the pier and with only a slight shift of viewpoint. The mood in this second painting is quite changed, however: the hush of evening has been replaced by an overcast midday light. The weather is dull and impassive, heavy clouds clamber up the sky pressing into the upper parts of the canvas. Here and there a ragged sun breaks through, catching along the rooftops, brightening the far horizon and sparkling on the bow waves of the fishing boats as they head for the open sea.

The dark mass of the headland and the distant shore of the river are reduced to a single horizontal band separating sky and sea. The tide is up and a stretch of muddy water fills the lower section of the picture, blotting out the foreground. A four-oared whaler is making its way around the head of the pier while seagulls swoop and squabble about its bows. Behind it are the smaller forms of two fishing boats, another stands off the lighthouse, while in the far distance are three tiny sails, reduced now to flecks of paint on the horizon. These boats are vital to Monet's painting, he has used them to introduce a sense of perspective on an otherwise flat plane of water, space and distance being emphasized in the diminishing scale of their hulls.

Monet's technique is clearly visible in this painting. Working directly onto the white ground of the canvas, he has painted in the whole picture with small tipped brushes; the chopped surface of the water, the buildings and even

THE LIGHTHOUSE AT HONFLEUR

1864

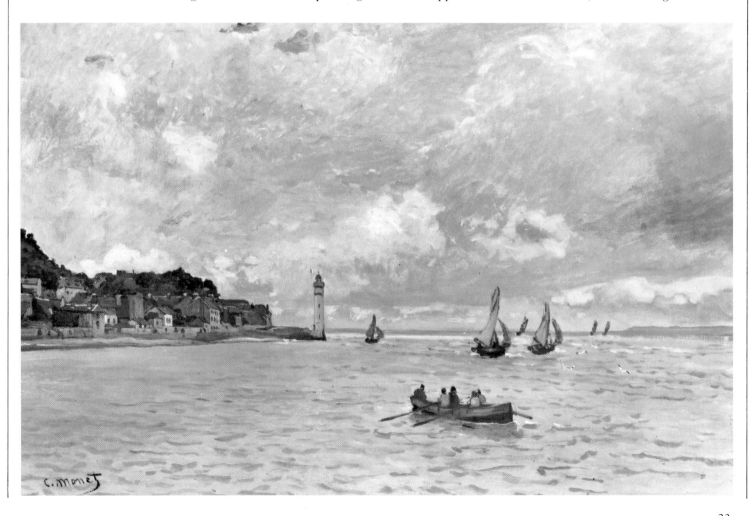

the great expanse of the clouds rolling overhead are hatched with delicate strokes. As with his earlier pictures, he has concentrated more on the variations of tone than on colour, restricting his palette to a range of blues and warm earths.

Monet stayed on in the estuary and worked on his paintings late into the summer. Gleyre's studio had closed down earlier that year, so there was no pressure on Monet to return to Paris and he moved instead to the family home in Sainte-Adresse. Here he started work on two large paintings, the first of Honfleur and the other showing the Cap de la Hève, the high ridge of cliffs that rise above Sainte-Adresse. These were *tableaux*, formal set-pieces designed specifically for public exhibition. Following the convention of the time, they were fully resolved compositions, developing and enlarging on the information in the studies, and consequently they were larger, more detailed and technically more polished than the pictures that Monet had produced in the open air.

The final tableau of the Hospice Lighthouse, entitled 'The Mouth of the Seine at Honfleur' (opposite), is similar to the second study in many ways: the spit of headland, the lighthouse and the play of light over the buildings have all been faithfully reproduced. The formation of clouds that break above the estuary is also a direct development from the study, although they have become brighter and warmer in the reincarnation.

It is in the foreground that Monet has made the most notable changes. The water is dark and rough, the waves are furrowed and flecked with foam, making the rowing boat's crossing considerably more precarious. The contrast is now between sea and sky, whereas in the study the two were almost identical in tone and it was the land that stood out in silhouette. Further boats have been added into the righthand side of the canvas, heeling and running before the stiff offshore breeze. One of these momentarily catches the light and its sails flash on the horizon; above it Monet has lifted the pattern of seagulls and set it against the clouds, enlivening the flat shadow with the sharp white notes of the birds' wings.

Dominating the lefthand side of the canvas is the single feature of a fishing boat. It lists heavily to one side so that the angle of its masts echoes those of the other boats on the far side of the canvas, binding the painting together and stabilizing the composition of the foreground. Monet's problem in constructing this part of the painting must have been how to persuade his boat to lean over at such an acute angle. He has not given it sails, which would have solved the problem, as these would obscure the view of the town behind. Equally it would be quite unrealistic to make the waves beneath the hull too violent as this would go against the mood of the painting; any sea that can throw a fishing boat on its side would be sure to swamp the little rowing boat completely. Monet has come up with a practical solution to the problem: he has the fishing boat resting at anchor while it lays out its nets. The heavy wooden otterboard that holds the trawl nets open has been swung overboard, suspended from the masthead, and it is the weight of this tackle, as much as the wind, that causes the boat to list so heavily.

Viewed overall, 'The Mouth of the Seine at Honfleur' represents a conflict of interests; Monet has found himself torn between two quite separate ambitions at the same time. On one side is his determination to be true to nature, not to idealize the subject or step beyond the bounds of realism. This had been fundamental to Monet's credo from the beginning; he had once said to Gleyre that he couldn't invent pictures and would paint only what he could see with his eyes. On the other was his burning desire to make his reputation in the Salon, to win himself official recognition, and to achieve this he had drawn on a wide range of influences and devices, melting them together in the privacy of his studio. The result is an ingenious compromise, a balance between the traditional painting techniques of the old masters and the direct observation of the new school.

Working at home soon led to difficulties. Monet had only moved over to Sainte-Adresse to prevent his family 'from turning sour' on him, but this diplomacy evidently failed. Within a few days he quarrelled with his father who, disapproving of his son's undisciplined life, immediately threatened to cut off his allowance. Faced with this possibility, Monet searched about for an alternative source of income. He sent three paintings down to Bazille in Montpellier with instructions that they be shown to the wealthy collector Aristide Bruyas, who lived nearby. In the

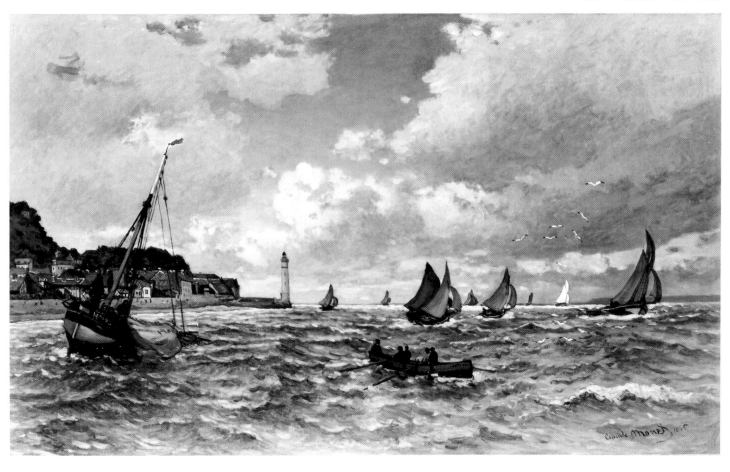

letter that accompanied them Monet went out of his way to stress his independence as an artist:

> One of these three canvases is a simple sketch which you saw me begin; it is based entirely on nature, you will perhaps find in it a certain relationship to Corot, but that this is so has absolutely nothing to do with imitation; the motif and especially the calm and misty effect are the only reasons for it. I have done it as conscientiously as possible, without having any painter in mind.

This is probably true; Monet admired Corot but it's fair to say that he never imitated him. In Monet's mind there was a clear difference between influence and imitation; one was the means by which an artist realized his own particular style, the other was for those who had none. As it happened Bruyas was not concerned with this distinction and politely declined all three of the pictures offered to him.

After only a few days at Sainte-Adresse, Monet devised a fictitious commission in Honfleur and left the family home once more. He resumed his work at the Ferme Saint-Siméon and late in that year, as winter was approaching, returned to Paris. He moved in with Bazille, who had rented a spacious studio in the Rue de Furstemberg which had once belonged to Delacroix. Here he completed his two large marine paintings and in the spring of that year, 1865, submitted them to the Salon.

Whatever Monet's motives had been with these two pictures, they succeeded. Both paintings were accepted by the Salon and provoked an enthusiastic response from the critics: 'the feeling for values, the striking point of view of the whole, a bold manner of seeing things and of forcing the attention of the spectator, these are qualities which

M. Monet already possesses to a high degree,' wrote Paul Mantz in the *Gazette des Beaux-Arts*. 'His 'Mouth of the Seine' abruptly stopped us in passing and we shall not forget it. From now on we shall certainly be interested in following the future efforts of this sincere painter'.

Even Monet was surprised by the reception his twin pictures had received at the Salon. Bazille told his parents that it was 'a much greater success than he expected. Several talented painters with whom he was not acquainted have written him complimentary letters.'

An anonymous critic who signed himself *Pigalle* described Monet as 'the author of a seascape the most original and supple, the most strongly and harmoniously painted, to be exhibited in a long time.' He did pause, however, to criticize the subdued colour: 'It has a somewhat dull tone, as in Courbet's; but what richness and what simplicity of view! M. Monet, unknown yesterday, has at the very start made a reputation by this picture alone.'

Encouraged by this success Monet spent the rest of the summer in the forest of Fontainebleau, preparing the way for a new painting. Progress was slow; the picture he had in mind was larger than anything he'd attempted before and he was constantly frustrated by interruptions and delays, not the least of these being that he broke his leg and was laid up in bed for several days, an unwilling patient for Bazille who was obliged to bring his medical knowledge out of retirement for the occasion. By autumn the picture was far from finished and Monet was forced to abandon it for the year and return to the estuary.

While he was there he revisited his old haunts in Honfleur and worked around the Ferme Saint-Siméon. From time to time he took the paddle steamer over to Trouville to visit Courbet, who was staying in this fashionable resort for the winter. Monet had known Courbet for over a year, but this was the first time he'd had the chance to spend any length of time with him and to watch him at work. In personality and appearance Courbet was far from attractive, a great vat of conceit and self-opinion whose admiration for his own paintings knew no bounds, but despite this he was capable of arousing fanatical admiration in the ranks of his disciples. Many of the younger generation of artists looked upon him as a symbol of the new age; they hung around the cafés where he drank, studiously imitating his ideas on both art and politics. Several of Monet's fellow students, particularly

Renoir, had been devoted followers. Courbet was the author of an uncompromising realism, a painter of everyday life as he saw it – warts and all. His intention was 'to be able to express the manners, ideas and aspect of my time ... in short, to produce living art'. He banished the time-honoured traditions of storytelling from his pictures; he had no time for the glories of France's history or for contriving scenes from the bible. 'How can I paint an angel,' he would ask, 'when I've never seen one?'

There is an undisguised brutality to Courbet's paintings: his still lifes are factual, his landscapes stripped of senti-mentality and his women built with the solidity of farm wagons. Added to this, his dislike of superficial prettiness led him to restrain the range of pigments on his palette, confining himself to the lower order of earth colours, and as

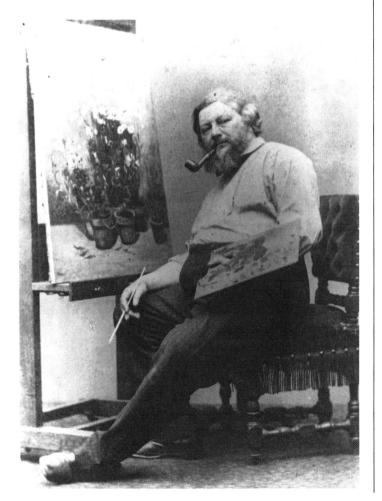

GUSTAVE COURBET

The determined realism of Courbet's painting exercised a hypnotic influence over the younger generation of landscape painters. They admired the thick, juicy texture of his paint and the factual subject matter of his pictures. Courbet was one of the first artists in France to stress the direct and unsentimental observation of nature. 'To paint a bit of country, one has got to know it,' he announced. 'I know my native countryside and I paint it. That woodland is near my home; that river is the Loue. Go and look at them and you will see my picture.'

a result many of his pictures are as dark as a creosoted log. He was, however, a superb technician and the paint on his canvases is manipulated with a savage mastery. He dragged and scraped the pigment, allowing it to break open in places so that the underlayers show through the torn colour. Often he used the flat blade of his palette knife, as well as the brush, to smear the colours onto the surface of the picture, making the most of the buttery texture of the medium.

Courbet lived life to the full; he had an insatiable appetite and an extraordinary capacity for serious drinking. Boudin had once spent a night out on the town with him and recollected afterwards that 'it was monstrously noisy. Heads whirled feverishly, reason tottered, Courbet proclaimed his creed, needless to say in a most unintelligible manner ... We sang, shouted and bellowed for so long that dawn found us with our glasses still in our hands. On the way home we made a din in the streets, which was very undignified.'

Monet enjoyed Courbet's company and learned a great deal from him during that summer. It was largely through Courbet that he gained the courage to do away with academic pretensions and paint contemporary life as he saw it, but the influence of Courbet wasn't always beneficial; his lack of colour was in many ways holding Monet back at this stage. Courbet conceived and measured his paintings in terms of shadow, staining his canvas down to a dark tone before beginning work: 'Courbet always painted upon a sombre base, on canvases prepared with brown,' Monet recalled, 'a convenient procedure, which he endeavoured to have me adopt. "Upon it," he used to say, "you can dispose your lights, your coloured masses; you immediately see your effect".' It was this 'old master' technique, with its tarred brown paintwork, that had deadened the colour of Monet's 'Mouth of the Seine at Honfleur', as *Pigalle* had been quick to point out.

For all his conceit, Courbet admired Monet's work and took a genuine interest in his career. He saw in Monet a fresh, determined originality; an artist not content just to paint angels. Courbet liked to work on a grand scale and he now pressed Monet to do the same. He loaned him the money to buy materials for his unfinished painting down in Fontainebleau, handing out advice freely and uninvited as he did so and even posing for one of the figures in it. Under his guidance Monet embarked on a canvas over twenty feet

long, 'a great tartine', according to Boudin, 'that'll cost him both an arm and a leg'. As it turned out, the painting was never finished; when work began in the spring of 1866 something went wrong with its design. It is possible that Courbet was to blame for this failure, that having put forward the money he tried to interfere with the way the painting was made, but there is no firm evidence for this. Later that summer the canvas was taken off its stretcher and rolled up, leaving Monet with precious little to show for two years' hard labour.

THE SEINE ESTUARY is treacherous. The current flows so slowly that the water loses its grasp on the silt and deposits it in the river mouth, choking the passageways and sealing off the entrances to the ports. Deep water becomes shallow, sand banks can spring up overnight and the channels between them alter direction without warning. In the past the fishermen of Honfleur had come to rely more on their eyes and instincts than on any chart as they made their way across its surface, and the uncanny skill they developed in the estuary made them into outstanding navigators. Over the centuries they had become legendary as explorers, rivalled only by the sailors of Dieppe, with whom they are often compared and confused. Sailors from Honfleur are said to have reached Labrador, Brazil and the Cape of Good Hope. Quebec was colonized from Honfleur and its fishermen were the first to trawl the Dogger Bank.

In 1866 Monet used the fishing fleet of Honfleur as the subject of a painting (page 29). The quayside that acts as both berth and marketplace is stacked with boats, their solid timber hulls riding above delicately patterned reflections. Monet has observed the details very closely; the registration marks on the prows and sails, the nets hauled up the masts to dry and the tilt of the gaff-rigged yard arms set out against the sky. Standing in a clearing in this forest of sails, a group of people examine the day's catch, while others work on board ship securing the tackle. The quayside was the nerve centre of Honfleur, noisy and crowded. Some years earlier a traveller had observed that 'the pier at high water presents all that a lover of coast scenery can wish for: old boats with well-mended gear, some containing vegetables and fruit, others turbot, soles and flounders and many laden entirely with shrimps, with which the market abounds, nets and lines of all forms and sizes, with baskets as various: old women and young, grotesque and pretty, of all colours, with baskets, tins and pans … a constant bustle and activity prevail in the place, every tide brings a ship laden with passengers, chiefly women, with their long white flapping caps, from Le Havre.'

That summer, while working on the 'Fishing Boats at Honfleur', Monet stayed in the Hôtel Cheval Blanc, which stands just to the left of the picture frame. Its position on the waterfront made it particularly convenient for travellers waiting to board the packet boat which moored up along the quayside each morning, 'smoking and hissing away opposite the hotel'. In the painting this boat can be seen making its way out to sea, trailing a dense braid of smoke from its stack, its hull half cut from view by the flight of stone stairs. The crossing was slow, the sea frequently rough and the Channel a natural emetic, as a large sign next to the hotel, advertising a patented remedy for seasickness, reminded passengers as they embarked.

'Fishing Boats at Honfleur', was designed specifically for the Salon. As a young man, Monet focused his whole attention on this annual exhibition, for it was here that he intended to prove himself as a painter. This being said, the painting is considerably more daring than anything he'd done before. In it the distinction between *étude*, the open-air study, and *tableau*, the formal set-piece, has become less clearly defined. Monet only made studies for details of the painting, such as the flock of boats against the quayside. Much of the overall composition was invented on the final canvas, without any rehearsal, raising the possibility that some of it might have been painted directly from the subject.

In 'The Mouth of the Seine' Monet had increased the drama of the weather, adding details and focal points to his composition back in the studio, all conventions calculated to seduce the Salon jury. It had been painted to please and in this respect had succeeded brilliantly. Here, two years later, he was searching for something simpler and more personal. His observation of the scene is intimate; there are no grand gestures from cloud formations and stormy seas. In their place Monet has analyzed precise effects of nature: the configuration of reflections on the slick of still water, the patchwork structure of the sails above and the bleaching of the tones as the afternoon light softens the middle distance.

There is a startling informality to this painting of Honfleur. Rather than arranging the scene to suit himself,

shifting the parts about the canvas like props on a theatre stage, Monet appears to have seized an instant in time, a chance moment in the everyday life of the port, and pinned it to his canvas. The painting fails to contain the scene; the paddle steamer is rounding the harbour wall, already parts of it are out of sight, and in a moment it will be gone completely. The rowing boats moored in the foreground have been amputated by the edge of the picture, as are the steps above. The picture has become a window, framing the view at random. Only a section of the subject can be seen; the rest of it extends on beyond the boundary of the painting.

What is equally clear is that the apparent informality of this painting is an illusion, planned and premeditated by the artist. Every detail of the composition has been carefully thought out. The main bulk of the picture, the fleet of fishing boats huddled alongside the quay, lies on the righthand side of the canvas. The boats are assembled into a single wedge-shaped design, exactly like the triangular motif painted on their bows, that reaches across to the far side of the painting, emphasized by the distant square-rigged ship and the direction of the rowing boat that lies almost motionless on the water. The focal point of this structure is the paddle steamer; all the rhythms of the painting converge onto it. The steamer, meanwhile, is heading out of view, about to ruin the carefully balanced design for ever.

'Fishing Boats at Honfleur' was destroyed during World War II: all that remains of it are black-and-white photographs. The autumnal reds and browns of the boats' sails, the exact nature of the sky and the colour of the water, which in Honfleur is as dense and green as detergent, can only be imagined. However, the photographs show clearly Monet's astonishing gift for surface pattern, the way in which he enriches the design, setting the dark line of an anchor chain against the flat expanse of water below, the sharp notes of registration marks, fenders and anchor against the deep shadow of a hull. The whole canvas is alive with invention. In this painting Monet began to discover a distinctive visual language of his own, shedding the burden of influence as he did so, trusting more and more to the evidence of his own eyes.

In the spring of 1867 the painting was sent to the Salon together with 'Women in the Garden', a large canvas that

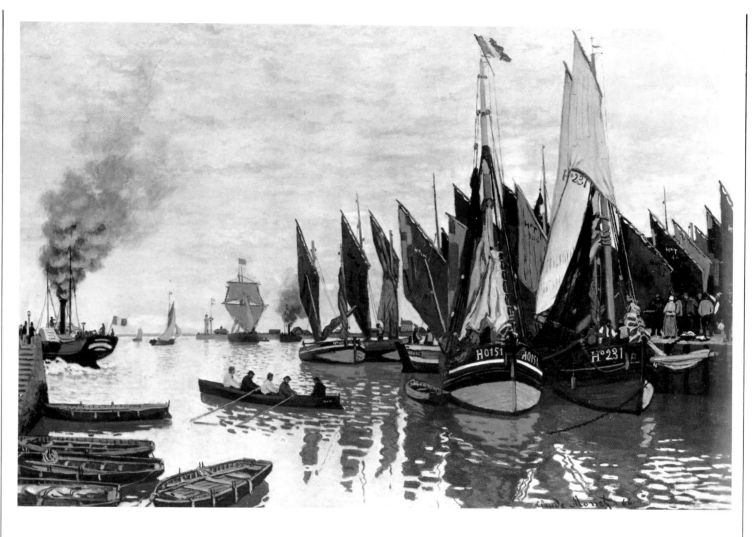

FISHING BOATS AT HONFLEUR

1866

Monet had been working on at his home in Ville d'Avray. It was the year of the World's Fair in Paris, and it was therefore more important than ever for artists to be represented in the Salon. Courbet wasn't risking the whims of the jury that year and built his own private pavilion where he could show what he wanted without interference. Monet had nothing to fear; he had every reason to assume his two pictures would be accepted. His track record so far had been outstanding: in 1865 he'd notched up a success with his two views of the Seine estuary. The following year, after the failure of his large painting in Fontainebleau, he had saved the day with a full-length portrait entitled 'The Green Dress' that had been widely admired. This year his luck ran out, however, for both his submissions were flatly rejected by the jury. In hindsight the reason seems clear enough; his paintings were still carefully made tableaux but in them the balance of intention had shifted slightly; instead of leaning towards the conventional they had become personal, 'experiments in light and colour' as Monet called them, and this, to the Salon jury, was incomprehensible. One member of the panel, thought to be Jules Breton, was afterwards asked whether he felt Monet was improving as a painter. Breton replied that it was for exactly that reason that he was rejecting Monet's work: it was the duty of the jury to save French art from the 'abominable practice of painting in the open air'.

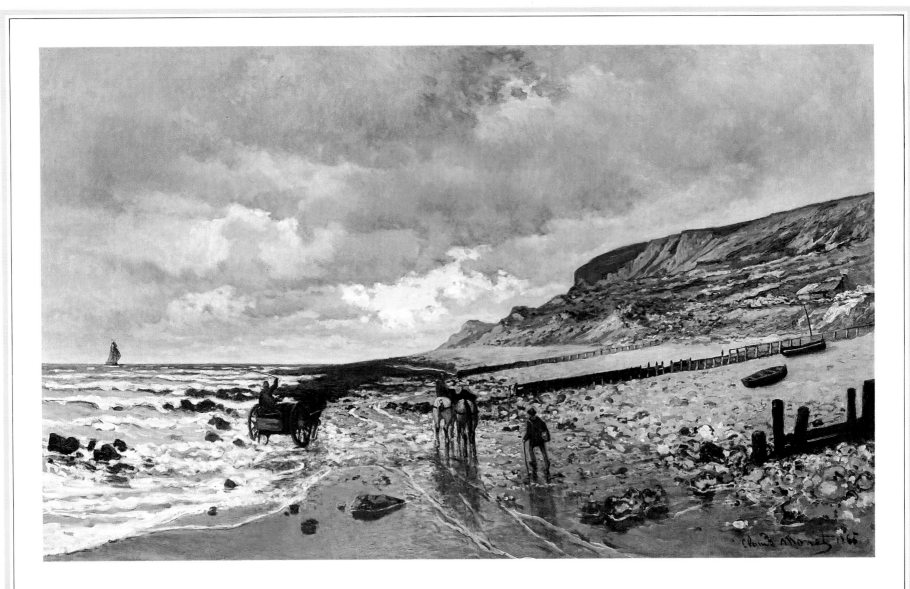

POINTE DE LA HÈVE, AT LOW TIDE

1865

The Seine Estuary

SAINTE-ADRESSE

1864–1867

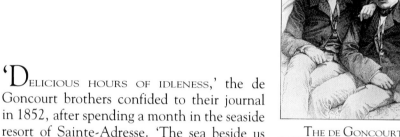

THE DE GONCOURTS

'DELICIOUS HOURS OF IDLENESS,' the de Goncourt brothers confided to their journal in 1852, after spending a month in the seaside resort of Sainte-Adresse. 'The sea beside us shone brightly and lulled us to sleep. Lunch led to dinner. There was no end to the nightcaps we drank.'

The de Goncourts were tireless chroniclers of their age, secreting away scraps of conversation, anecdotes, observations and witticisms in the pages of their nightly journal, penning in grotesque and often vicious thumbnail sketches of their friends and acquaintances. The journal is at once a history of their times, an intimate confession of their private lives and a stab in the back for their literary colleagues. That summer the two brothers had been staying in Sainte-Adresse with a man 'whose mania was hospitality … It was a sweet, charming, lazy life, as calm as the sea, the life that he led and we led with him. He had a little house, a little garden, a mistress, two or three rowing boats which we would take out to sea, and a wooden bathing house on the beach where we played all sorts of games and smoked and chatted.'

Sainte-Adresse was a suburb of Le Havre, a sickle-blade bay on the northern shore of the river mouth. It was a place for the respectable, the wealthy and the retired, set away from the congestion of the city and the clamour of the commercial docks. Sometimes called 'the Nice of Le Havre', the town boasted a church with a blue-slate steeple and splendid views from the platform of the lighthouse. Hotels, holiday villas and terraced gardens were perched on the hillside above a pebble beach where in the evening the fishing boats were pulled up away from the tide.

Although the majority of the residents were French, there was also a colony of English families living in the town. Their reasons for being in Sainte-Adresse were purely practical, as one of their group pointed out: 'A great number of English abroad, especially in sea-ports, are obliged to live in France, from embarrassment, or prudential and laudable motives, to retrieve their fortunes by rigid economy, which they find easier to practice when away from the remarks and scrutinies of their neighbours, with whose expenditure they previously kept pace.'

MONET HAD SPENT much of his childhood at Sainte-Adresse, in Tante Lecadre's home overlooking the Seine estuary. It was probably here that he had drawn many of the caricatures and where he had taken his first steps as a landscape painter, filling his sketchbooks with timid drawings of the ships making their way towards the harbour walls of Le Havre. In 1864, while he was staying in Honfleur, he had brought Bazille over to Sainte-Adresse to meet his family. Fortunately his friend's polite, well-spoken manner and easy grace had won them around and Bazille was able to report back to his parents: 'I had lunch with Monet's family, they are charming people. They have at Sainte-Adresse, near Le Havre, a delightful place … I had

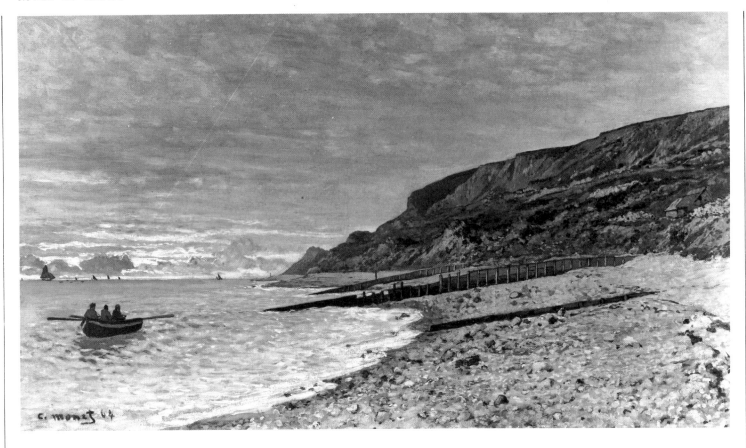

POINTE DE LA HÈVE

1864

to refuse the hospitable invitation they made me to spend the month of August there.'

The Monets could afford to be generous; business was as good that year as ever it had been. The outbreak of the American Civil War, far from strangling trade, had improved it. Le Havre had allied itself to the southern Confederate States, shipping over supplies and munitions at extortionate prices in exchange for cotton and tobacco. That summer the war had come a great deal closer to home, however, when the Confederate ship 'Alabama' had taken refuge in Cherbourg, just along the coast from Le Havre. Eventually it had been forced out to sea again where it was destroyed by the larger and more heavily armed Union ship, the 'Kearsarge'. All France had buzzed with the news; Edouard Manet had hurried to the scene and, hiring a fishing boat, had witnessed the battle. Returning to Paris he dashed off a painting and immediately exhibited it in public, hot as a newsflash.

The beach at Sainte-Adresse ends in a cliff, a massive outcrop of rock called the Cap de la Hève. This marks the furthest extremity of the Seine, where the hard spine of chalk that marches along the upper bank of the river's course through Normandy turns out to face the sea. White and crumbling, picked clean by the battering of the Channel seas, these cliffs then stretch unbroken from the point of the Cap de la Hève along the coastline to Dieppe, rising and falling above the water in a graceful switchback rhythm. Gulls wheel and dive about the impassive elevations and fishing ports lie in the cradle of each hollow.

'Pointe de la Hève, at Low Tide' (page 30) was exhibited in the Salon of 1865 together with 'The Mouth of the Seine at Honfleur'. The painting is dark; waves break relentlessly on the shore, running out over the beach in frothy patterns. Heavy-bellied clouds roll overhead, parting briefly to silhouette the headland. A wagon with two carthorses led beside it makes its way through the surf,

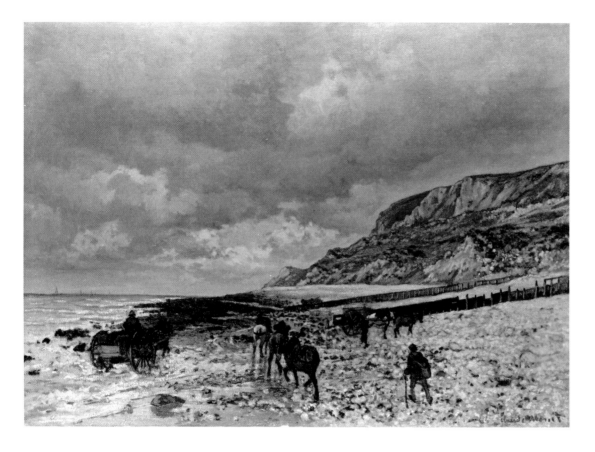

HORSES AT POINTE DE LA HÈVE

1864

this the only significant alteration is in the weather. Monet has again whipped up a storm for the benefit of his audience; sharp lights play over the sea and shingle, flickering between the shadows, accenting the picture surface and heightening the drama of the scene.

This flagrant romanticism was an intentional move on Monet's part, calculated to appeal to Parisian taste. The violence of the elements running unchecked was more exciting to art-lovers than calm seas and fair sailing. Nature's outbursts of bad temper were considered to be picturesque, provided they were confined to the space within a gilt frame. The reality was considerably more brutal. The Cap de la Hève was one of the notorious wrecking grounds on the northern coast of France as it took the full brunt of the Atlantic swell. The headland marked the grave of several ships that had been making for the safety of the Seine estuary in high seas, but which had gone aground to be pounded to matchwood within sight of the harbour walls. There is an ingenious if fanciful theory that this hazard gave the town of Sainte-Adresse its name; sea captains caught in a storm off the lee shore of the Cap de la Hève, and finding the crew on their knees praying for salvation, would flog them to their feet once more telling them that it was not God who was going to save their skins but *Sens et Adresse* (roughly translated as 'common-sense and skilful sailing').

avoiding the pebbles higher up, but despite this foreground activity, the painting is dominated by the headland of the Cap de la Hève. Huge and tumbling as the ruins of a castle, it fills the middle distance, a single amorphous mass jutting out into the canvas. Hard bones of chalk show through the tatters of its vegetation and weather-blackened breakwaters reach down towards the seashore, dividing the shingle into sections.

The painting is based on two studies that Monet had made in the autumn of the previous year (above and left). Elements have been taken from both: the figures, the low tide line and the stormy skies are taken from one, with only slight modifications, while the topographical details of the Cap de la Hève itself are closer to the other, more tranquil version. The best of both has been run together in a single conglomerate painting. Inevitably the final tableau is much larger than the studies; the canvas is over twice the size and the brushwork is correspondingly more precise. It is also broader and spans a wider section of the scene. Apart from

In 1867 MONET was back home on probation. The two paintings on which he had staked so much hope that year, 'Fishing boats at Honfleur' and 'Women in the Garden', had both been rejected from the Salon. His experiments in open-air painting had been declared an abomination to French art and his use of colour described as putrescent. However, the real bone of contention among the family that summer was his mistress, Camille Doncieux, who had been living with him in his house in Ville d'Avray. Monet had met her two years earlier in Paris and later that same summer had persuaded her to join him in the forest of Fontainebleau, where she can be seen in the existing fragment of his large painting 'The Picnic', sitting beside Courbet in a sunlit puddle of summer skirts. She had been the model for Monet's Salon success 'The Green Dress', and had then taken the title role in 'Women in the Garden', posing in different dresses for all four figures.

Following the rejection of his two paintings in 1867 Monet had found himself on the verge of bankruptcy. He had managed to sell a still life of flowers for 200 francs and Bazille, stretching his own budget to its limits, had agreed to buy 'Women in the Garden' for 2500 francs, payable in monthly instalments. Despite this, Monet's cash flow had drained to a trickle, hardly enough to support one person, let alone two. To make matters worse, Camille had discovered that she was pregnant. Eventually, when the situation became desperate, Bazille wrote to Monet's father explaining the predicament and asking for his help and understanding. The reply from Sainte-Adresse was simple and to the point; there was no question of money or any other financial assistance from the family, but if Monet cared to return home he could have a room and meals for the summer. Camille was not invited and Adolphe Monet politely but firmly recommended that all association with her was severed. It was not that he necessarily disapproved of the affair himself, he explained, it was Tante Lecadre's feelings that must be considered. Faced with this ultimatum Monet had no choice but to comply and, leaving Camille with a friend of his, he left Paris and returned to face the combined disapproval of his family in Sainte-Adresse.

The fact that Adolphe Monet was in exactly the same situation as his son at that moment, and had recently given his mistress the bonus of an illegitimate child, can only have rubbed salt into the wound. The difference was that he had kept the indiscretion to himself – his sister hadn't been allowed to hear of it – and therefore, in the eyes of society, no impropriety had been committed. The canons of middle-class morality may not have been quite fair, but they were perfectly well understood.

WHILE HE WAS AT HOME that summer, Monet painted the view from a first-floor window of the house, looking out over the garden terrace to the estuary beyond (opposite). Surrounded by barricades of gladioli and geranium, Monet's father sits in his wicker chair staring directly into the morning sun, his face shaded by a panama hat and his walking stick planted out in front. Beside him is a woman, presumably Tante Lecadre, with her back turned to the artist and quite invisible behind her parasol. Two of Monet's cousins lean on the trelliswork beyond, silhouetted against the ringing blue water.

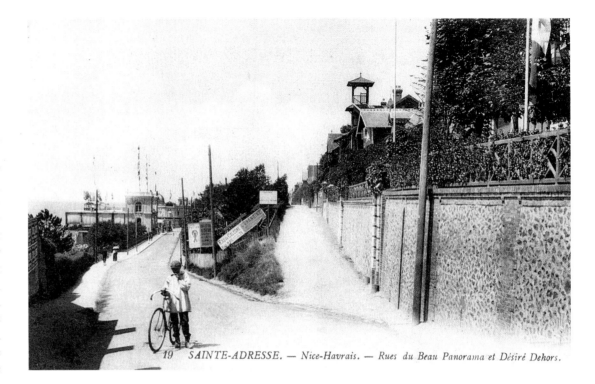

19 SAINTE-ADRESSE. — Nice-Havrais. — Rues du Beau Panorama et Désiré Dehors.

The sea is calm and untroubled; an offshore breeze rustles up small waves, scoring the surface with tones of deep jade. A fishing boat passes by, its sails dark and jagged against the sea, while in the distance a catalogue of shipping is strung out across the horizon, funnelling in towards the harbour walls of Le Havre which lie just to the left outside the picture frame. Beyond them the far shore of the river is reduced to a smudge of blue-greys.

Twenty years after this picture was painted, Guy de Maupassant was to describe exactly the same view in the opening chapter of his novel *Pierre et Jean*:

Other vessels could be seen, similarly capped with smoke, heading from every direction towards the short, white jetty that swallowed them up like a mouth, one after the other. And fishing smacks and big sailing ships with delicate masts and spars shining against the sky, hauled by invisible tugs, were all coming in faster or slower towards this devouring ogre, who now and again seemed sated and vomited out into the open sea another fleet of liners, brigs, schooners and three-masters, their spars a thicket of tangled branches. Steamers hurried off to right and left over the flat belly of the ocean, while sailing ships, abandoned by the tugs that had towed

STREET IN SAINTE-ADRESSE

The resort of Sainte-Adresse was built on a hillside that rose up sharply from the shingle beach, offering each house a commanding and uncluttered view of the Seine estuary. Monet took advantage of this elevated viewpoint when painting the 'Terrace at Sainte-Adresse' from a first-floor window of the family home.

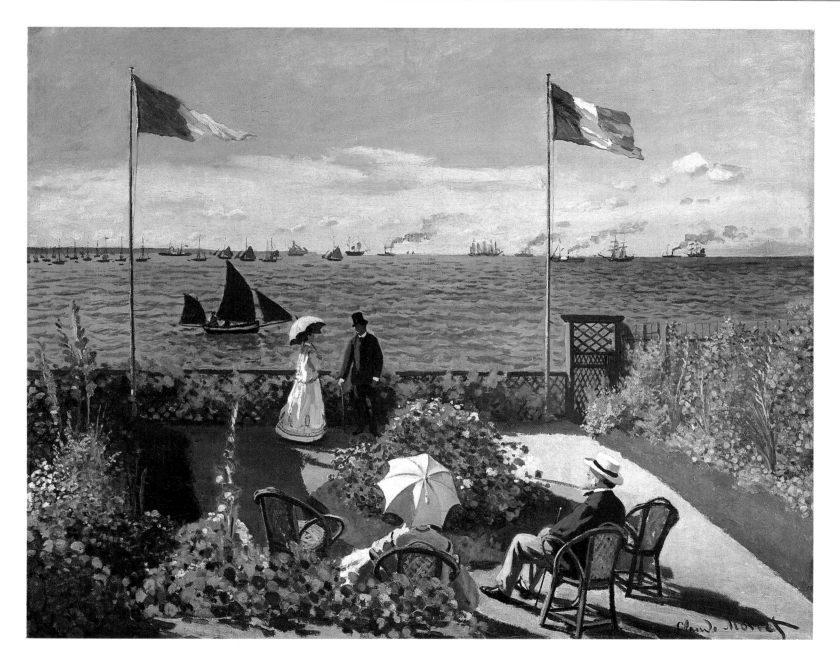

TERRACE AT SAINTE-ADRESSE

1867

them, stood motionless while donning from maintop to topgallant the white canvas or the brown that seemed red in the setting sun.

Several of the landscapes that Monet painted appear again in Maupassant novels, translated into passages of descriptive prose and recorded with the same meticulous attention to detail that he shows here. This was not plagiarism but simply a coincidence; Maupassant had been born near Dieppe in 1850 and as a result he often returned to the Normandy coast in the summertime. He shared Monet's love of the Seine. During the course of his short life, Maupassant was to frequent many of the same places as Monet and used them as the settings for his stories, paralleling the painter's work with his words. They eventually met some years later in Etretat, the seaside resort that lies a few miles further up the coast.

THE COLOUR IN 'Terrace at Sainte-Adresse' is rich and magnificent. The dark tones that had been the chrysalis of Monet's development have fallen away to be replaced by brilliant lights. Bright dabs and blobs of paint stand out against the shadows. Spears of sunlit flowers are built from pools of saturated pigment, patches of high-pitched colour collide with each other, creating forms and suggesting outlines that seem to dissolve away again on closer inspection. Monet's brush stabs and stammers across the canvas, rippling the surface of the sea with little quivering strokes that set it in motion. Touches of colour dashed down beside each other become flags and ships and the shadows beneath the clouds.

Monet makes it clear that this painting is not a group portrait. He has given very little significance to individual likenesses: his cousins face the viewer, but have practically no features; Monet's father is looking out to sea and his aunt, if that is who she is, exists only as a device. The figures are just elements in the picture, part of the overall composition. By turning their backs to the viewer, Monet invites us to look beyond them to the flags, the ramparts of flowers and the open sea.

It is the quality of light that takes the leading role in Monet's painting. The woman silhouetted against the sea may have no recognizable features, but the geometry of light and shade on her dress is carefully analyzed, divided into two flat patterns that lock together with no half tones

between to soften the impact. Monet has had the impudence to conceal Tante Lecadre's face completely, but in its place he has made a detailed study of the light playing over her parasol, testing the density of the shadows behind each rib, faithfully recording every shift and nuance of colour that he sees before him and treating the convex surface with the same respect as if it were a portrait.

The subject matter of this picture has begun to slip into second place. Monet is no longer interested in what he looks at, only in what he sees: in this sense it makes little difference to him whether he paints his aunt's portrait or her parasol. What is quite evident is that light has now become a physical presence in the painting. The shadows that stretch out behind his father's chair are as solid as the wooden legs that cast them. Monet makes no attempt to separate the reality of one from the transitory effect of the other, but paints them both exactly as he sees them.

Possibly the most remarkable feature of this painting is its viewpoint. It has been painted from an upper-floor window looking down on the terrace. As a result the background is not behind the foreground pictorially, but above it. The rows of flowers, the figures, the sea and the distant ships are now separately layered up the painting. Instead of the landscape queueing up in rank, it is spread over the surface of the canvas. The sky that had played such an important role in 'Pointe de la Hève' is reduced to a narrow band along the top of the canvas.

Monet has almost certainly borrowed this ingenious device from a Japanese print. Hokusai, Hiroshige and Utamaro, all of whom Monet in particular admired, had frequently used these bird's-eye perspectives to throw their designs evenly across the page. Japanese art had become extremely fashionable in France but there was some disagreement as to who could claim to have been the first to have discovered it, though the de Goncourt brothers gave themselves much of the credit: 'The taste for things Chinese and Japanese! We were among the first to have this taste. It is now spreading to everything and everyone, even idiots and middle-class women.'

Among the rival claimants was the painter Félix Bracquemond who had come across a volume of Hokusai prints back in the 1850s, which he insisted was being used as the packing tissue around a shipment of china. Shops selling oriental curiosities, such as the Porte Chinoise in the Rue de Rivoli, had opened at much the same date.

Monet didn't actually make a collection of Japanese prints until he was in Holland a few years later, but he was certainly aware of them at this time, as the 'Terrace at Sainte-Adresse' demonstrates. He had seen examples at the Paris World's Fair earlier that year, although the American-born painter James Whistler had probably introduced him to them eighteen months before, when the two artists had been staying in Trouville together. Whistler was fascinated by Japanese prints and gradually absorbed the lessons he learned from them into his own pictures.

During the course of that summer Monet wrote to Bazille, who was staying with his family in Montpellier: 'I've cut out a lot of work for myself; I have about twenty canvases on the way, some stunning marines, and some figures, gardens and finally, among my marines, I'm doing the regattas at Le Havre with many people on the beach and the ship lane full of little sails.'

Le Havre was famous for its regattas. The shipyards, the docks and the town's long association with the sea made it a natural centre for yachting. In Monet's painting (page 38) the yachts are drawn up on parade, shaking out full sail in the morning light. They appear to be closely related to the *Picoteux*, the boats of the fishing fleet, the arrangement of their sails and spars an adaptation of those of their working cousins. Above them, battalions of small clouds fleck the sky. The beach streaks away into the middle distance where the whitewashed buildings of Sainte-Adresse stand sharply defined in the sunshine, surmounted by a single terraced building perched on the headland.

Tante Lecadre viewed these new paintings of Monet's with grave suspicion. In her opinion they were too sketchy, too quickly painted to be treated as serious works of art. To allow the marks of the painter's tools to show on the canvas was, to her way of thinking, slightly vulgar. The surface of the painting should be mirror-smooth and hard as tortoise-shell. There was a saying in those days that a painting was only finished when it was 'no longer possible to make out the means by which it had been created'.

The problem of 'finish' was to haunt Monet all his life. Even in the 'Pointe de la Hève' the handling of the paint had caused some raised eyebrows and one writer had observed that Monet lacked 'that finesse that is only to be gained at the price of long study'. Monet resisted the con-

vention, however; in 'Regatta at Sainte-Adresse' the sea is studded with little brushstrokes, each one a delicate calibration of colour, that collectively suggest the translucence of sunlit water. The morning light catches on the sails of the yachts in thick juicy strokes of paint, the high stratum of clouds above is scumbled across the blue in long veils of white pigment, dragged with the tip of the brush until they crumble and break open. This is not lack of finesse, but an essential part of Monet's technique, his own personal handwriting, individual and distinctive as a signature.

Monet's exploration of atmospheric change led him to repeat this scene in a sibling picture, 'The Beach at Sainte-Adresse' (page 39), painted from a few yards farther back along the beach. The plump hulls of rowing boats fill the foreground, lying on the hip of the shingle above pools of deep shadow. The sky is overcast and the soft lustres of the clouds are pieced together from tough little brushstrokes. The town of Sainte-Adresse is stretched out along the circumference of the bay, reaching out to a narrow promontory. Beyond this, the jetty and chimneys of Le Havre can just be seen behind the irregular polygons of the fishing boat's sails.

In his letters to Bazille that summer Monet referred to several paintings that no longer exist today. In particular he mentioned a large picture of a steamship that he was preparing for the Salon and which he described as 'very curious'. However, his one overriding concern during these months was Camille, who had given birth to a son that July.

'Camille has given birth to a large and handsome boy,' he told Bazille, 'whom despite everything – I don't know how – I feel I love; I suffer to think that his mother has not enough to eat.' Monet hadn't been able to afford the train fare to Paris and so had not been with her at the time. Unable to give any help himself, he had pestered Bazille for money: 'I would be terribly unhappy if she were to give birth without what is proper'.

These new worries, coming at a time when his career seemed precarious, seem to have affected his eyesight and Monet found himself temporarily blinded. He recovered quickly from this mysterious affliction and that autumn when Bazille offered him the use of his studio in the Rue de la Condamine, he accepted and escaped the confinement of the family home at Sainte-Adresse to return to Paris.

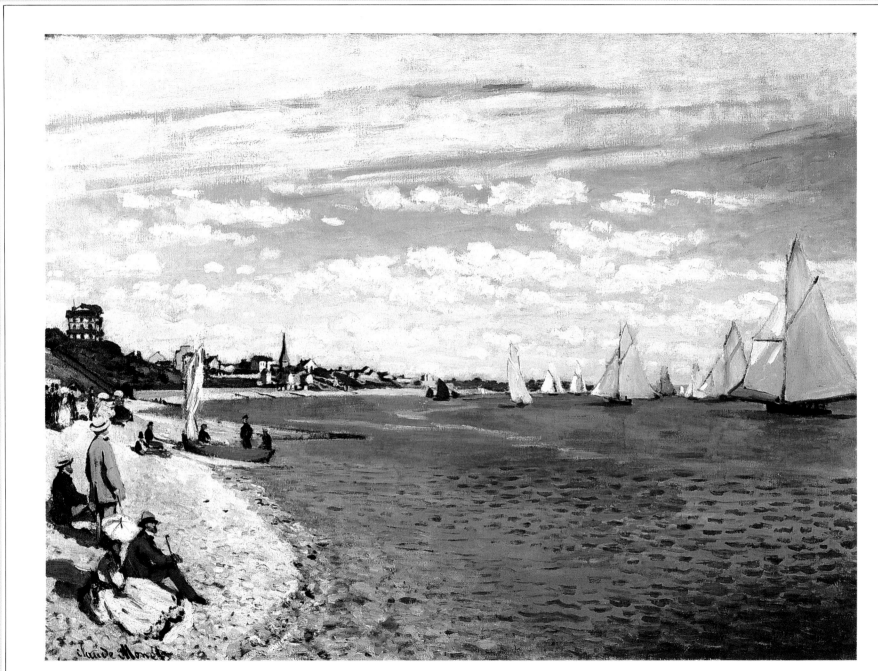

REGATTA AT SAINTE-ADRESSE

1867

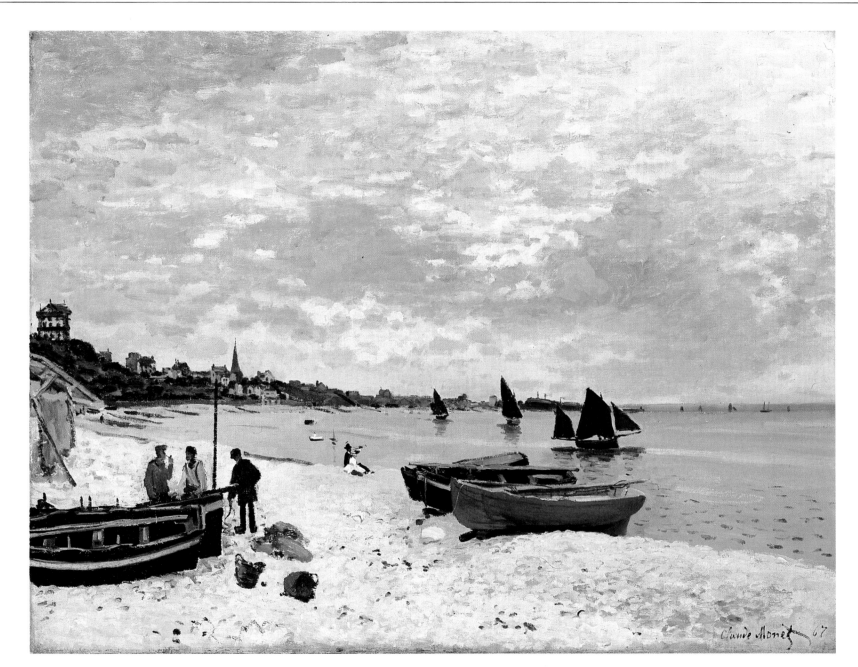

THE BEACH AT SAINTE-ADRESSE

1867

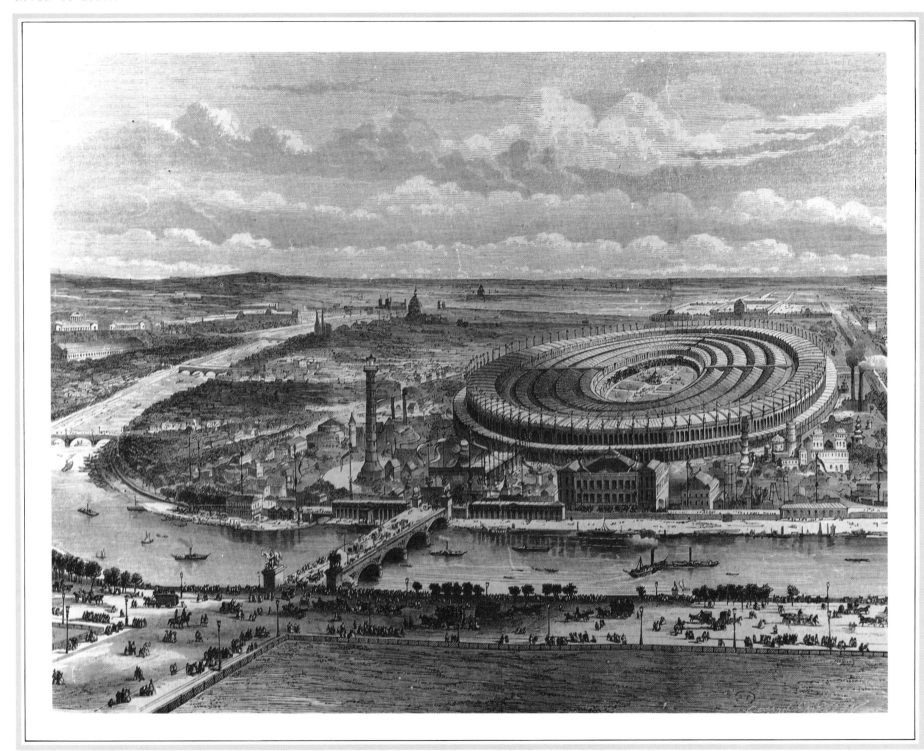

PARIS

1867–73

This was the second and largest of the great exhibitions staged during the reign of Napoleon III. The site was the Champ de Mars, the military parade ground set in a curve of the river to the west of Paris. The exhibition was opened by the Emperor on 1 April 1867, and the entrance gates recorded over seven million visitors during that summer. Though a special service of paddle steamers was commissioned to ferry visitors to the show by river, many others arrived by carriage and omnibus, and the congestion on the Pont d'Iena, the bridge in the foreground of this view, was so bad that angry letters of complaint were sent to the newspapers.

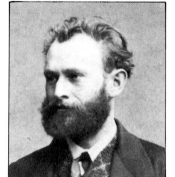

EDOUARD MANET

THE PARIS WORLD'S FAIR opened in 1867 on the banks of the Seine. The site for this great spectacle was the Champ de Mars, a military parade ground on the west side of the city where the Eiffel tower now stands. There were precedents for this choice: twelve years before, following the success of the Great Exhibition in the Crystal Palace in London, there had been a similar exhibition in Paris on the Champ de Mars, and it had earlier been the site of a significant festival during the Revolution, when Robespierre had staged his sacrifice to the 'Supreme Being'. This new project, however, was to be larger and considerably more extravagant than anything Paris had seen before.

In the centre of the show was a massive gallery, roofed over with the latest technology of glass and cast iron, and built along the lines of a giant railway station. Around it were dotted smaller pavilions, villas and towers, laced together with gravel paths. The river Seine was an integral part of the whole machine; its water was pumped up into the grounds and directed into lakes, streams and cascades. Man-made grottoes were flooded to become subterranean aquariums where rare fish swam behind glass walls and oysters were cultivated for the restaurants. From the landing-stage on the edge of the Seine, divers walked on the river bed. English steam boats, Hungarian yachts and Turkish caiques were demonstrated along with gondolas and patented life-rafts. A miniature clipper that had sailed the Atlantic was put on show and naval gunnery was hauled about by mechanical lifting devices.

Inside the huge disposable amphitheatre every craft and product of French ingenuity was put on display: pipes were carved, diamonds ground and ivory tusks whittled into ornaments. Sèvres porcelain, *haute couture* and French wines were given prominent positions. Scented water spouted from fountains and Vichy water was on tap. False teeth were made on the spot for waiting customers, as were dolls, hair nets, chocolates, shoes and artificial flowers. Every provincial district was given its own street where local skills, from forestry to rope-making, were shown off, and each of the colonies was given an individual pavilion. But it was the *Galerie des Machines* that took pride of place for here, in the largest of the halls, everything that could be pulled or pushed by steam was lined up, polished and gleaming and ready to be applauded. There were steam trains, saws, and pumps, even a steam-powered cathedral organ. It was not all French machinery by any means; foreign countries were also allowed to contribute to this mechanical wonderland: the Swiss were represented by telescopes and clocks, the English by pot-bellied steam cranes, and the Prussians unfortunately chose to display a range of siege cannons – the very ones that were to bombard Paris three years later.

It was the largest exhibition of its kind; a magnificent affirmation of national pride. The Emperor officially opened it on 1 April, a date that might have been better chosen, and visitors came from all over the world to take part. They arrived at the site on paddle-boats, the forerunners of the modern *bateaux-mouches*, that ran a regular service from the Quai d'Orsay. From there they walked through the maze of steets and galleries; they took the steam omnibus around the perimeter to see the balloons rising on their tethers and parachutes coming down from wooden towers. In physical terms the Fair was a marathon, and those too old or tired to stay the course could pay to be towed about in three-wheeled bath-chairs that had been designed especially for the occasion.

The visual arts, still France's greatest export, were equally well represented. In the Paris Salon, situated on the other bank of the river and linked to the main show by ferry boats, a special exhibition had been put together. Over five thousand paintings and several hundred tons of sculpture were collected there beneath one roof.

Despite this opportunity, the new school of painters had failed to have their pictures accepted. Monet's two pictures had been rejected, as had those of Bazille, Renoir and Pissarro. Courbet's exhibition in his private pavilion received nothing but bad press, even from the camp of the Realists. 'Nothing, nothing, nothing at all in this exhibition of Courbet's', complained the De Goncourt brothers: 'Ugliness, and more ugliness. And ugliness without any of its grandeur, ugliness without the beauty of ugliness.'

Although he had nothing on show, Monet remained in Paris to witness the exhibition. It was not a sight to be missed, and he and Camille were just two of the seven million spectators who pressed through the entrance gates that spring. Monet was fascinated by machinery; he often included paddle-steamers and trains in his paintings and was later to become an enthusiastic supporter of car-racing, although he never learnt to drive himself. Another exhibit that caught his attention at the Fair was the display of Japanese prints, in which he particularly studied the high viewpoint that these artists used to spread out the composition. Intrigued by the possibilities of this system, Monet at once obtained permission to work from the gallery that runs around the rim of the Louvre, and from this vantage point he painted three canvases, one of the church of Saint-Germain l'Auxerrois and the other two showing views across the Seine.

'Quai du Louvre' (opposite) is a study of textures: the soft haze of spring foliage, the dry biscuit tones of the road and the sharp counterpoint of light and shade playing over

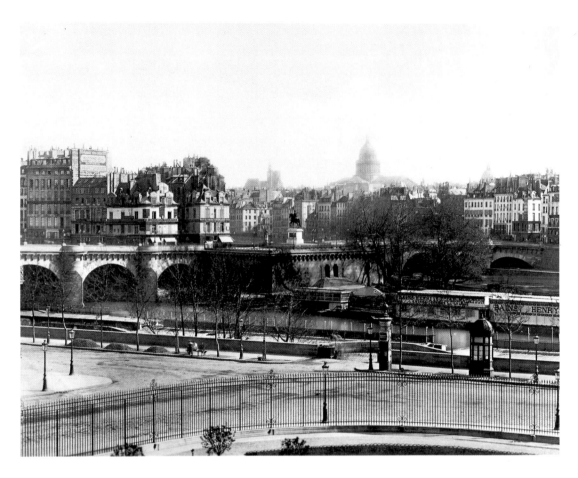

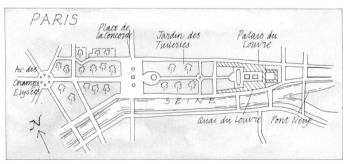

garret roofs, windows and shutters. The figures in the street below have become insignificant, reduced in scale to mere details in the picture, standing above the patches of shadow like lead soldiers on their stands. The bottle-green water of the river is just visible in the deep trench of its embankment. The Seine was becoming increasingly industrialized: according to Zola 'strange masses peopled the river' in this

PARIS FROM THE BALCONY OF THE LOUVRE

This early photograph of Paris is framed around exactly the same view as Monet's painting of the Quai du Louvre, although the slow time exposure of the camera has stripped the scene of all pedestrians and passing traffic. To the left of the picture is the Pont Neuf, and in the distance, rising above the rooftops, is the dome of the Pantheon which acted as the focal point for both the paintings of the river which Monet made from the balcony of the Louvre.

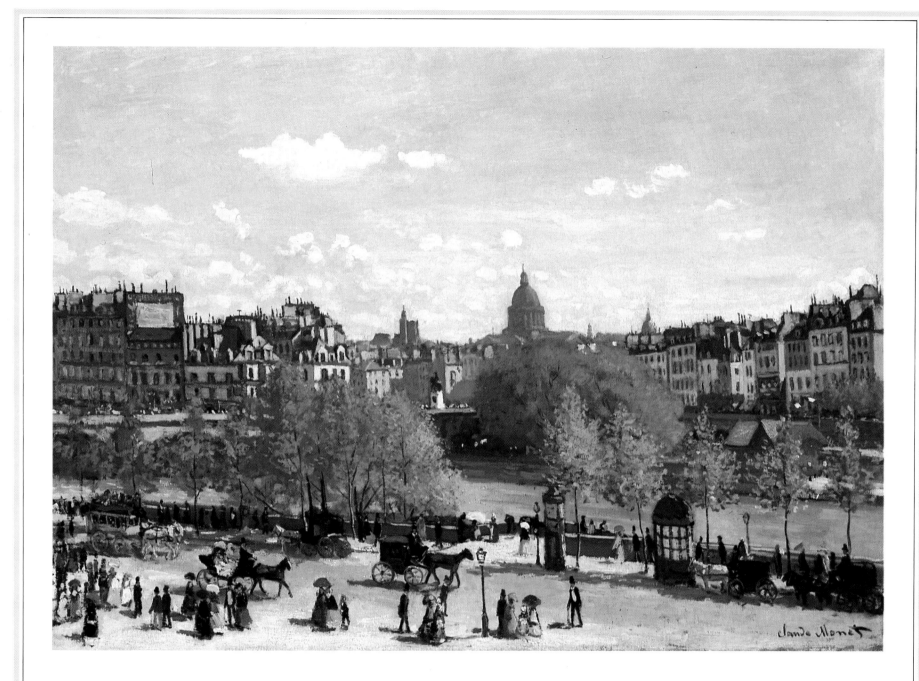

QUAI DU LOUVRE

1867

part of Paris, there was 'a sleeping flotilla of small boats and yawls, a floating wash-house, and a dredger moored to the quay … against the bank were lighters laden with coals, and barges full of mill stone, dominated as it were by the gigantic arm of a steam crane.'

Partially hidden behind a screen of trees is the solid bulk of the Pont Neuf which, despite its name, is the oldest surviving bridge in Paris and the first to be built without a clutter of houses along each side. At the time of its construction the Pont Neuf was used as a boulevard as much as a crossing point, the streets of Paris being so dark and tangled that Parisians walked across the bridge just to breathe in the fresh air. Over the years this open space had become a fairground, a jumble of stalls and barrows where mountebanks sold patented medicines, beggars held out their hands for alms, and acrobats and jugglers performed.

By the time Monet painted the bridge all this had changed; the only traces of a street-market were the bookstalls that still clung to the banks of the river. On every side the slums and backstreets of Paris were being torn down as the Emperor, Napoleon III, feared they were a breeding ground for insurrection. Having swept into power on the incoming tide of a revolution, he had no wish to leave on its ebb. The new city that he had ordered in the place of the old was designed by Baron Haussmann to be elegant, ordered and, above all, easy to police.

'Quai du Louvre' and 'Garden of the Princess' (right) are variations on each other, the same scene framed in different shaped canvases. One spans the view horizontally in the conventional landscape format, the other takes a vertical slice of the city, reaching down from the sky to the manicured gardens at the foot of the Louvre. Both compositions are tethered to the distant stump of the Pantheon, whose dome rises above the rooftops of the Left Bank. Dedicated to St Genevieve, whose remains lie beneath its foundations, the Pantheon had been completed only months before the Revolution, at which time it had instantly been siezed and redesignated a Temple of Fame, an atheist necropolis for the graves of those who had died in the name of the new liberty. Although none of the painters of this generation were to be buried there, several of its writers, particularly Zola and Victor Hugo, were to have their last remains stored beneath its dome.

What made the gallery of the Louvre particularly attractive as a location was its seclusion. In the previous few

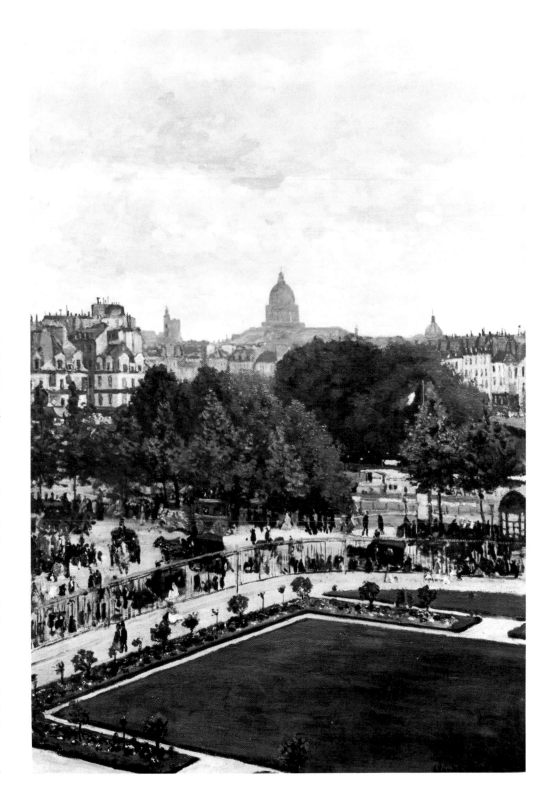

months Monet had been grappling with a purely technical problem; his ambition was to construct large and carefully thought-out paintings, which at the same time were worked with all the verve and spontaneity of a rapid sketch. What he was looking for, therefore, were sites where he could have a direct view of the subject but which still offered him the privacy of a studio. For 'Women in the Garden' it was the walls of the garden that had provided him with this seclusion, and later at Sainte-Adresse he painted the terrace view from the window of his upstairs studio for the same reason. Here in Paris he now found a balcony lifted far above the bustle and commotion of the streets, where he could work in peace, unmolested by the eyes of the curious and the opinions of boulevard critics.

From this open-air studio Monet was able to work on his paintings for some length of time, contemplating the effects of light over the city at his leisure; but despite this he has still managed to capture a sense of restless activity, as if the picture has been achieved in an instant. Cross-currents of pedestrians, carriages and horses confuse the flow of traffic in the street, their outlines faintly smudged as they hurry past. Monet's brush just avoids formulating the contours of these forms and they appear transient and blurred.

Monet used his bird's eye perspective to increase the groundplan of his design, stacking the cityscape in layers on the canvas and reducing the area of the sky. His isolated position above the street gave him the opportunity to study his subject undisturbed, but nothing could stop the clouds from shifting and altering around him. Traditionally, landscape artists had grasped at a fleeting effect of the sky in a quick sketch thrown together on the spot, and then developed the representation at leisure in the studio; but for Monet this technique lacked the authenticity of direct observation and relied too much on the fallibility of memory. Unlike Boudin, therefore, he very rarely allowed the sky to dominate the composition and, at this stage, was inclined to simplify it. In 'Garden of the Princess' he provides very little meteorological information; the luminosity of the sky has been touched with rapid brushstrokes that capture the intensity of the light without defining the exact contours of the individual clouds. Monet appears less interested in the source of the light than in its effect on the elements of the cityscape below, and as a result as much space has been given to the flat, featureless surface of the lawns as to the sky above.

GARDEN OF THE PRINCESS

1867

WITH THE SALON already under way that year, Monet arranged for 'Garden of the Princess' to be put on show in the window of Latouche's gallery on the corner of the Rue La Fayette. Here it excited some attention: the painter Diaz, whom Monet had met down in Fontainebleau, admired the audacity of its composition and paused to compliment him on its realism, but the cartoonist Daumier stormed into the gallery demanding that this 'horror' be taken out of public view. Edouard Manet passed by with a group of friends and, seeing the little knot of spectators assembled there in front of the window, was heard to comment: 'Just look at this young man who attempts to do *plein air!* As if the ancients had ever thought of such a thing.'

This is a particularly revealing remark of Manet's which exposes the prejudices of his own mind more than those of Monet, for in both technique and composition, Manet relied on the old masters. Many of his pictures had been bred from masterpieces of the past, and he said himself that as a student he learned more copying from the paintings in the Louvre than from his teachers. Consequently, elements of Venetian, Italian and, above all, Spanish art can be found in his paintings. His famous 'Olympia', which had caused such a scandal in the Salon two years before, had blended together influences of Goya and Velázquez with those of Titian and Giorgione. Yet what made the painting so shocking was its setting in the contemporary world; it was a mythology in modern dress which for all its classical precedents left no doubt that this its subject was not a goddess but a little Parisian cocotte, tense and alert as a bird.

The Salon of 1865 witnessed a bizarre encounter involving the two painters. In that year, following a series of complaints and accusations of favouritism, it had been agreed that all the paintings would be hung in alphabetical order. As a result, Monet's 'Mouth of the Seine at Honfleur' and 'Pointe de la Hève, at Low Tide' were positioned on either side of Manet's 'Olympia'. The names were so close, being only separated by a single vowel, that the hanging committee possibly had not even noticed that these pictures were painted by two different artists. When Manet arrived at the Salon on the opening day, eager to discover how his new painting had been received by the critics, he was astounded to find himself condemned on one hand for his own work, and on the other praised for two marine paintings which were nothing to do with him. 'I am being

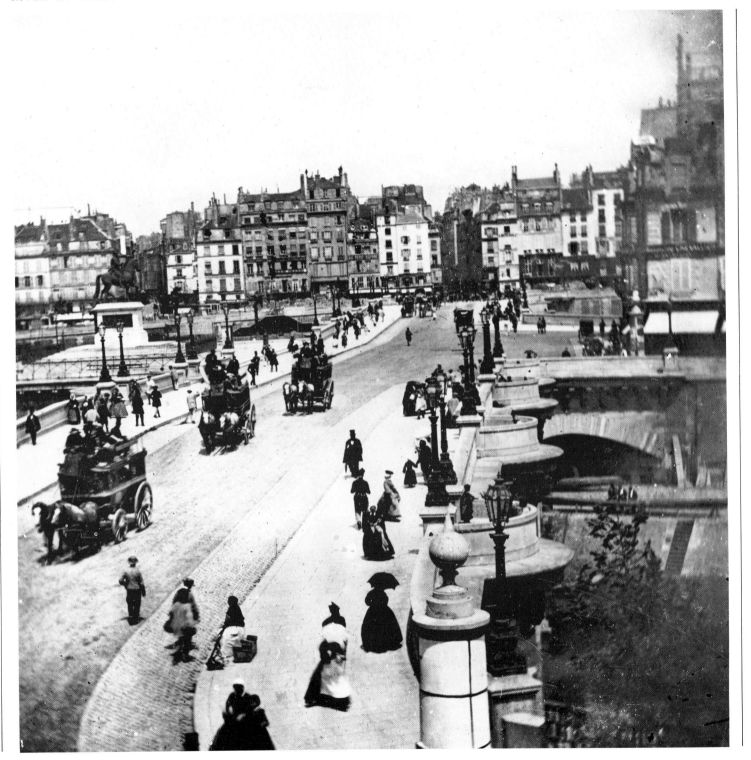

THE PONT NEUF

Despite its name, this was the earliest surviving bridge in Paris. In medieval times it had been one of the few open spaces in the city, and as such was often used as a marketplace, the wide pavements with their semicircular niches making a natural setting for stalls and sideshows. This nineteenth-century photograph of the bridge was taken from the Left Bank, looking towards the Beaubourg district of Paris. It is the opposite view from that taken by Monet in his painting of 1872, and the window from which he worked is visible at the centre of the picture.

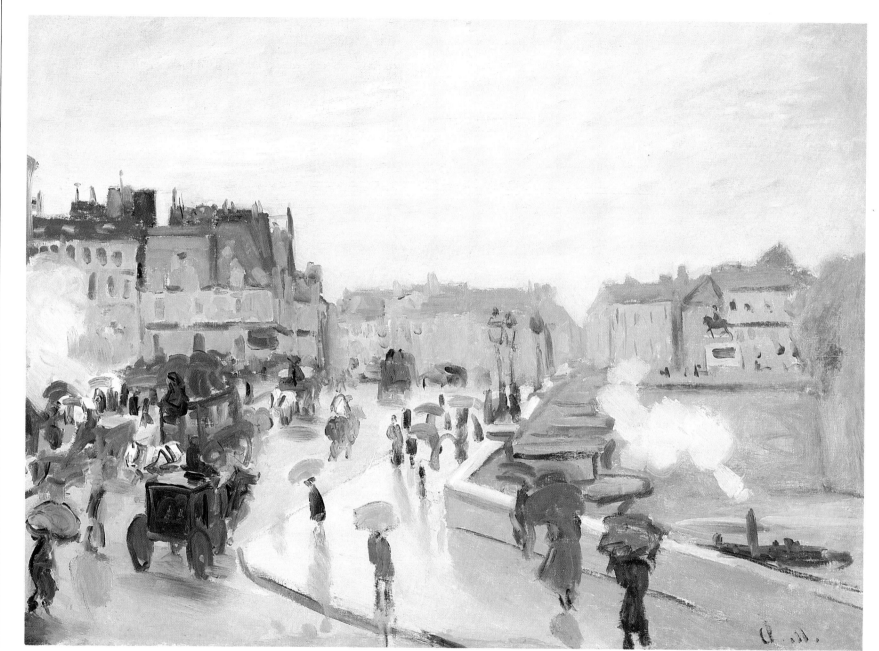

THE PONT NEUF

1872

complimented only on a painting that is not by me' he told his friends, 'One would think this to be a mystification.' He couldn't really believe that Monet existed and assumed that the name was some sort of practical joke. 'Who is this Monet who wishes to steal my thunder?' he wanted to know. As soon as they'd spotted the error, the critics were quick to see its potential and milked the pun for all it was worth: 'Monet or Manet?' asked André Gill, 'Monet. But it is to Manet that we owe this Monet. Bravo, Monet! *Merci,* Manet!'

Monet had admired the astonishing technical mastery of Manet's pictures for some years, but what impressed him more than anything was Manet's subject matter; for here was a painter of Parisian life, an artist who drew his inspiration from the everyday world of the streets around him. As a student, despite his fascination for classical painting, Manet had once paid the nude in his life class to put her clothes on again so he could paint her in contemporary dress. In his painting of the World's Fair, made later in the summer of 1867, he concentrated not so much on the engineering of the show as on the people sauntering past it. Beyond them, dashed in with a handful of brushstrokes, stretches the huge exhibition reaching out to where the Seine throws a shackle of water around the showground.

Courbet had constructed his pavilion from solid materials and at the end of the exhibition he offered it up for rent. It was probably Bazille who came up with the idea of taking it jointly as a group and exhibiting there together, as he explained in a letter to his parents:

> We have therefore decided to rent each year a large studio where we'll exhibit as many of our works as we wish. We shall invite painters we admire to send pictures, Courbet, Corot, Diaz and Daubigny … With these people, and Monet, who is stronger than all of them, we are sure to succeed.

They couldn't raise the money, however, and the plan failed. 'Bleeding ourselves as much as possible,' Bazille wrote, 'we were able to collect the sum of 2500 francs, which is not sufficient.' Through lack of finance for a collective exhibition, the idea was laid aside and the launching of the new 'group' was delayed by a further seven years.

At times the Seine glides through Paris so slowly that it scarcely appears to be moving at all; in a stiff breeze the surface of the river can even be made to turn back on itself and flow upstream. Considering how often Monet was in Paris, it is perhaps surprising that this part of the Seine's course does not feature in his paintings more often. In all his days in the capital he never once painted on the river bank as he did elsewhere, nor did he add his name to the list of artists who have stood on the quayside below Notre Dame, looking up at the body of the cathedral that crouches between the spider's legs of its buttresses on the island in the Seine.

In 1872 Monet painted the Pont Neuf once more (page 47), this time from a window above a café. It is raining and the colours are a smudge of sullen greys; the coaches and carriages and the figures hidden beneath their umbrellas are washed into the wet paintwork of the bridge with a few perfunctory strokes, the hasty brushwork marvellously capturing the drizzling weather. A tugboat passes

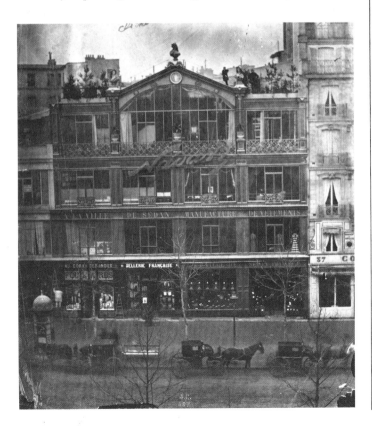

The Studio of Félix Nadar

The photographer Nadar was a friend of the artists who frequented the Café Guerbois, and regularly joined the gatherings at the cafe. His studio on the first floor of this building on the Boulevard des Capucines was lent to them in 1874 for the group exhibition which later became known as the First Exhibition of the Impressionists. Nadar was a man of varied talents and flamboyant personality, best remembered today for his aerial photographs of Paris which he took from a balloon tethered above the city.

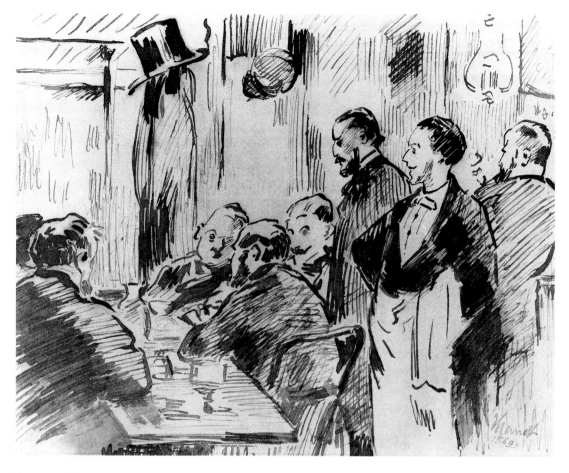

EDOUARD MANET: CAFÉ
INTERIOR, 1869

Although it bears no
inscription, it is more than
likely that this pen drawing
represents the interior of the
Café Guerbois where Manet
was a regular customer. It stood
at No. 11 Grand-Rue des
Batignolles and was decorated
with ornate tiles and glass
mirrors in elaborately
carved frames. Waiters in white
aprons pushed their way
between marble-topped tables,
serving drinks in an atmosphere
thick with cigar-smoke and
discussion.

underneath, its smoke drifting lazily ahead in the motionless air. Above it the statue of Henri IV, who had been
responsible for completing though not commissioning the
bridge, stands out against the rain-dulled buildings of the
Left Bank. This picture had probably been inspired by a
canvas that Renoir had painted from the same position in
the summer before. This shows a wider span of the same
scene with figures strolling by in the sunlight. Renoir had
posted his brother Edmond on the bridge while he worked,
to stop passers-by and ask the time, the way or anything
else he could think of that would arrest the crowd for a few
moments so that Renoir, standing at a window, could
quickly rough in the poses on his canvas.

Renoir liked to paint sunlight, which reflected his own
optimistic nature, but good weather was not essential to
Monet's painting. Any condition, however overcast, had
its possibilities for him. The colours of a sunlit day were

different from those when it rained but not necessarily
better; both had their merits. Rain turned the bridge into a
mirror as though it was the surface of the river itself.

With THE OPEN countryside only minutes away by train,
Monet rarely painted in the city: nevertheless, Paris
remained the centre of his world. In 1869 Manet invited
him to attend the meetings at the Café Guerbois of a select
group of painters, writers and critics, 'revolutionaries to a
man, and all animated by the same passionate love of art',
who every Thursday converged on this café in the Rue de
Batignolles. 'There I met Fantin-Latour and Cézanne,'
Monet recalled, 'Degas who had just returned from a trip to
Italy, the art critic Duranty, Emile Zola who was then
making his debut in literature, and several others as well.
I myself brought along Sisley, Bazille and Renoir.'

These meetings at the café made a profound impression
on Monet. 'Nothing could be more interesting than the
talks we had, with their perpetual clashes of opinion,' he
said later. 'You laid in a stock of enthusiasm that kept you
going for weeks on end until you could give final form to
the idea you had in your mind.'

Manet would sit with his elbows planted on the marble-
topped table and his hat pushed to the back of his head,
conducting the debate in his sharp Montmartre accent.
Conversation in the café was animated, often excited; the
painters 'reproached Corot for reworking his landscapes in
the studio. They vomited on Ingres.' Discussions frequently
became heated, arguments broke out and, on occasion, the
group were even reduced to blows. Manet and Duranty
quarrelled so badly one evening that they actually came to
fighting a duel, although neither managed to inflict much
damage on the other.

It may seem curious that a formal invitation was needed
to join a group such as this, but Café society in the latter
part of the nineteenth century was governed by a strict
protocol. So rigid was this discipline that Balzac was able to
assert that 'you can know a man by the café he drinks in.'

The Café Guerbois was to prove vital to the evolution of
the new school of painting; it was the common factor that
linked a group of artists many of whom were stylistically
quite different from each other. 'From these meetings,'
wrote Théodore Duret, 'sprang the powerful development
of art which was soon to go by the name Impressionism.'

49

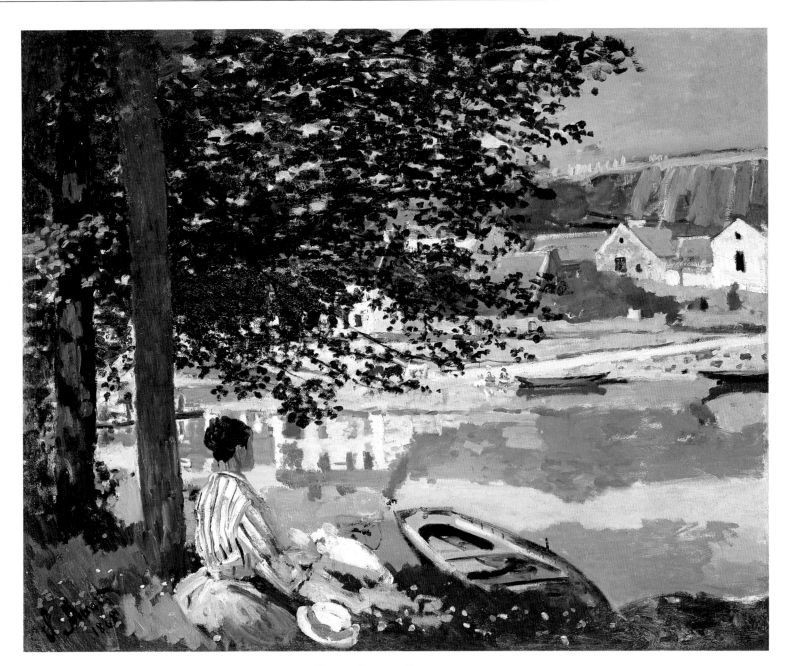

ON THE SEINE AT BENNECOURT

1868

BENNECOURT

1868

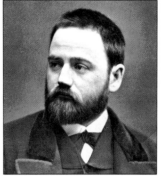

EMILE ZOLA

IT TOOK OVER TWO HOURS to reach Bennecourt from Paris by rail. The steam train out of the Gare Saint-Lazare stopped at Bonniéres-sur-Seine and from there a ferry-boat 'that creaked and grated against its chain' crossed over the river to where the village stood on the opposite shore. Bennecourt was a rural backwater, a row of hard, yellow-stone buildings strung out along the water's edge. From the river it was half hidden from view behind the small islands that lay, tufted by trees and under-growth, in the current of the stream.

Monet spent the summer of 1868 at Bennecourt with Camille and their son Jean, who was then approaching his first birthday. They stayed at an inn 'with a little grocery business attached, its large common room smelling of soap-suds, and its spacious yard full of manure, on which the ducks desported themselves'. The cooking, Zola described as 'exquisite': the omelettes overdone, the sausages greasy and the bread so hard that it was painful to cut.

Only one painting remains to commemorate this brief summer holiday in the country: 'On the Seine at Benne-court' (opposite). In this little canvas Camille sits in the long grass, her hat off and her skirts cushioned out around her waist. She stares across the calm mirror of the water to where the sturdy buildings of the village castellate the distant riverbank. Above her head the trees spread out their fronds of shadowed foliage, filtering the sunlight and forming a pattern on the canvas as dark and intricate as the pierced woodwork of a cathedral screen.

This meditative and peaceful picture was made on an island in the river, looking over towards Le Gloton, a hamlet that joins, with no perceptible break, to the village of Benne-court. The boat that brought Monet and Camille over lies tethered to the shore. Monet had prob-ably rented this for the summer so that they could enjoy the tranquillity of the Seine, 'living on its waters for days together'. Twenty years later, in his novel *L'Oeuvre*, Zola described just such a couple 'rowing about, discovering new countries, and lingering for hours under the willows on the banks, or in the little creeks, dark with shade. Between the islands scattered along the stream there was a shifting and mysterious city, a network of passages along which, with the lower branches of the trees caressingly brushing against them, they softly glided along, as it were, in the world, with the ringdoves and the kingfishers.'

Peeping through the foliage at the centre of the painting, its reflection lying unbroken on the still water beside Camille, is the inn where Monet and his family stayed that summer. It was probably Zola who had recommended the place to them, as only a year before he had spent some weeks there with his friend Cézanne. This connection is particularly relevant, as in *L'Oeuvre* Zola was to describe an artist coming to Bennecourt with his girlfriend, just as Monet had done that summer. This painter, Claude Lantier, is a cunning mixture of Manet, Monet and Cézanne: in fact, he seems to grow from one into the next as the book progresses.

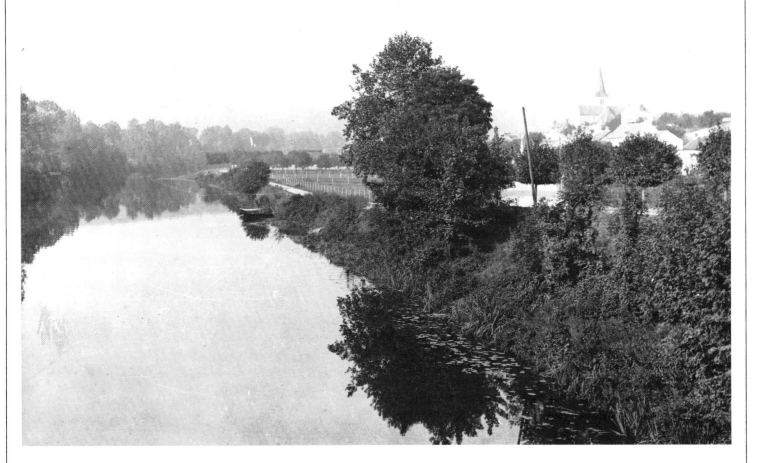

In the summer of 1868, Monet and his future wife, Camille, stayed for several weeks in the village of Bennecourt. It was a small rustic village on the border of Normandy; there was no bridge over the river and the only way to reach it from the far shore was by chain-ferry. Monet's single painting commemorating the visit was made on the island which lies to the extreme left of this photograph, from a viewpoint looking in towards the village.

Monet's painting is vibrant with invention. Bright eyes of light wink through the shaded foliage; the extremities of the foliage are scribbled in across the middle distance with wicked little strokes of the brush. In the sky and water broad patterns of flat paint are accented by sharp touches of colour around about them. The picture appears hasty and impulsive, but it is more deliberate than it may seem; the canvas was not dashed off in the inspiration of an afternoon. The thick paintwork of the buildings was already dry when the screen of foliage was added; this is demonstrated by the fact that the dark pigment in some of the outer leaves has torn as it was dragged across the rough texture beneath. Monet built the painting up over a period of days,

deliberating on the overall design, calculating and reworking effects of colour and brushwork.

What lends the painting its vital, sketchy appearance is Monet's technique of leaving the colours as they came from his palette, not modifying them with glazes. Oil paint is versatile; it can be either opaque or translucent depending on how it is mixed. The raw colour as it comes from the tube tends to be translucent; thinned with turpentine it is reduced to a fine stain that just tints the canvas. The same colour mixed with lead white, however, becomes opaque and fat as butter, a thick layer of pigment that covers the canvas and obliterates the preparations beneath it. In the past the old masters had used both these possibilities of the medium, modelling the lit areas of their pictures in a crust of solid paint and then developing the shadows with glazes of transparent colour floated into place when the underlayers had dried. These glazes enriched the surface of the painting, producing deep and mysterious colours that glowed like a stained-glass window in the darkness. But there was also a danger that they might soften the clarity of the drawing and destroy the impact of its colour; it used to be said that glazes 'eat the light' in a painting. Monet had gradually rejected the use of glazes, impatient with the fact that they had to be worked in preplanned stages over a period of time and did not allow for any immediate response to the landscape. In 'On the Seine at Bennecourt' there is no transparent paint. Monet has mixed each of his colours on the palette and then touched them in directly on the canvas.

> When you go out to paint, try to forget what objects you have in front of you, a tree, a field. Merely think, here is a little square of blue, here is an oblong of pink, here a streak of yellow, and paint it just as it looks to you, the exact colour and shape until it gives you your own naive impression of the scene.

The technique as described by Monet sounds simple enough, but it requires painstaking concentration, as each tone and colour must be exactly right before it reaches the canvas. The effect, however, cannot be matched; it is fresh and spontaneous and gives the illusion of having been effortlessly achieved.

The light generated on the water is a masterpiece of observation. Monet has analyzed each colour in turn, dissecting the overall effect with the precision of a surgeon. Few artists before could claim to have stolen the afternoon light with such skill, but here Monet and his contemporaries had one advantage over the landscape painters of the past. This was the new zinc paint tubes, originally invented to hold toothpaste but quickly adapted to take oil paint. Previously, preparation of the paint colours, the mixing of pigments and oils, had been a laborious part of the process of painting. With the new tubes of prepared colour, Monet was able to stand on the banks of the Seine and study the light for days on end. He was no longer tied to the studio; he could carry his painting out into the countryside each day and work there at leisure without having to return for fresh paint. None of the paintings of Corot, Boudin or Jongkind would have been technically feasible before the invention of the paint tube although, in the early part of the century, various attempts had been made to make oil colours more portable. Leather pouches of pigment that had to be pricked with a pin had been tried, as had stainless steel syringes packed with paint. None of these systems had worked too well, and as a result it had been the watercolourists who had monopolized open-air painting.

The various photographs and paintings of Monet at work show that he never took out more equipment than he needed and kept his materials down to the bare necessities. He carried a light folding easel, a wooden box of paints that also held his brushes, and a square sketching palette. As a young man he preferred to stand as he worked, shading the canvas with a large umbrella when the sun was shining on its surface.

In 'On the Seine at Bennecourt' there is a subtle alteration in focus, a shift of emphasis so slight, so seductive that we are scarcely aware of its insistence. Camille sits in the long grass gazing at the scene before her, engrossed in a daydream. She acts as a signpost in the composition, redirecting the focus of the painting. Instead of holding our attention, she deflects it towards the sun-drenched village on the far shore. The dark screen of leaves, the filtered light and the direction of her gaze all combine to thrust our interest away from the foreground into the whole area of the painting until we too, like her, become absorbed in the powdery light beyond.

It is perhaps fitting that Camille has her face turned away, for she remains a strangely indistinct figure in Monet's life. She frequently appears in his paintings, sometimes staring out of the canvas at the viewer but more often in the distance, an anonymous figure with a parasol standing on the banks of the river, or walking through the meadows and poppy-fields of the Ile de France, added to the picture as a colour detail. There is no indication of what sort of life she led with Monet, how she coped with his driving ambition, whether she saw him as the leader of a new school or simply as an artist with incomprehensible ideas, the painter of pictures that wouldn't sell. It would be convenient if Claude Lantier's girlfriend Christine, who sat on the island at Bennecourt 'with parted lips, her eyes watching the blue sky', were a portrait of Camille. It may be that, like her fictional counterpart, Camille was puzzled by the painter's colour, his bright water and blue-tinted trees and felt secretly that 'there ought not to be any blue trees in nature'.

IN MONET'S LETTERS there are references to other pictures painted during that summer in Bennecourt, but only this one has survived. Its subject somehow evades definition, for it is not about a figure, a village or a landscape. It is about a moment in time, a few drowsy hours of sunlight that have been arrested and preserved on canvas. As if it were a page torn from a diary, Monet offers us a fragment of his own life and it is this that makes the picture so appealing. Instead of contriving a fiction, Monet allows the picture to become autobiographical, holding it up as a window to his life. The subject of his painting has become as portable as the materials that create it.

Monet's intensely personal view of the world around him could be looked upon as an aspect of Realism were it not for the fact that it has none of the overtones, none of the aggressive fatalism that Zola, Courbet and the others of that calling have discharged into the title. Back in 1863 Castagnary had noted a new spirit emerging in landscape painting and had named it 'Naturalism': 'The naturalist school,' he announced, 'declares that art is the expression of life under all phases and on all levels, and that its sole aim is to reproduce nature by carrying it to its maximum power and intensity: it is truth balanced with science. The naturalist school re-establishes the broken relationship between man and nature.'

During the course of his life, Monet was to be called a Naturalist, an Intransigent, an Actualist and finally an Impressionist. He acknowledged each of these titles in turn, although he appeared to set little store by any of them. It was the attitude of mind that concerned him, not the name it was given, and as an old man he was proud to announce: 'I have been, I am, and always shall be, an independent.'

THE HOLIDAY IN BENNECOURT came to an abrupt end when Monet ran out of money and was turned out of the inn. In a letter to Bazille, he complained:

> I was certainly born under an unlucky star. I have just been thrown out of the inn, naked as a worm. I have found a roof for Camille and my poor little Jean for a few days in the country. This evening I am leaving for Le Havre to see about trying something with my collector. My family have no intention of doing anything more for me. I don't even know where I'll sleep tomorrow. Your very harassed friend – Claude Monet.
>
> P.S. I was so upset yesterday that I had the stupidity to throw myself in the water. Fortunately, no harm came of it.

Whether the postscript really signifies that Monet tried to do away with himself it is hard to say; the story sounds rather melodramatic, especially as the remark was only added to the letter as an afterthought. It may be that he was exaggerating the incident somewhat in the hope of prompting money from Bazille by return of post.

The collector that Monet refers to in this letter was a ship builder called Gaudibert, who had recently bought some of his landscapes. Earlier that year Monet had taken part in a large marine exhibition in Le Havre, along with Courbet, Boudin and Manet. The show had gone off well enough, although it had done little to relieve his acute financial problem: 'I'm getting very low,' he'd confided to Bazille. 'Disappointments, insults, hopes, new disappointments – you see, my dear friend. At the exhibition in Le Havre, I sold nothing. I possess a silver medal worth 15 francs, some splendid reviews in local papers, there you are; it's not much to eat.'

To make matters worse, his creditors had swooped down on him at the end of the exhibition and carried off his remaining pictures. These had been sold off for next to nothing and it was in this way that Gaudibert had come to buy them so cheaply. Gaudibert was not insensitive to the artist's problem, however, and when Monet wrote to him from Bennecourt he came up trumps. He commissioned a portrait of himself and his wife and, in the meantime, he put Monet on a small allowance.

'Thanks to the gentleman of Le Havre who comes to my aid, I am enjoying the most complete tranquillity.' he was able to tell Bazille a few weeks later from Fécamp. 'Consequently, my wish would be to continue in this way in a hidden bit of quiet nature. Frankly I don't envy you being in Paris ... One is too much taken up with what one sees and hears in Paris, however firm one might be; what I'm doing here will have the merit of not resembling anyone, at least I think so, because it will simply be the expression of what I shall have felt, I myself, personally.'

LA GRENOUILLERE

1869

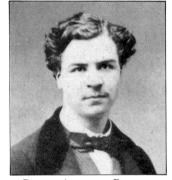

PIERRE-AUGUSTE RENOIR

Hᴀʟꜰ ᴀ ᴍɪʟᴇ ʙᴇʟᴏᴡ Bᴏᴜɢɪᴠᴀʟ, in the slack curve of a bend in the river, lay the café of La Grenouillère. It floated on the edge of the Seine, shaded by poplar trees and tethered to the banks of the Ile de Croissy. Noisy and high-spirited, bustling with weekend crowds, La Grenouillère provided an antidote to the claustrophobia of city life: summer dresses, parasols and top hats mingled with rowing caps and striped vests. Women chatted, boats scudded about the water and dogs dozed in the sunlight.

In the 1860s boating was all the rage. Fresh air and exercise were a new discovery, and the river Seine had become the playground of Paris. Rowing clubs were formed, races and regattas organized; the same spirit that put three men in a boat on the Thames brought the Parisians tumbling out of the city on Sunday afternoons. It was to this passion for outdoor living that La Grenouillère owed its popularity. The railway track to Saint-Germain had made it easy to reach, as trains from the Gare Saint-Lazare stopped at the Chatou bridge. The 'American Omnibus' ran a service from Paris to Bougival and ferries crossed over regularly to the island from the mainland.

Monet came to La Grenouillère in the summer of 1869. He had moved into a house nearby, in the village of Saint-Michel on the hillside overlooking the river. As usual he was impoverished, and in an attempt to rustle up business he wrote a grovelling letter to Arsène Houssaye, who had recently bought his portrait of Camille:

The settling in is finished and I'm in very good condition and full of courage for work, but alas the fatal rejection has almost taken the bread out of my mouth. I have thought, and I hope you will excuse me, that since you formerly found a canvas of mine to your taste, you might like to see the few that I have been able to save, for I thought that you would be good enough to come to my aid a little, since my position is almost desperate and the worst is that I can't even work.

It was a well-aimed letter but it had no effect. Houssaye was not to be persuaded into buying any more pictures and within weeks Monet had not only run out of paint, he had nothing to eat either.

Fortunately Renoir was living not far away. He was equally impoverished and cutting down on expenses that summer by staying with his parents in Louveciennes. He came from a quite different background to Monet; born in 1841, the son of a tailor from Limoges, Renoir had been brought up in the rabbit warren of congested streets around the old market of Les Halles in Paris. At the age of fourteen he was apprenticed to a porcelain works and earned a living painting decorative designs onto dinner plates. A few years later he lost this job to a machine and instead turned his talents to painting ladies' fans, and murals on café walls. With the money he made from this work he enrolled in Gleyre's classes, and it was here that he met Monet. The introduction had been brought about by Bazille who, having watched Renoir draw one day, decided that he was 'really somebody'.

Good-natured, sensual and charming, Renoir was gifted with an irrepressible love of life that was quite infectious; he used to describe himself as a cork, never fighting against the stream but always bobbing along with the current. He disliked theories and high-blown ideas on art. He once told Gleyre that he painted simply to amuse himself, and consequently his fame as a pioneer of modern art remained something of a mystery to him:

> While others shouted, broke window panes, teased the models and disturbed the teacher, I was very quiet in my corner, very attentive, very docile, studying the model, listening to the teacher... And yet it was I whom they called revolutionary.

Renoir's attitude, during this summer on the banks of the Seine, was one of philosophical acceptance: 'We don't eat every day,' he wrote to Bazille, 'yet I'm happy in spite of it because as far as painting is concerned, Monet is good company.' The letter went off without a stamp.

Poverty was a way of life for Renoir and he was able to give Monet expert tuition on how to cope with it. He obtained an allotment and planted it with potatoes; in the evenings, as a more immediate measure, he would walk down to Monet's house with his pockets stuffed with scraps of bread that he had collected from his parents' dinner table. Monet hated living in these reduced circumstances and he found it hard to be on the receiving end of such charity: 'Renoir is bringing us crusts from his home so that we don't starve,' he told Bazille bitterly. 'For eight days now we've had no bread, wine, fire to cook on or light – it's horrible.'

For several weeks, in the late summer of 1869, Monet and Renoir worked together at La Grenouillère. It was an ideal subject; colourful and gregarious, it served them as both an open-air studio and a dive where they could drown their sorrows. The café itself was built on the shallow hull of an 'enormous raft' which lay a few yards offshore. A wooden superstructure of trelliswork and shuttering supported tarred roofs trimmed with bunting. There was nothing unusual about this construction: contemporary photographs of the river show that the Seine was once cluttered with every sort of floating contraption; houseboats, converted barges and dance floors set up on rickety pontoons.

The inside of the café was strictly functional: bare floors, scrubbed tables and hard benches. According to Maupassant this inner room was the haunt of 'journalists, show offs, young men with private incomes, scoundrels, degenerates and rogues'. There were dances on Thursday nights, and at weekends the interior was a bustle of activity and crowded as a railway carriage. 'The customers seated at the tables swallow red, white, yellow and green liquids ... a swimmer appears on the roof each second and jumps into the water, splashing those nearby, who respond with wild cries.'

Running from the prow of the raft was a gangplank linking La Grenouillère to a tiny island. This was round and slightly humped, with a single tree sprouting from its centre, which had earned it the name of the 'Flower-Pot'. Beyond it was the swimming area, the water here being deep enough to take the bathers as they hurled themselves off the roof of the café. By all accounts it was only the men who indulged in these acrobatic feats; the ladies had discovered more graceful ways of submerging themselves:

> To those who have not witnessed the gambols of the French ladies in the water, the mode of bathing is very curious: they often form a circle, taking hold of each others' hands, and dancing or rather bobbing up and down in the water, without ever wetting the head, which is bonneted, for two hours together in the afternoon ... Nor is this excessive bathing confined to the lower orders, or those in rude health. Delicate ladies and their children generally bathe twice a day and remain no inconsiderable time splashing in the water.

In writing his memoir of his father, Jean Renoir caused some confusion about La Grenouillère. He, like the dealer Vollard before him, assumed it to be another name for the Fournaise Restaurant, but this is not the case; the two were quite different. Fournaise's restaurant was a solid brick building further upstream on the island of Chatou, not far from the railway bridge. It was altogether more respectable than La Grenouillère, a place to linger over lunch and let the day slip by in the warm shadows of the red-striped awnings. Renoir was often there as a young man and was given free meals in exchange for his paintings; when he pointed out that they had practically no market value, Fournaise would reply that he needed the canvas to cover the damp patches on his walls. It was here, on the first floor terrace overlooking the river, that Renoir later painted his famous picture of the 'Déjeuner des Canotiers'.

Despite this misunderstanding, Jean Renoir did explain how La Grenouillère came by its name. It translates literally as the 'frog-pond' but this does not simply mean that the place was crawling with frogs. There was a *double entendre* here, an in-joke that would have been well understood at the time. In the late nineteenth century a 'frog' was a particular breed of professional flirt, quite distinct from the Parisian prostitutes who patrolled a set beat on the city pavements. The Grenouillères were freelance cocottes who gave their favours easily, going where the fancy took them and drawn to the gaiety of the riverside cafés like moths to the flame of a candle. According to Renoir, the Grenouillères were usually 'good sorts'; they brought a suggestion of sensuality with them to the café, a current of excitement and flirtation, and in turn they gave the place its name.

MONET'S AMBITION, while he was working at La Grenouillère, was to paint a large exhibition piece for the next year's Salon. As with all his previous tableaux, he set about it methodically, testing out the subject in a series of experimental paintings. These preparatory paintings of La Grenouillère were not really studies in the literal meaning of the word, but were more like dress-rehearsals for the final performance, real indicators of the major work to come.

The first and the most remarkable of these preparatory paintings (opposite) was made on the riverbank looking directly across at the Flower-Pot island. The network of gangplanks around La Grenouillère formed a natural compound for the boats: splinter-sharp sculls, rowing boats and the more graceful skiffs with carved seats in their sterns were held here and could be hired from the ticket office at

THE SEINE AT CHATOU

In the late nineteenth century, when Monet and Renoir were working on the Seine, the suburbs of Paris were still semi-rural. The islands were heavily wooded and the towpaths used as allotments or for grazing cattle. Floating in the foreground of this view is one of the many houseboats that used to clutter the riverbank. Its construction is similar in many ways to the cafe of La Grenouillère which was situated two miles upstream. Stretched across the far horizon is the Chatou railway bridge which carried the track out to Saint-Germain-en-Laye.

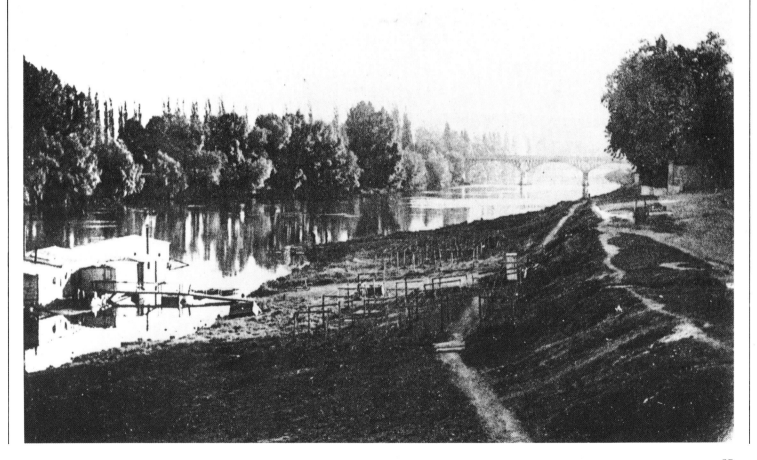

the entrance to the café. It is this enclosed pool of water that fills the lower margin of Monet's picture. Part of the words *'location canotage'* can clearly be seen stencilled to the parapet of the café that juts into the righthand side of the canvas, while the poster pinned to the bows below is probably an advertisement for a regatta in Bougival.

Monet once said that he wished he had been born blind and only gained his sight when he became a painter, so that he could observe the colours before his eyes without having any previous knowledge of their identity. In this way he felt he would be able to study nature without any preconceptions, with no prejudice, no expectation of the subject before him; his mind would be as blank as the film in a camera and the painting would record only what his eyes reported.

This idea illustrates Monet's determination to analyze nature objectively, and it was this principle that he managed to put into practice in his painting of La Grenouillère.

RENOIR: LA GRENOUILLÈRE

1869

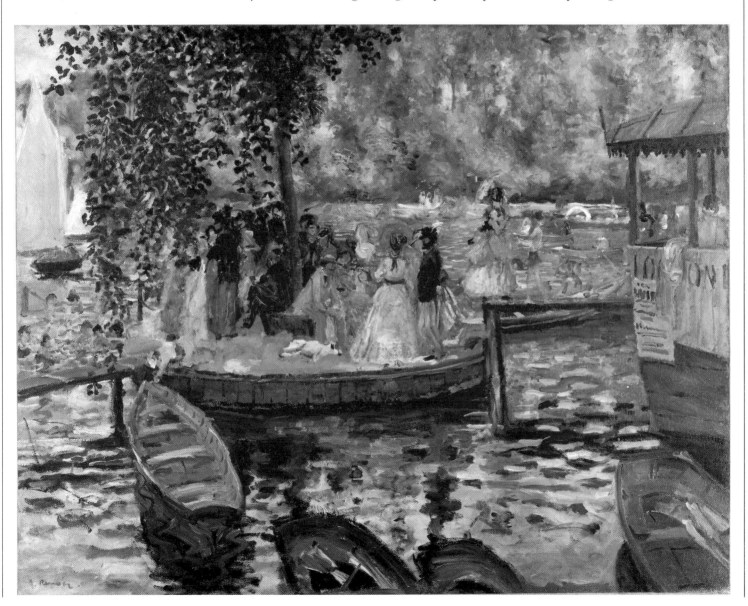

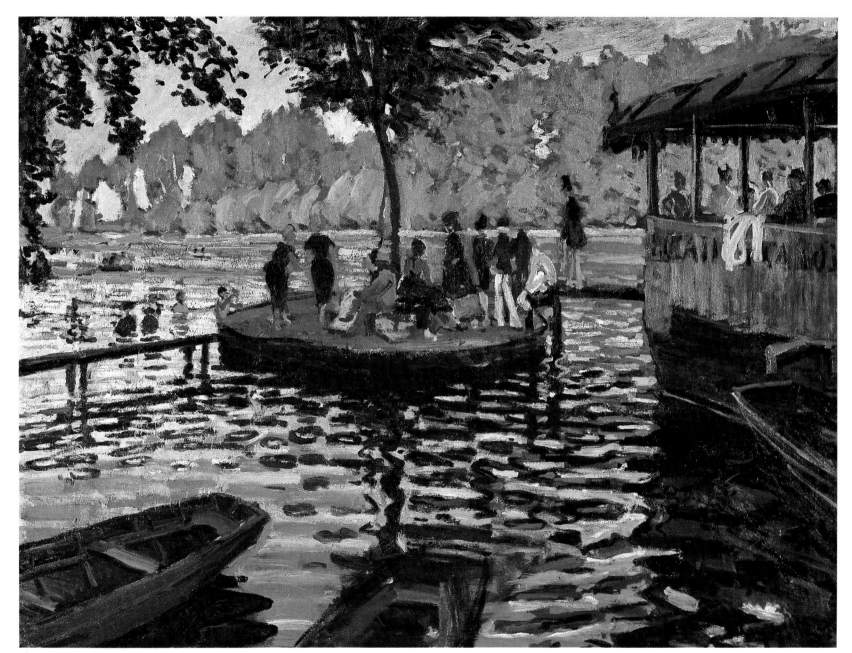

LA GRENOUILLÈRE

1869

The brushwork is rapid and confident; Monet seems to write down the whole picture in a series of short, blunt strokes, quickly jotting in the details as if they were an afterthought. Ignoring his knowledge of the subject, he paints only what he can see with his eyes at any given moment. The distant trees have been sculpted from light and shade without any attempt to imitate the texture of summer foliage. Figures are included in the painting, but Monet has not tried to make them the focus of the picture; they are no more important to the composition than the silhouette of the foliage above or the timbers of the café beside them. The great mackerel-skin of water dominates the painting; slabs of white and blue paint laid down beside black, interrupted by notes of warm ochre, miraculously become rippling water in our minds. The complex image of light sparking and winking off the river has been converted into a vibrant patchwork of broken colour.

In this picture, made in the late summer of 1869, Monet sowed the seeds for much of his later work. It has all the qualities we associate with him: the uncontrived view of contemporary life, the optimism, the broken brushwork and, above all, this miraculous alchemy of colour in which sunlight is translated into touches of paint.

Renoir, meanwhile, had made a painting of exactly the same scene. In his canvas the arrangement of the Flower-Pot island, with the tip of the café on one side and a section of the catwalk running back towards the shore on the other, is almost identical to Monet's. The handling of the paint, however, is by no means the same. There are subtle variations of technique and design that reveal two very different artists at work. Renoir is more involved with his subject; he was a natural portrait painter and could not resist elaborating the figures in his picture. Dappled sunlight plays over long dresses, straw hats and fluttering ribbons. Instinctively, Renoir has brought the little crowd of people to the centre of attention, so that we can almost hear the buzz and chatter of their voices. The trees behind them are painted softly, the structure of their leaves dissolved in a haze of brushstrokes. Less concerned with the water that laps around the boats in the foreground, Renoir has cropped it off a few feet from the hull of the café. The picture is enclosed and in many ways more intimate than Monet's. By reducing the foreground and lifting the trees into the upper reaches of the canvas he has compressed the overall sense of space, enveloping his figures in a cocoon of summer foliage.

Despite the differences of temperament between the two painters, the compositions of these two paintings are fundamentally the same; though not identical in every detail, they are clearly twins. It is often said that they were painted together, using the same subject on the same day and that their similarity grew from this spontaneous creative combustion. There is no reason to doubt this, although the two painters were not actually standing as close as it might appear. Monet was working at the water's edge and his composition reaches down to within a few yards of his feet. Taking bearings on the swag of leaves hanging down in the foreground of his painting and comparing it to the other, it appears that Renoir was standing about six yards to his left. More importantly, it is clear that he was higher up than Monet – the horizon line in Renoir's picture is well above the heads of the figures whereas in Monet's it is at shoulder height. This suggests that Renoir was standing further back on the island, possibly on the balcony of one of the changing rooms. From there he could have stretched his picture to include the whole scene: the framework of the café, the boat compound and even Monet working on the edge of the river; but he has chosen to take a small section of what he sees, as if looking down a telescope the wrong way.

The similarity between the two paintings cannot be a coincidence; it must have been contrived. It is unlikely that two painters working at their canvases from different positions and angles would by chance come up with identical compositions. One of the paintings must have been started first, if only by a few minutes, and the other based on it. This may seem an insignificant point, but it betrays intriguing evidence of collusion between the two artists. Far from working independently, they appear to have collaborated on their pictures, adopting the same composition as a conscious experiment, as though they too wanted to compare their respective styles.

Monet made another of these preparatory paintings (page 63), presumably from the gangplank that ran across the water to the main hull of the café. It looks downstream towards Rueil, a little village beyond Bougival, on the far shore. Figures teeter along the long catwalk that links the Flower-Pot island to the shore, their beetle-black bodies silhouetted against the bright water, while others splash about the river. The determined horizontal of this catwalk cuts straight through the long avenue of the river, dividing

BOATS ON THE BANKS OF THE SEINE

The enormous popularity of boating gradually transformed the Seine. Pontoons such as the one in this photograph were constructed along the riverbanks, sculls and rowing skiffs were hired out by the hour, and waterside cafés sprang up to cater for the crowds of Parisians who invaded the river at weekends.

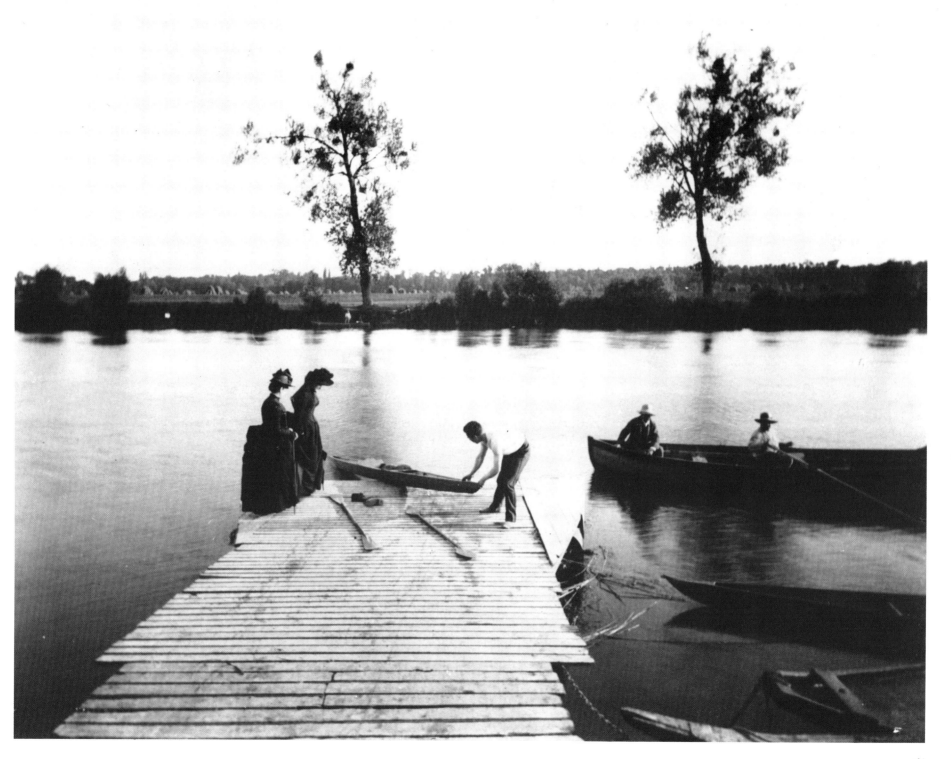

it halfway up the picture and interrupting the continuity of its perspective. Unlike Sisley and Pissarro, who often created deep tunnelled compositions, Monet preferred to measure space in width and very rarely allows our attention to drift away into the far distance. In this case, he has ruled off the foreground with the thin line of the catwalk, placing three figures against the water, strategically positioned to disrupt the view of the river beyond.

By the end of September Monet was ready to start work on the final painting, but he could not afford the materials to do so. He was beside himself with anger. All his life he had had nothing but contempt for money and he couldn't now believe that anything as petty as the lack of a little ready cash should stand in the way of his ambition:

'Here I am again stopped for want of paint,' he complained to Bazille. 'Lucky soul, you will at least be able to bring back lots of canvases. Only I will have done nothing this year. It makes me furious with everyone. I am wickedly jealous, I am in a rage: if only I could work everything would be alright.'

Bazille should have been sending him fifty francs a month for 'Women in the Garden', which he had bought from Monet on the understanding that he would pay by instalments. However, Bazille was feeling the pinch as well that summer; he had recently been forced to pawn his watch and was now falling behind on his payments. Monet was not pleased by this delay, but what really incensed him was that Bazille had suggested that instead of begging, Monet would do better to earn himself some money by cutting wood.

'You say that it's not fifty, or a hundred francs that will get me out of this,' Monet continued in the same letter, 'that's possible, but if you look at it in this way, there's nothing for me to do now but to break my head against a wall because I can't lay hands on an instantaneous fortune. I had a dream, a tableau, the bathing place at La Grenouillère for which I have made some rotten sketches, but it's only a dream.'

Despite this gloom, it seems that he managed to find the money, for a final picture of La Grenouillère was made. The composition was based largely on the first study, extended to include the catwalk that features in the second. The finished picture was submitted to the Salon of 1870

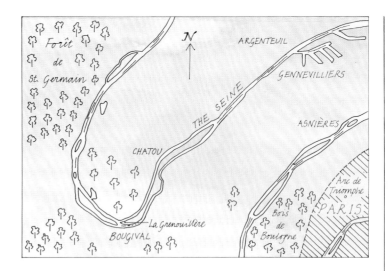

and rejected. Seventy years later it was destroyed in a Berlin bank vault, along with 'Fishing Boats at Honfleur'.

Nothing remains of La Grenouillère today. The café caught fire and was burned down. By the turn of the century all that remained was the Flower-Pot island, the 'Camembert' as it came to be known. For several years it was still a place for picnickers to moor their boats at weekends. Apollinaire visited it in 1912 and later wrote:

From the island's shores one sees
the empty canoes bumping one another
and now
neither Sunday nor the days
of the week
Neither the painters nor Maupassant
walk there
in shirtsleeves accompanied
by plump women as silly as
cabbages.
Little boats you make me so sad
From the island's shores.

Eventually the Flower-Pot disappeared also when the Seine was dredged and its banks widened to take the new diesel-powered barges. The café has gone, but its name has survived; it has been inherited by the golf club on the Ile de Croissy that overlooks the pool of water where the café once floated.

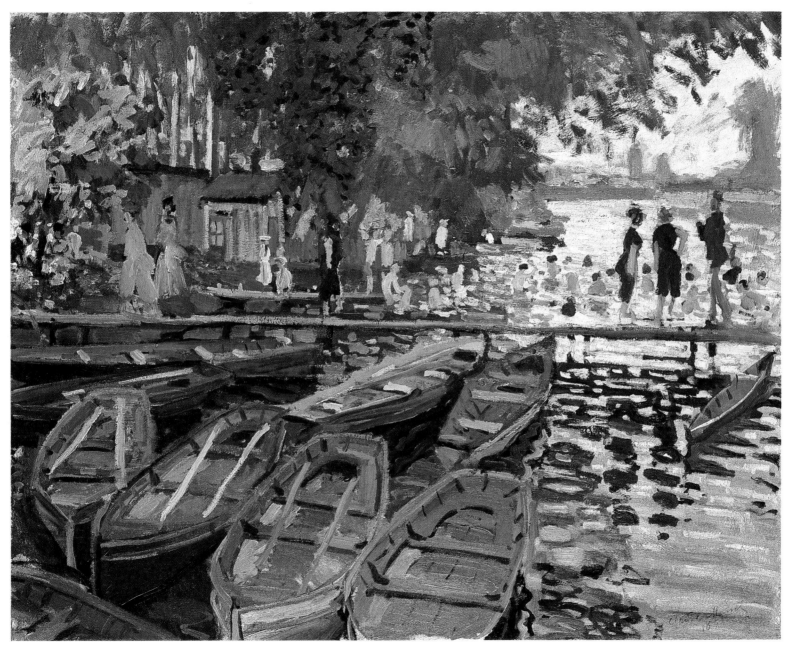

<u>B</u>ATHERS AT <u>L</u>A <u>G</u>RENOUILLÈRE

1869

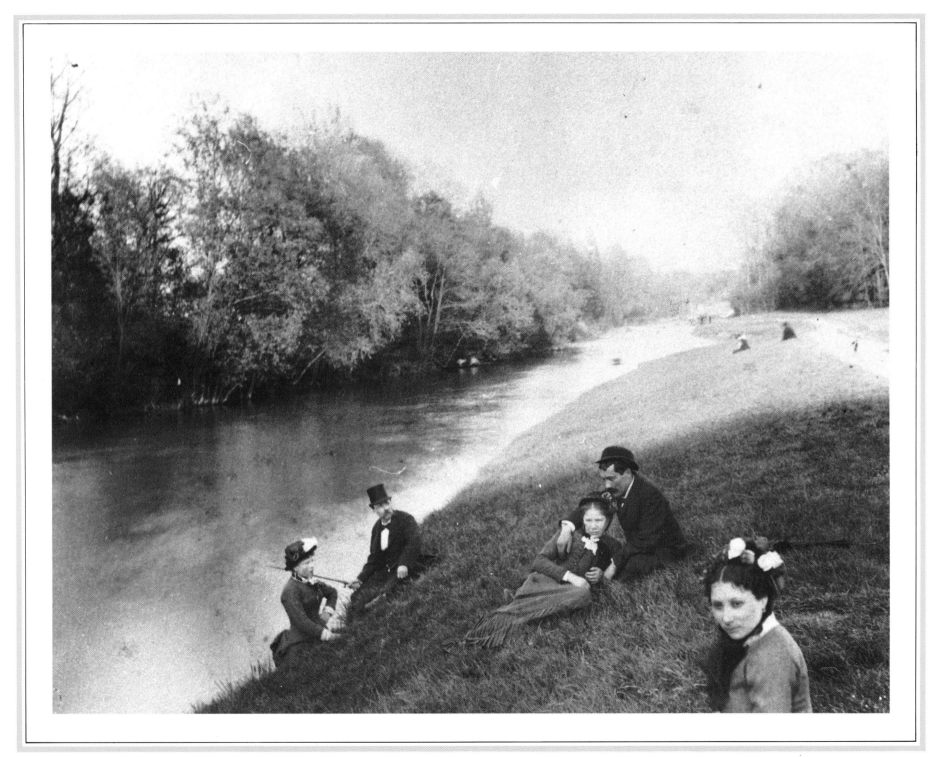

BOUGIVAL

1867-1870

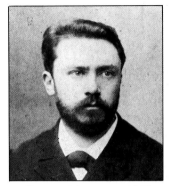

CLAUDE MONET, C. 1868

BANKS OF THE SEINE

The railway track to Saint-Germain-en-Laye and the new service of 'American' omnibuses opened the upper reaches of the Seine to Parisians. It took only fifteen minutes from the city to reach the station at Chatou, from where there was easy access to La Grenouillère and Bougival. At weekends the towpaths along the river, once the domain of the bargees, became crowded with picnickers, fishermen and courting couples.

To THE WEST OF PARIS the Seine appears to lose its sense of direction. Twisting and turning, drawing back in serpentine coils, it aimlessly searches between the villages of the Ile de France. So vague is its path that from the air its course resembles a piece of stretched elastic that has suddenly snapped. Before the nineteenth century navigation was not easy, for although Paris is only a hundred and ten miles from the coast as the crow flies, a barge following the line of the river was forced to travel over twice that distance before reaching the city. The current could also be erratic, as the riverbanks had been artificially narrowed in places to raise the level of water over the shallows. These passes, as they were known, made the water accelerate and as a result it could take up to forty men and women, as well as horses, to tow a boat through the bottle-neck. At one time there had been villages in the Seine valley whose entire population made a living from the single task of hauling barges in this way.

Eventually, an ambitious system of locks was planned to control the flow of the river as it made its way out towards the sea. In 1838 the first and largest of these was built at Bougival, a small town on the outskirts of Paris. The water-gates took advantage of the natural terrain of the river, ingeniously corking up the gaps in the vertebrae of small islands that divided the central stream, while a weir further down at Bezons acted as a safety valve and prevented the river from flooding its banks.

These waterworks had put Bougival on the map and lent the place an air of importance, but the river had brought other activities to the town. Often at weekends, the town was decked out with bunting for the regattas. There were classes for rowing skiffs, sailing boats and steam pinnaces. Bazille had won a race there in 1865 in a boat called 'La Cagnotte', but discovered to his annoyance that, just as racehorses are given more credit than their jockeys, so the name of the boat was reported in the newspapers rather than his own.

La Grenouillère was only a short walk away, floating on the slack water created by the Bougival locks. It was to become the most famous of the cafés on the Ile de Croissy but it was not there alone. Inns and drinking houses littered the island, wooden balconies overhung the water, boats were tied to wooden jetties, and pontoons led from one establishment to the next. There were cafés and guinguettes, separated from each other by flimsy fencing. At Bougival was to be found the 'Bal des Canotiers', later the setting for a painting by Renoir, with its trellised arms embracing a tiny patch of ground where the oarsmen danced with their girlfriends. These cafés were simple, half rustic places but Renoir, always eager to look on the bright side, saw only their grace and endowed them with an Olympian charm that they possibly did not deserve. Zola's vivid image of a waterside café, although describing a point on the river two miles closer to Paris, is probably nearer to the truth:

They took a table on a sort of wooden terrace belonging

to an eating house that reeked of fat and wine. The place was full of shouting, singing and the clatter of crockery, and in each private and public dining room there was some club outing shouting away, and the thin partitions adding a vibrating sonority to the din. The stairs shook as the waiters ran up.

Out on the terrace the river breezes dispelled the odours of burnt fat ... To right and left stretched a double row of cafés and booths, and looking through the scant yellow foliage you could make out bits of white tablecloth, black coats, and bright coloured skirts; people were going up and down bare headed, running and laughing, and the dismal strains of the barrel organ were mingled with the bawling of the crowd. A smell of fried fish and dust hung in the still air ... And beyond all this the serene beauty of evening was falling over the Seine and its hills, vague bluish vapours bathing the trees in transparent mist.

Riotous living on the islands in the river was confined to weekends and summer months, however, and hardly ruffled the placidity of Bougival. In the 1860s it was well known as a suburb on the fringes of Paris, a quiet town where the plastered buildings, with their wrought iron gates, shuttered windows and high garden walls, breathed an air of privacy. Bougival lay in the cleft of two hills, its main street reaching down from a dusty church square towards the river. Trees lined the waterfront, shading the slate-roofed houses behind with limbs that had been pollarded so sternly over the years that they had come to resemble the candlesticks in a synagogue. Bougival's situation in those days was ideal, as it was within easy reach of the city by omnibus and yet still untouched by the industrialization whose stain was spreading out from Paris along the line of the river.

The district had its share of celebrities: Bizet had lived there for some years and Saint-Saëns composed in the little village of Voisins, on the hillside above the river, despite the fact that the locals thought he was deranged and treated him with grave suspicion. Alexandre Dumas had built himself a massive house, the Château Monte Cristo as it became known, between Bougival and Port Marly. Here he had succeeded in squandering the enormous royalties earned from his novels: construction alone had cost him a small fortune. The ground was too soft for the foundations and it was necessary to build the house on an elaborate system of cellars, complex as a Piranesi print, that reached down to the bedrock. To satisfy Dumas' love of the exotic, two turbaned architect-slaves, once the property of the Bey of Tunis, had been imported from Africa to decorate the rooms with Moslem designs. As soon as the chateau was finished it was opened to the public, and sightseers flocked from all over Paris to take a look at this remarkable folly with its sculpted facades, fluttering pennants, wrought iron balconies and weathercocks. There had been English gardens, fountains, artificial streams and avenues of trees named after the characters in the author's novels. Dumas had worked, meanwhile, in a Gothic pavilion guarded by a stone dog, with the motto *Cave Canem*, and a moat flooded with water pumped from the river. It had been open house on all occasions and at mealtimes Dumas had often confessed to his friends that he couldn't introduce them to the other guests as he didn't yet know them himself. Inevitably, the house had ruined him; even the tide of romantic novels that had flowed from the moated grotto failed to wash away the debts and in the 1850s Dumas had been forced to sell up.

Monet's first pictures of Bougival were made in the hard winter of 1867. Standing on the shore, looking down towards La Grenouillère, he painted two canvases of the frozen river. The landscape is quite still, the sky a flat gun-metal tone of grey. Ice-floes, solid and geometric as the unformed parts of a Chinese puzzle, rest becalmed in the water. Small figures stand out against the ground as they scratch about the banks, boats lie locked in the snow and the splinters of bare poplars are mirrored in the river below. It's not clear what it was that brought Monet to Bougival in the depths of winter. There would have been no boating at that time of year and the riverside cafés would all have been closed. Several of his friends lived in the area, however. Pissarro had a house at Louveciennes as did Renoir's parents; Sisley was living further up the valley, where he had painted pictures of magical luminosity in the woods around Celle Saint-Cloud. It was possibly while on his way to one of these homes that Monet had discovered the river at Bougival.

These two pictures of the ice-bound river have claim to being the first paintings that Monet made from the banks of the upper Seine, but they are by no means the first he painted in the snow. In the past Monet had often worked in the winter, taking his canvas out into the snow-laden lanes

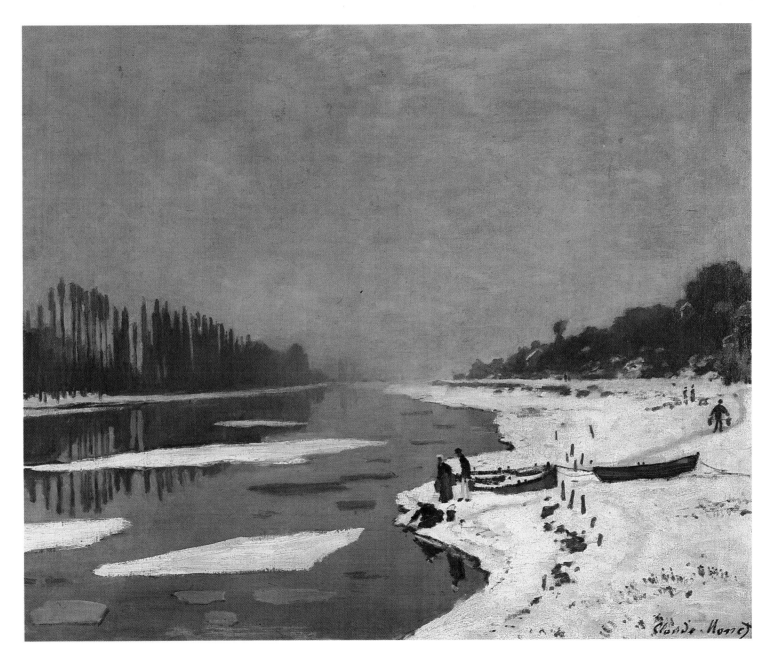

ICE-FLOES ON THE SEINE AT BOUGIVAL

1867

around the Ferme Saint-Siméon. Painting in the open air is a great deal less romantic and therapeutic as a pastime than it may sound; in summer there are mosquitoes, sudden gusts of wind, and cows whose dull-witted curiosity prompts them to nudge the easel and lick the paint; in winter there are the vicissitudes of the cold to contend with, and the artist's fingers turn as blue as the shadows on the ground. Monet was quite impervious to the weather, however; during the course of his life he worked in heat waves, blizzards and rainstorms without apparent discomfort. In winter he would carry a bottle of warm water in either pocket, and by occasionally warming his hands on these he could continue work on his picture undistracted.

Monet never lived in Bougival itself, but in the summer of 1869 he rented a house in Saint-Michel, a village on the hillside above the town. This was a period of experiment in his life, the beginning of the summer in which he would work so closely with Renoir at La Grenouillère. Also during this time, Monet would sometimes walk up to Louveciennes to paint alongside Pissarro. There he tested out the older artist's love of plunging compositions, in paintings of the wooded pathways and the perspective of village streets.

In 'The Seine at Bougival' (page 70), Monet has returned to one of his own favourite devices, leading the viewer into the scene along the banks of the river and bringing the composition to rest on the clutter of houses in the middle distance. Sharp interchanges of light and shade draw the separate elements of the painting together. The aqueduct that stretches out its arches against the sky appears to be the fragment of some Roman structure, but is in fact undamaged and dates from a much later period. It was built by Louis XIV to provide the head of water for the legion of fountains in his gardens at Versailles and Marly-le-Roi and beneath the aqueduct, on the banks of the river at Port Marly, was a pumping station. It consisted of a series of hefty paddle-wheels which revolved in the current, driving the water up a ladder of canals that had been cut like steps into the hillside. Louis had such a love of fountains that he had ordered that they should be playing at all times: unfortunately, not even this formidable feat of seventeenth-century engineering could supply enough water to keep them all going at the same time, and so the king became the victim of a minor deception: the fountains were switched on wherever he went and off again when he had passed. The pump-house at Port Marly was adapted and

improved over the years; the building that Monet would have known, and which was often painted by Sisley, was a magnificent Second Empire palace that jutted out into the river, carried on six arches, with paddle-wheels between each span. It no longer exists today and only the stump of one arch has survived to mark its position on the shoreline.

During this brief, experimental period at Bougival it is clear that Monet was searching for a greater simplicity to his pictures. His intention was to clarify the design; to take a fragment of nature, almost at random, and set it to the rhythm of an overall pattern. He was not concerned with the formulas of the past, the extravagant theories and measurements that had burdened the compositions of the old masters, but sought in its place a simple logic that would bind the picture together.

Possibly the most fluent of these arrangements is to be found in the painting of 'The Bridge at Bougival' (page 71), an iron-framed structure that leap-frogged the water in two separate spans. Monet worked on it from the island in the river, looking towards the town over the swell of one arch. Two hills frame the background and the houses of Bougival lie in the valley between like water that has collected in a gutter. The focus of the painting is on a point at the far end of the bridge, for here all the lines of the picture converge and meet: the shadowed pavement, the intersection of the two hills, the trunks of the trees and the sunlit road on the far shore. It's as if all the separate parts of the painting have collided in this one area of the canvas. Even the figures are turned away from us and direct their attention towards the core of the painting.

What makes the composition so successful and so tantalizing, however, is that Monet has made not only the painting's structure converge in the centre of the canvas, but also its space. The picture focuses on a strangely ambiguous point in the landscape where much of the town is actually out of sight, obscured behind the hip of the bridge. As a result, the perspective of the road leads straight into the distant hills, welding the foreground to the background and compressing the sense of space between them. A year before, on the banks of the Seine at Bennecourt, Monet had used Camille's profile to thrust the viewer's attention into the sunlit composition; here at Bougival he has used the bridge, with its figures facing inwards, in exactly the same way, forcing us to look beyond the foreground and into the heart of the painting.

VIEW OF BOUGIVAL

This picture was taken from the Ile de Croissy looking over towards the outskirts of the town. The pollarded trees and the buildings that line the far shore are the continuation of those that appear on the lefthand side of Monet's 'Bridge at Bougival'.

Like so many of the great landscape painters of the past, Monet had begun to understand light in associations of warm and cold colours. In 'The Bridge at Bougival' the canvas is bustling with subtle interchanges between the two: the warm, putty colour of the dusty road against the cool purple of the shadows, the rich peat brown of the foliage against the overcast sky and the juicy greens of the distant trees against the cold slate blue of rooftops. The picture never tires, never becomes dull; ragged patches of shade stand out against the light, tiny leaves accent the broad expanses of the sky, and thick strokes of paint punch out the reflections on the water.

'The Bridge at Bougival' is dated 1870, although the leaves still clinging to the trees suggest it may have been painted in the previous autumn. It could not have been later than this, as by the following summer Monet and Camille had moved up to Trouville. Here, in the last days before the Franco-Prussian War, Monet painted along the seafront of this famous resort where the English tourists sat taking the ozone in their deck chairs.

On 18 July 1870, three days after the declaration of war with Prussia, Monet and Camille were married in Paris. It was a brief legal ceremony to which only a few of his closest friends were invited. The newly married couple continued to live in Trouville until, later that summer, Monet happened to cross over to Le Havre one day. He found the town seething with rumours of invasion and conscription; crowds of people, anxious to leave the country, milled about the quaysides, others queued for tickets and jostled for spaces on the packet boats. Faced with this alarming spectacle Monet panicked and, without pausing to consider, he boarded a ship and sailed for England. It was left to Camille to collect together their belongings, book passage for herself and Jean on another ship and follow him to London.

The artists at the Café Guerbois all reacted differently to the news of war. Pissarro moved over to London, as Monet had done: Sisley, who was half English by birth, was not involved with the fighting. Manet signed up but was disgusted to find that even in the army he couldn't escape the politics of the art-world; he was promoted to the rank of captain only to discover that his colonel was Meissonnier, the very painter whose Salon pictures he so disliked. Renoir joined the cavalry; that he had never ridden a horse in his life didn't seem to trouble him. Degas failed his medical; he was told that his eyesight, which had served him as an artist well enough, wasn't up to aiming a rifle.

At the outbreak of war Bazille had returned to his parents' house in the south, but when he heard of the terrible losses the French army was suffering at the hands of the Prussians, he returned to Paris and signed up. For several weeks he was marched around the city: on 28 November 1870 he was shot in the back and killed, while retreating along a road not far from Fontainebleau where he and Monet had spent so many happy days together.

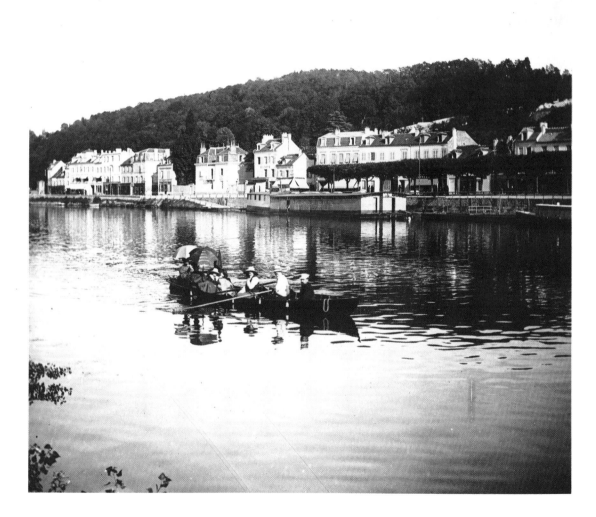

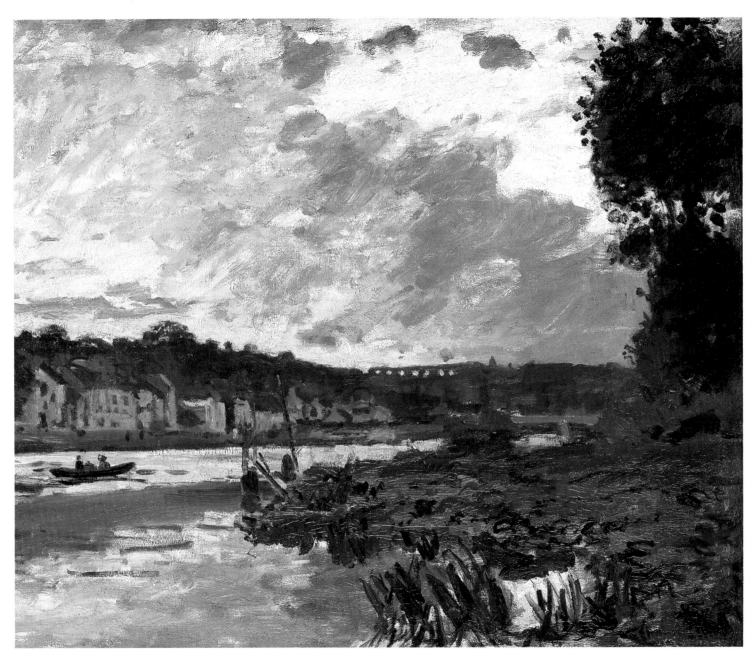

THE SEINE AT BOUGIVAL

1870

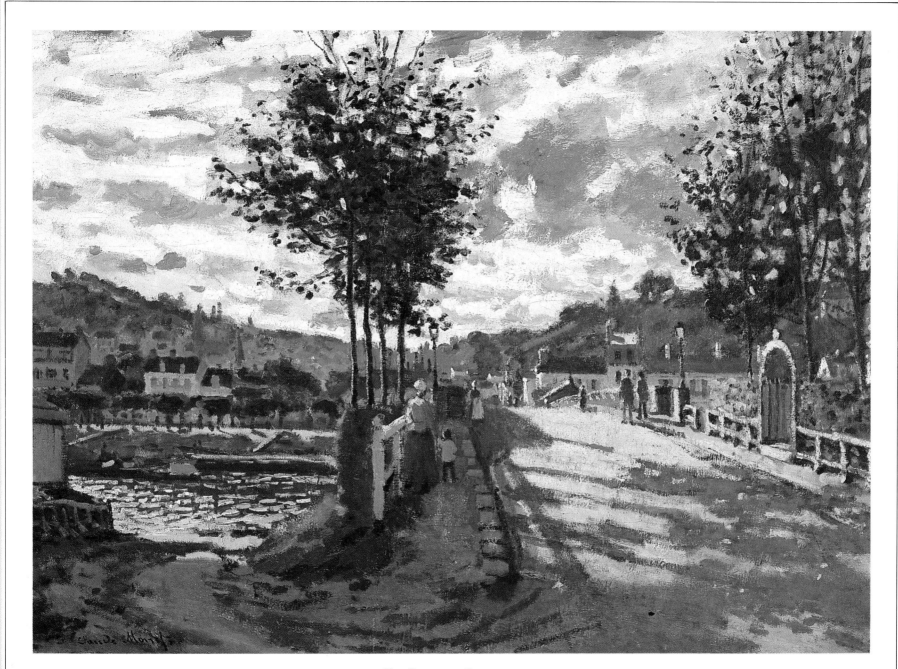

THE BRIDGE AT BOUGIVAL

1870

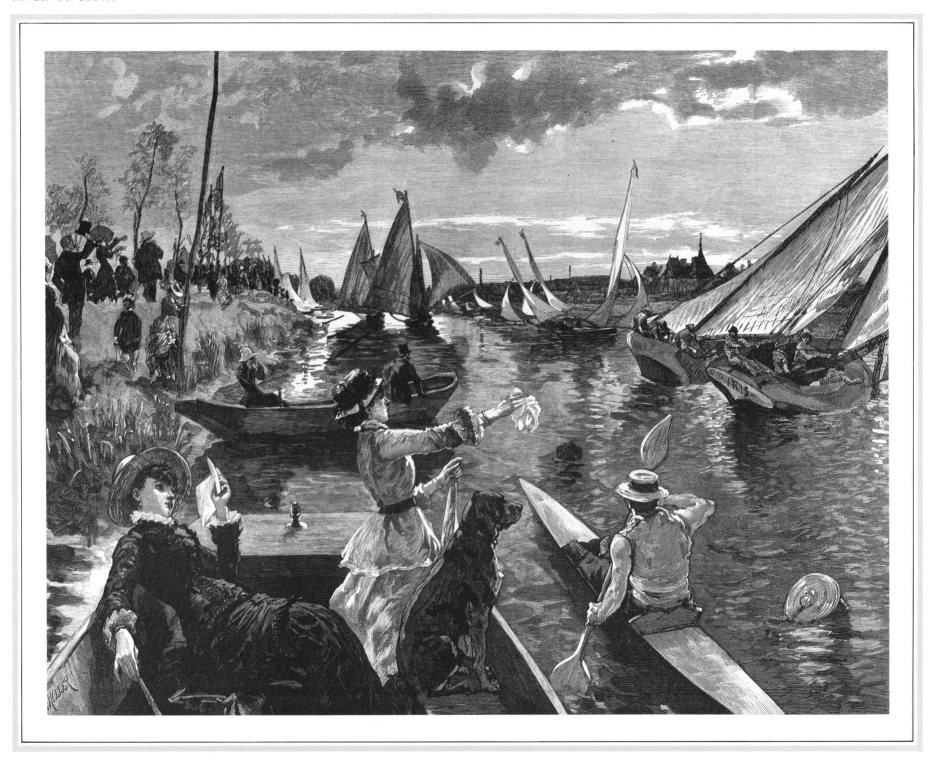

ARGENTEUIL

1871–1877

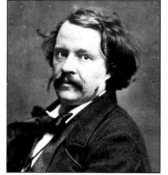

FÉLIX NADAR

REGATTA AT ARGENTEUIL

In 1867 the Paris World's Fair staged its boat races at Argenteuil, and after that the town was well-known for its regattas. It had the advantage of a comparatively straight stretch of water which allowed the spectators to watch the full course of the race. Although this engraving, like the paintings of both Monet and Renoir, shows only sailing boats competing, there were also competitions for sculls, rowing boats and even steam pinnaces.

In November 1870, a Prussian soldier climbed onto the roof of Argenteuil church and directed his telescope towards Paris. From this crow's nest he could see over the hastily built ramparts and earthworks into the heart of the city, which had now been under siege for over a month:

> You can see the beleaguered city so well that you might fancy a short and harmless stroll would take you to the Arc de Triomphe – the chiselled figures on it we can trace most minutely with a good field glass. There is a busy life going on inside. The engine of the railway round the city is dashing to and fro; smoke issues from all the chimneys. It is a huge and strong ring that runs round poor Paris, and no human being is allowed to pass through our lines. Yet Paris is not cut off from all communication. Balloons come and go – they are rich in the power of invention, the French – and, despite our great vigilance, we frequently notice that they are holding communication with the outer world through lighted beacons and whatnot.

Inside the barricades life was becoming grimmer by the day. Soldiers bivouacked in the Champs Elysées, the Salon had been turned into a hospital and the trees in the Bois de Boulogne had been cut down to the ground.

'Hunger is beginning, and famine is on the horizon,' observed Edmond de Goncourt. 'And elegant Parisians are beginning to turn their dressing rooms into hen-houses. People calculate and count and wonder if, with all the waste, all the scraps, all the scrapings, there will be some-thing to eat a fortnight hence.'

With food supplies running dangerously low in the city, French ingenuity was soon stretched to its limit and the Parisians, already famous for discovering delicacies in the most improbable places, were forced to try out any substitute for meat that came their way. Horses became part of the regular diet and appeared on restaurant menus described as beef. Cats and dogs were next, and within weeks the relative merits of their flavours had become a topic of conversation: it was generally accepted that poodle was the most tender, spaniel quite acceptable, bulldog was gristly and to be avoided. Soon anything that moved was eaten; rats and mice were at a premium and Daumier drew cartoons of Parisians politely queueing at sewer holes in the streets. The spirit of free enterprise led inevitably to a black market and food prices became extortionate. Ration books were issued and there were bread riots in the streets. It was not only stomachs that were feeling the pangs of starvation, however; morals had also begun to wilt in the siege. Honour became a luxury for the well-fed, and society ladies of previously untarnished reputation found it in themselves to exchange their favours for a string of sausages or a leg of mutton.

After the signing of the Armistice on 28 January 1871 the Prussians removed themselves from Paris, but its problems were far from over. The city fell into the hands of the Commune, a group of revolutionaries who seized power and held the capital for three months. Fighting broke out, the

Marseillaise was revived and liberty became the well-worn excuse for anarchy. Barricades blocked the streets once more, and mortar shells rained from the sky as they had done all through the winter – the only consolation for the Parisians being that these were now fired from French guns.

Courbet, whose politics had always been flavoured with insurrection, had become the revolution's official Minister for Arts and it was in this capacity that he helped to pull down the column in the Place Vendôme which carried a statue of Napoleon I, an unacceptable symbol of imperial tyranny. Ropes and pulleys were attached to its balustrade, a section was hacked out of its base and it fell 'with a dull and mighty crash, in the middle of a blinding cloud of dust'. Following this flagrant act of vandalism, for which Courbet later denied all responsibility, the Parisians began to fear for their art treasures and spirited away anything else that might fall prey to the Commune: 'The Venus de Milo is hidden – guess where – at the Prefecture de Police. All the same, it is thought that Courbet is on her track, and the silly employees fear the worst if the fanatical modernist lays his hands on the classical masterpiece.'

Monet waited until the fighting was over, and the Communards either imprisoned or executed, before returning to France. One of his first missions on arrival in Paris was to visit Courbet who, following arrest and trial, had been temporarily moved from his cell in Saint-Pélagie jail to a nursing home. Monet obtained permission to see him there and together with Armand Gautier, himself a member of the Commune, was granted a brief audience with the realist painter. They found him in a pitiful state, shrunk in both body and spirit but pathetically pleased to see the few friends he had left.

Monet did not stay in Paris for long: the place was gutted, buildings pitted and roofless, cafés closed and many of the great palaces damaged beyond repair, burned to the ground by the Communards as a final act of defiance before their capture. Retaining his studio in the Rue d'Isly, Monet moved out to Argenteuil, a growing suburb that lay on one of the coiled springs of the river a few miles outside the city. It was Manet who had recommended Argenteuil; he knew the town well as his family had been living at Gennevilliers, on the opposite bank of the river, for several generations. Using his influence in the district, he managed to find Monet a house in the Rue Pierre Guienne. This was in the old part of town, near to the railway station and just a few minutes walk from the riverbank. It belonged to a Mme Aubry-Villet, a woman of some importance in Argenteuil as she was both sister to the writer Villet and widow of the town's last mayor. She agreed to rent out the house for a thousand francs a year, to be paid quarterly. With this settled, Monet moved in during December of 1871 and a month later held a house warming party to which Boudin, among others, was invited.

Monet had never worked in Argenteuil before, but he would have known it well enough since the town, with its avenue of trees and sparkling water, lay on the track of the Western Railway and he must have glimpsed it from a carriage window on several occasions in the past as he rattled through on his way to Le Havre.

Argenteuil was going through a crisis of identity at that time. Like so many of the towns that clung to the apron strings of Paris it was changing fast; parts of it were still quite rural, but others had become heavily industrialized. Steel-workers lived next to wine-growers, open fields were fenced in by factory chimneys and the river reflected the plumes of smoke that rose from their stacks. Argenteuil was a modern landscape in every sense, but what attracted Monet in particular was that it was also famous for its sailing. There were jetties, moorings and marinas where boats could be hired; regattas were a regular feature and in the summer the river was bristling with masts.

Argenteuil had paid heavily for its part in the war. The Prussians, who used the town as an observatory for their artillery, had extracted a fine of over 15,000 francs from the inhabitants on leaving. The town's factories had been closed down and both its bridges destroyed. The road-bridge, which led directly into Paris, had been burned down by the French army as it was retreating towards the capital in the autumn of 1870. The railway bridge, which crossed the river a few hundred yards upstream, had gone the same way. At the outbreak of war it had been unceremoniously blown off its concrete pillars and lay in the water throughout the winter, its cast-iron girders limp and sagging as if the frame had been built from damp cardboard.

Monet's first picture of Argenteuil (opposite) was made on the banks of the river almost directly opposite his new home. Painted just a few days after his arrival, it shows the roadbridge undergoing reconstruction. Wooden scaffolding

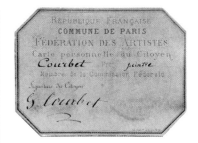

COURBET'S CARD AS A MEMBER OF THE COMMUNE

The Paris Commune seized control of the city in the summer of 1871. Shortly afterwards, Courbet was elected as the Commune's official Minister of Arts, and it was for his activities as a member of this revolutionary movement that he was later tried, jailed and eventually exiled from France, so having to pass his last years in Switzerland.

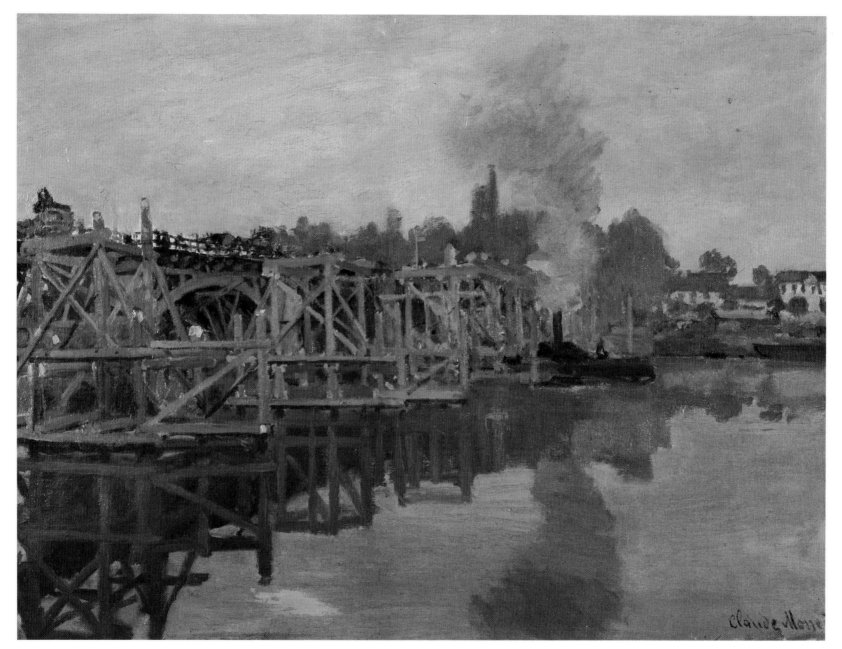

ROADBRIDGE UNDER REPAIR

1872

cocoons the stone piles, the sky and water around it are dull and passive and only the muted warmth of the heavy timbers stands out against the cold, bruised tones of winter. Although not completed, the roadbridge is open to traffic once more; figures and carriages make their way across the river while, down below, a tugboat feels its way between the latticework of timbers.

From this same position on the shore Monet painted a second picture of the unfinished bridge (below), this time looking straight through the window of one arch. It is a composition of great simplicity and audacity, quite un-

precedented in Monet's earlier work. The dark framework of the scaffolding is perfectly reflected in the water below and together the two images frame the distant view of the river. The stark symmetry of the design is stripped of all miscellaneous detail: on the far horizon is a single building, the block of the houseboat and a moored yacht lie on either side, while a horse and coach are positioned directly above.

By the summer of 1872 the repair work was completed and, in the brilliant sunshine of a Sunday afternoon, Monet painted the new bridge stretched out across the river (opposite). His easel has been set up on the promenade, the

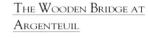

THE WOODEN BRIDGE AT ARGENTEUIL

1872

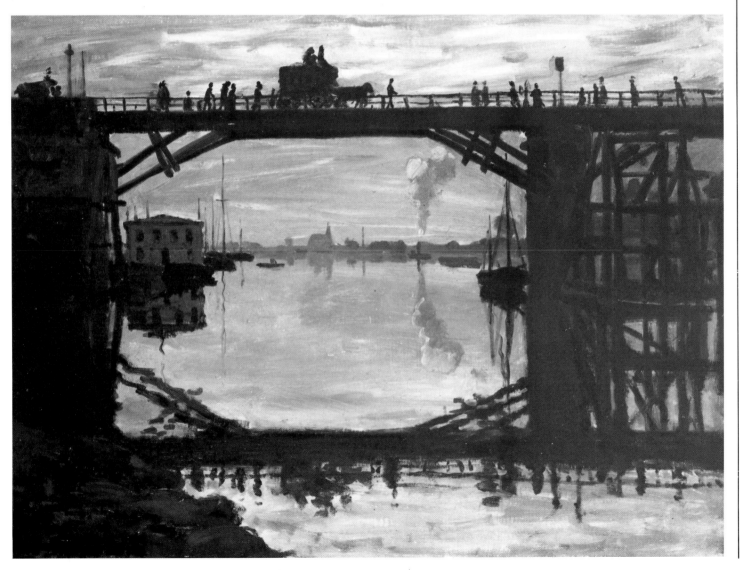

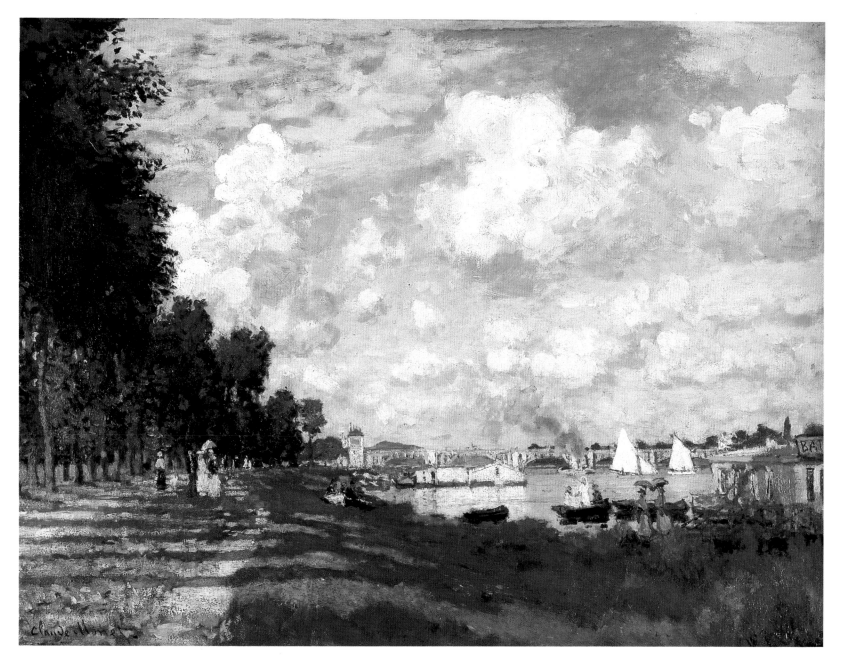

SUNDAY AT ARGENTEUIL

1872

avenue of trees that fringed the town, and from there his picture embraces the whole basin of Argenteuil. Figures dressed in their Sunday best stroll along the banks of the river. Trees darken the lefthand side of the canvas, their shadows barring the path as they reach out towards the water. Yachts with sails as crisp as newly laundered linen scud about the calm water while the smoke of a steamer drifts lazily against the sky. The flotilla of houseboats that can be seen moored to the shore below the bridge were public wash-houses. The one nearest, on the far right of the picture, was a 'bain chaud', the new, improved model that boasted both hot and cold water; the first few letters of this title can just be made out above the doorway.

Monet was not a countryman. He was not interested in painting the joys or hardships of rustic life, preferring the more urbane pleasures of weekends in the open air; a world of rest and relaxation. The few figures who walk in the shade of the promenade at Argenteuil, or sit on the river-bank gazing out at the great expanse of water, are not peasants but city-men out for the day with their wives and girlfriends. 'As a true Parisian he brings Paris to the country,' Zola had pointed out. 'He cannot paint a land-scape without including well-dressed men and women. Nature seems to lose its interest for him as soon as it does not bear the stamp of our customs.'

The arrangement of 'Sunday at Argenteuil' is much the same as that in 'The Roadbridge under Repair'. A sharply receding perspective on the left of the composition, ruled off in the middle distance by the horizontal of the road-bridge, creates an enclosed space on the canvas, a stage set that contains the whole landscape. But the composition has an ingenious twist to it for in terms of tone and colour alone, the canvas is divided into two distinct parts and falls into a simple pattern. The dark mass of the avenue and riverbank occupy the lower territory of the picture, rising on either side of the canvas to cradle the sunwashed blues of sky and water above. The borderline of these dense greens sweeps down across the canvas in a graceful, semi-circular rhythm, beginning in the line of the trees, picked up in the curve of the river and then lifting again with the shadow that separates the nearest of the wash-houses. There is nothing arbitrary about this motion; Monet has arranged it all with great care, even touching a shaft of light onto the corner of the wooden houseboat to complete the gentle parabola of his composition.

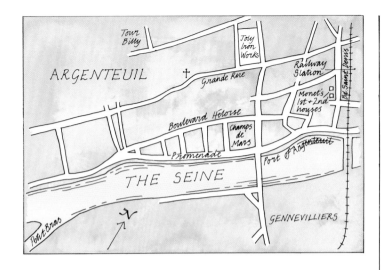

Fat and lazy clouds fill the sky; these are not the romantic storms of Monet's early career, but puffs of cumulus cheerfully butting their way across the picture. Monet has exchanged drama for charm. Five years earlier, in his paintings of Paris, he had simplified the cloud formations, but now he has allowed them back once more, jotting down their bulk in quick, sure strokes and scribbling in the luminous purple-grey shadows beneath their bellies with the tip of his brush. His technique has become increasingly rapid and his control of the medium more certain as he translates the landscape into equivalent colours on the canvas. The sunlight that plays across the sky and water, warming the upper sides of the clouds and feeling its way across the framework of the bridge below, has been pressed into the picture in thick strokes; warm colours worked over cool; touches of gold on a ground of enamelled blue.

The promenade, the 'Champs Elysées of Argenteuil' as it was sometimes called, was one of the town's finer points and invariably warranted a mention in descriptions of the area. Its appearance is so natural that it comes as something of a surprise to realize that it was, in fact, an artificial addition to the town. The promenade had originally been an island, separated from the shore by a narrow channel of water. Unfortunately, in the heat of summer this arm of the river had often become stagnant or dried up completely, plaguing the town with a terrible smell. Successive out-breaks of malaria were blamed on its brackish water, where mosquitoes hatched in their thousands, and eventually work had begun on filling it in with rocks. The town walls,

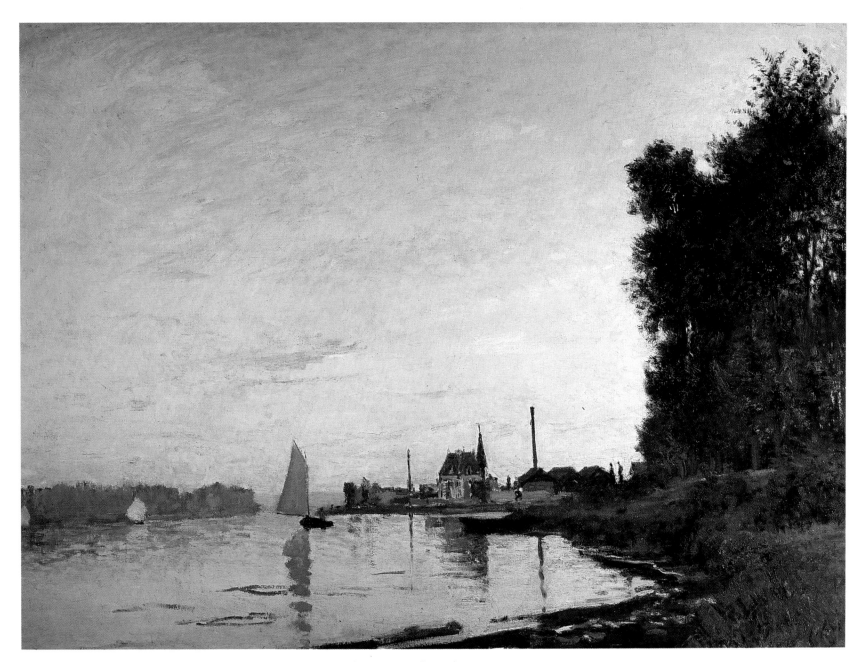

ARGENTEUIL, LATE AFTERNOON

1872

built during the wars of religion, were knocked down and shovelled into the river until, by 1818, the island had become an extension of the town. Planted with an avenue of trees, it was quite an attraction and formed a natural park, screening the town from the open river.

For all its industry, Argenteuil was an ancient place and many of its roads and paths traced out the boundaries of buildings that had long since passed away. Its importance as a town dated back to the seventh century, when a nunnery had been built on the banks of the river in a place then known as 'Argentoïalium'. Héloïse had taken sanctuary there after her ill-advised love affair with Abelard and later, when the nunnery was made over into a monastery, it came under the control of Abbot Suger, whose enthusiasm for building, in his own cathedral at Saint-Denis, had helped to pioneer the new Gothic movement in architecture.

The 1789 Revolution saw the last of the monastery, but by the time Monet came to Argenteuil, its skeleton could still be seen littered about the countryside. Stumps of crumbling masonry stood in the fields and vineyards around Argenteuil defining the boundaries of the ancient building without giving any clear idea of its appearance. The nunnery's most famous protégée had lent her name to the Boulevard Héloïse, the main road that cut in behind the promenade on what had originally been the banks of the river.

The only remnant of the seventeenth-century fortifications that Monet would have known was a single turret to the north-west of town known as the 'Tour Billy'. The rest of the walls had been demolished and were now serving as the foundations for the new promenade, but Argenteuil had retained one direct link with the past and that was a relic. In the ninth century the Emperor Charlemagne had given the nunnery a Holy Tunic, said to have been part of Christ's wardrobe. This had somehow survived the Revolution and had been transferred to the town church where it lay on the altar. At Pentecost each year it was taken down and paraded about the streets, with a good deal of chanting and incense-burning to heighten the effect. Over the centuries this annual ceremony had grown and improved until it eventually became the excuse for a fete, a three-day celebration in the Champ de Mars which Monet made the subject of a painting when he first arrived in Argenteuil.

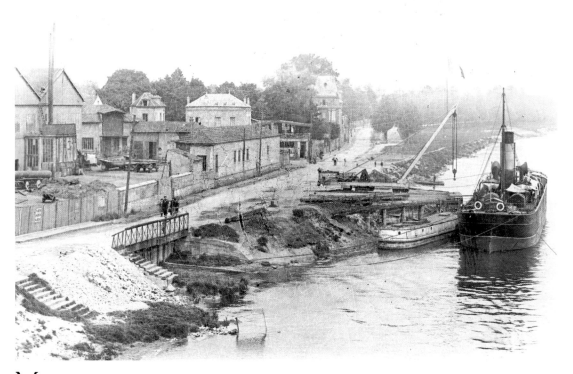

Monet never repeated the view of the river that appears in 'Sunday at Argenteuil' but, turning about and facing in the opposite direction, he made several paintings of the promenade looking downstream (pages 79 and 81). These are peaceful paintings with wide, empty skies mirrored in calm water. The towpath leads seductively into the heart of the picture, sails with the freshness of white card stand on the river, and knots of women make their way along the promenade. The illusion of open countryside is broken, however, by the pencil-thin chimneys that trickle their smoke into the still atmosphere. They belonged to a carton factory that had just reopened for business after the war. Argenteuil was supporting a wide range of industries at this time: there were tallow shops, tanneries and chemical plants. Artificial dyes were produced in the town, as were bottles of carbonated mineral water. A heavy sawmill was situated on the banks of the river where it provided lumber for the building trade. Among the most successful of these businesses was the Joly iron works in the centre of the town, which started out as a small blacksmith's shop and

FACTORY BY THE RIVER AT ARGENTEUIL

In Monet's day, industrial development was rapidly encroaching on the town of Argenteuil. This factory, and the little manor house beyond, appeared in the background of Monet's paintings when his easel was set up on the promenade stretching away behind the moored boats. The road curving in towards the town is the Boulevard Héloïse, named after the heroine of the famous medieval love story.

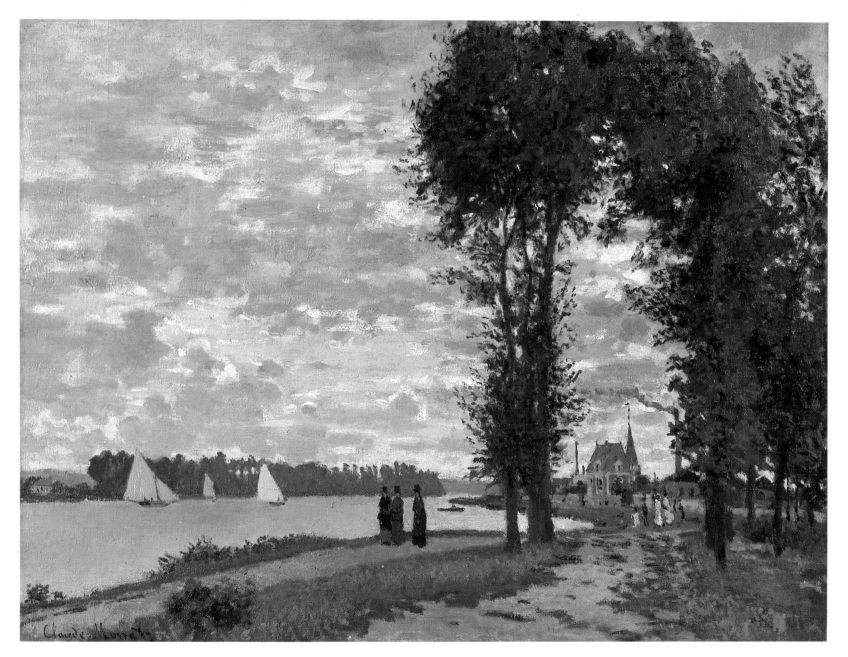

PROMENADE ALONG THE SEINE

1872

grew into one of the country's largest manufacturers, exporting cast-iron bridges, barges and construction parts all over the world. It had provided the wrought ironwork for the famous market place in Paris, Les Halles, and had forged the steel for Argenteuil's own railway bridge. The town also manufactured lighter domestic articles such as crystal glass, silk and artificial lace, and not all its industry was modern: the town had been mining gypsum – better known as 'plaster of Paris' – since the Middle Ages, although the introduction of steam-driven machinery, coupled with the enormous demand for plaster during the rebuilding of Paris, had recently put these mines on a different scale of operations.

With the coming of the railway the population of Argenteuil, which had remained remarkably unchanged for two hundred years, doubled in two decades. Industry brought a new standard of living to the town, but there were objections, the foremost of these being the smell. The tallow factory opposite the church had let off such obnoxious fumes that it was eventually forced to close down. The tannery was no better; one of the local residents complained that the stink from the drying hides was so frightful that his house was uninhabitable and his tenants were refusing to pay their rent. Nor were the new factories too safe, as the town had discovered to its cost when the distillery exploded in 1869, bombarding the nearby houses with flying debris.

Monet's attitude towards the industry in Argenteuil is not clear. He never attempted to disguise it; in his paintings of the promenade, factory chimneys poke out from behind the high roof of a Louis XIII style chateau, but it does not appear that Monet was passing comment on the uneasy alliance between the two. To him they are both part of a landscape and he paints them as he sees them, treating the thin column of the chimneys as he might the trunk of a tree or the mast of a sailing boat.

It is interesting to note that Monet, who frequently included industrial sites in his landscapes, practically never showed men working, even in the fields. The one notable exception to this is the painting known as 'Men Unloading Coal' (above), which he painted further upstream at Asnières in 1875. It is a painting of stark geometry. Beneath the portal of one cast-iron arch, coal barges with hulls as heavy and clumsy as wooden clogs line the river-bank. Like a scene from Puccini's *Il Tabarro*, rows of steve-

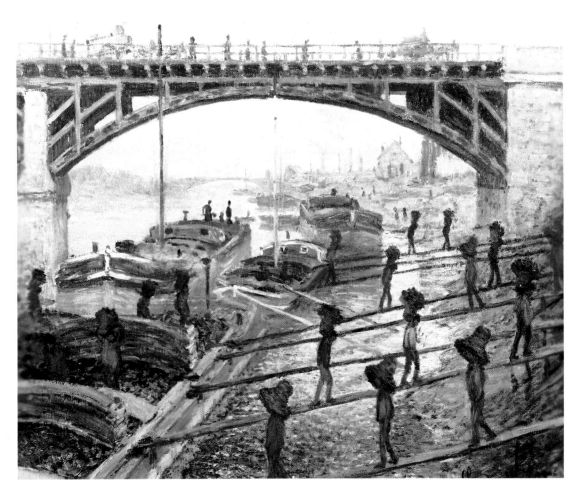

dores work back and forth humping coal up the narrow gangplanks above a slick of glassy water. Of all Monet's pictures this is the one that comes closest to the social realism of Zola's novels, his demi-monde of embittered and downtrodden individuals crushed by the weight of their own circumstance. Yet Monet's painting does not radiate social injustice; his figures are just outlines and quite anonymous. The overriding impression is not of protest but of intricate design. What is so striking about his stevedores is the mesmerizing rhythm of their movement across the canvas. Monet has no intention of expressing indignation at the conditions of this work; his painting is first and foremost a composition, a delicately balanced piece of machinery. It anticipates the remark made by Maurice Denis some years later, that a painting 'before being a war-horse, a social anecdote or a nude woman, is firstly colours

MEN UNLOADING COAL

1875

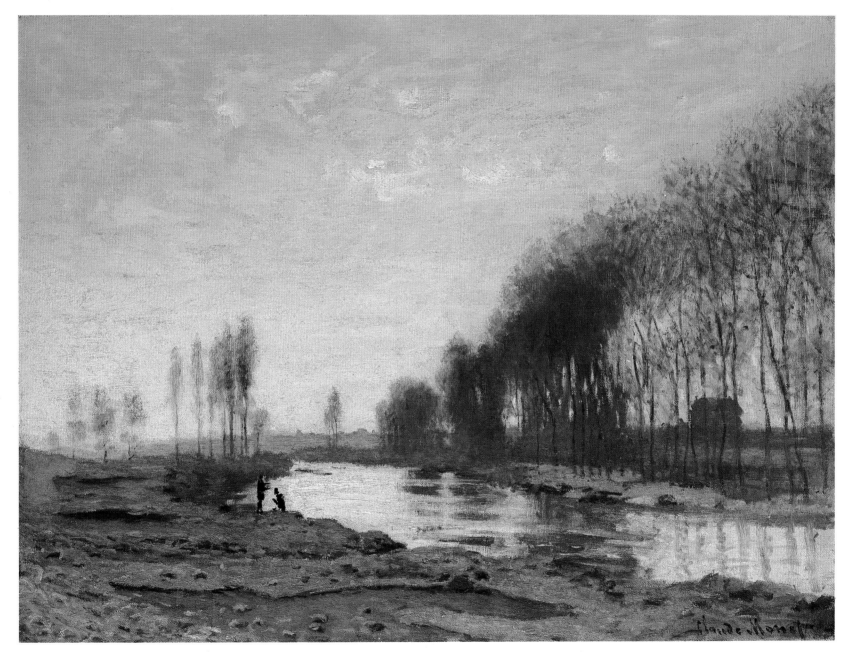

THE PETIT-BRAS IN SPRING

1872

laid on a canvas and arranged in a certain order'.

Monet's genius, demonstrated so clearly in this painting, was that he could find his arrangement of colour in the most unlikely locations. He had a keen eye for surface pattern; a row of chimneys serves him as well as an avenue of trees, a plume of factory smoke no differently from a summer cloud and, as a result, it may be unwise to read too much into his subject matter. In his paintings of the promenade along the Seine, Monet has included the factory chimneys simply because they are there. He forges them into an integral part of the composition, their tall brick columns falling into sequence with the vertical rhythm of the tree trunks, the tiny weathercock and standing figures.

There were times when Monet turned his back on the progress evident in Argenteuil's industrial sites and looked for a more idyllic landscape. The trees that appear in the background of 'The Promenade along the Seine' grew on a small island in the river and behind this, tucked away out of sight, was a narrow arm of water known as the Petit Bras. Monet discovered it when he first arrived at Argenteuil and painted it in 1872, just as spring was beginning to stir the land (page 83). Two figures stand on the riverbank, silhouetted against the water, but despite their presence there is an air of privacy about the painting. The channel of water that makes its way beneath the haze of winter branches is undisturbed and clear as a chalk stream on an English estate. The island on the far shore, the Ile Marante, was quite deserted when Monet painted it, as was the house that appears between the trees belonging to the village of Bezons on the other side of the Seine, but this had not always been the case by any means. In the eighteenth century Louis Watelet, an artist, writer and garden designer, had built himself a farm on the land, complete with windmill and milking parlour. It was a romantic ideal more than a practical undertaking, a fantasy of rustic life where guests dressed as shepherds and shepherdesses skittered about the place in ribbons and bonnets as though they had dropped from a painting by Boucher.

The trees along the Petit Bras sheltered the water from the stiff river breezes, and in winter its entrance made a natural mooring for the boats. Monet often painted them as they lay at anchor in the lee of the island. There is a melancholy to these paintings, a sense of time dragging its heels.

In his painting of 'Pleasure Boats' (page 102) the yachts are unmanned, their sails down and stowed away. Long ripples crease the river, slapping at the hulls and adding a slight vibrato to their reflections on the water. The fine black lines of the masts cross-cut the painting, echoed on either side in the church spire, mooring posts and factory chimneys. Monet has intersected horizontal with vertical and emphasized only the static elements of the composition. The picture is completely still and somehow lonely – like a holiday resort out of season.

In summer the Petit Bras was transformed; the trees grew heavy with foliage, the views of the distant hills vanished and the little channel of water became a chasm of leaves. As the season turned, the colours caught fire. In another painting of the Petit Bras, 'The Seine at Argenteuil in Autumn' (opposite), painted in 1873, Monet confronts the spectator with an unbroken web of paint. There are no firm outlines to the painting; the scene has been treated as a single unity. Slabs of cobalt blue float above golden reflections, trees lose definition, and images dissolve in the mesmerizing surface of the picture. The paint is dry and as porous as plaster, built up in tiny flickering strokes and so thick that in places Monet has had to scratch at it with a knife to regain the tooth of the canvas. The picture has been worked and reworked until it glows with the intense satisfaction of the elements in close proximity; sun-baked earth beside cool water, dense foliage beneath open sky.

This image of the river is echoed in a description written by Maupassant of just such a scene:

> For ten years my great, my only absorbing passion was the Seine, that lovely, calm, varied stinking river, full of mirages and filth. I think I loved it so much because it gave me the feeling of being alive. Oh, those strolls along the flower-covered banks, with my friends the frogs dreamily cooling their bellies on lily pads, and the frail, dainty lilies among the tall grasses, which parted suddenly to reveal a scene from a Japanese album as a kingfisher darted past me like a blue flame!

The Petit Bras offered Monet the scenery and something of the seclusion of the open countryside but he could have found a dozen sites as good, if not better, further downstream. The reason that he stayed on in Argenteuil for so long was simply that it was near to Paris. Monet had moved out to the suburbs but his life still centred on the city. He still worked in his studio in the Rue d'Isly and every Thurs-

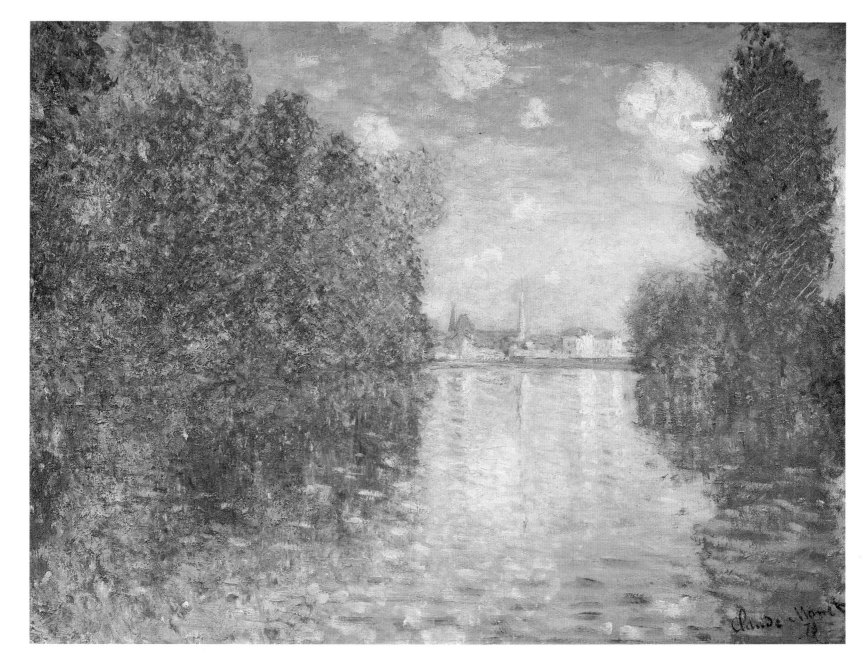

THE SEINE AT ARGENTEUIL, AUTUMN

1873

day evening he would be sure to turn up at the weekly meetings at the Café Guerbois: 'they kept our wits sharpened, they encouraged us with stores of enthusiasm that for weeks and weeks kept us up, until the final shaping of the idea was accomplished. From them we emerged with a firmer will, with our thoughts clearer and more distinct'.

It was the railway that made these visits possible. Monet's house at Argenteuil was a only a few minutes walk from the station, and from there the journey into Paris took no more than fifteen minutes. The railway had always been vitally important to Monet for, until he built his studio-boat, this was the only practical way he had of travelling around the countryside. It was the railway that had taken him to Le Havre, Fontainebleau and Bennecourt, and consequently it was only a matter of time before it became a theme in his work. In 1869 a steam train made its debut in his pictures, contentedly trundling along the horizon trailing a string of smoke-filled carriages. Later at Argenteuil, the trains began to appear more frequently in his paintings, either standing waiting in the station near his home or rumbling out across the cast-iron bridge, firing smoke rings into the sky as they went. Monet's interest in trains increased until eventually, before leaving the district, he was to commemorate his weekly pilgrimages into Paris in a series of pictures of the Gare Saint-Lazare.

The railway track to Argenteuil had been opened in 1851 and was largely responsible for the town's rapid indus- trialization over the next few years. At the time of its arrival the steam-train was looked upon as something of a mixed blessing; to some its invention meant progress and profit while others subscribed to Ruskin's heartfelt belief that trains were 'the loathsomest form of devilry now extant, animated and deliberate earthquakes, destructive of all wise, social habits and possible natural beauty, carriages of damned souls on the ridges of their own graves'.

Argenteuil's railway bridge had also proved controversial. Its clean, uncomplicated line was not universally appreciated among the town's residents, who felt that the addition of a few swags of decoration might improve its gaunt appearance; functionalism was not regarded as an excuse for ugliness. The Joly iron works had provided the construction materials, and many were of the opinion that it should have been allowed to design the bridge as well.

Monet's first picture of the railway bridge at Argenteuil (opposite) emphasizes, if anything, the severity of the design. The hard box-girder construction, perched on its concrete pods, streaks straight across the canvas, dwarfing the sailing boats and the two figures on the shore. Land, smoke and bridge zig-zag across the picture, slashing it apart with sharp diagonals. The abrupt realism of the painting is reprieved, however, by its captivating use of colour, for despite the complexity of the scene, the whole landscape is a series of variations on the single colour blue. The bridge reflects the water, the shadowed pillars inherit its colour, and the little yachts dip their white sails in ultramarine as they pass beneath. The smoke that billows from the train has absorbed the cool tones of the river and pumps them into a sky of thinly painted cobalt. Monet does not allow

THE RAILWAY BRIDGE AT ARGENTEUIL

The railway track to Argenteuil was built in 1851 and can be held partly responsible for the town's dramatic change of character during the next twenty years. From a quiet rural district, famous for its asparagus and wine-making, it became a modern industrial suburb of Paris. The box-framed iron bridge was demolished at the outset of the Franco-Prussian war, but reconstructed in the following year. From this view, the railway station providing the vital direct link to Paris would lie just to the left of the bridge; both the houses which Monet rented while he was in Argenteuil were within walking distance of it.

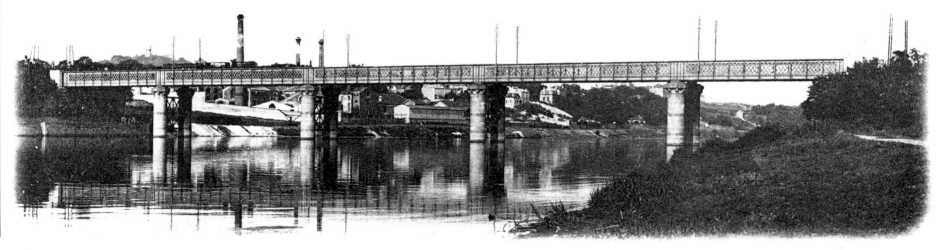

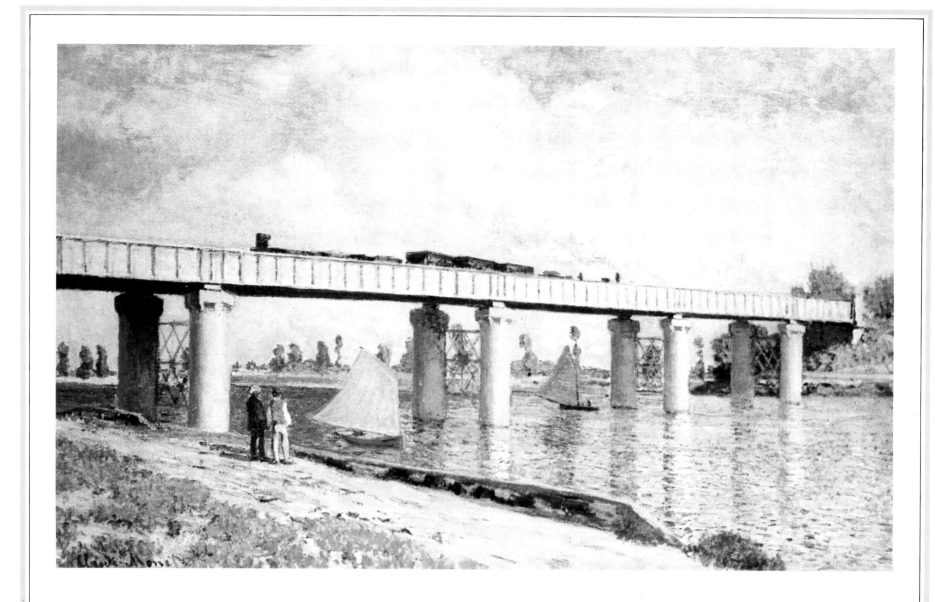

THE RAILWAY BRIDGE AT ARGENTEUIL

1874

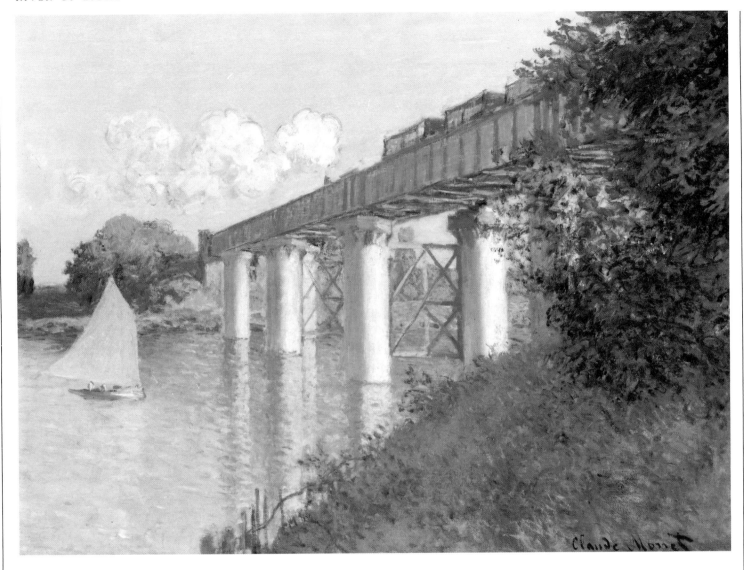

these dominant blues to become too glacial, however, but cunningly modulates the surface with sparks of yellow and summer greens. The sky he has warmed with nothing more than the buff tone of the canvas, the bare unprimed fabric, which he allows to show through between the brushstrokes.

'Railway Bridge at Argenteuil' was painted in 1873 on the riverbank almost directly below his home. The following year Monet returned to the subject, this time tucking himself under the bridge on the other side of its embankment (above). A wedge of land fills the foreground, a blurred mass of grass and foliage. Beyond this the bridge

recedes into the middle distance, cold and uncompromising as the nave of a cathedral, vanishing into the spongey material of the far trees. The painting is a fascinating study in textures, constantly offsetting hard against soft, the solid against the transitory. This is a favourite device of Monet's and, during the same year, he repeated it in his painting of 'The Roadbridge at Argenteuil' (opposite). Here the arrangement is almost identical: a triangular wedge of bushes in the foreground; the bridge, with its little turrets standing sentry at one end, running back in sharp perspective to the horizon of the far shore. Again it's the balance of

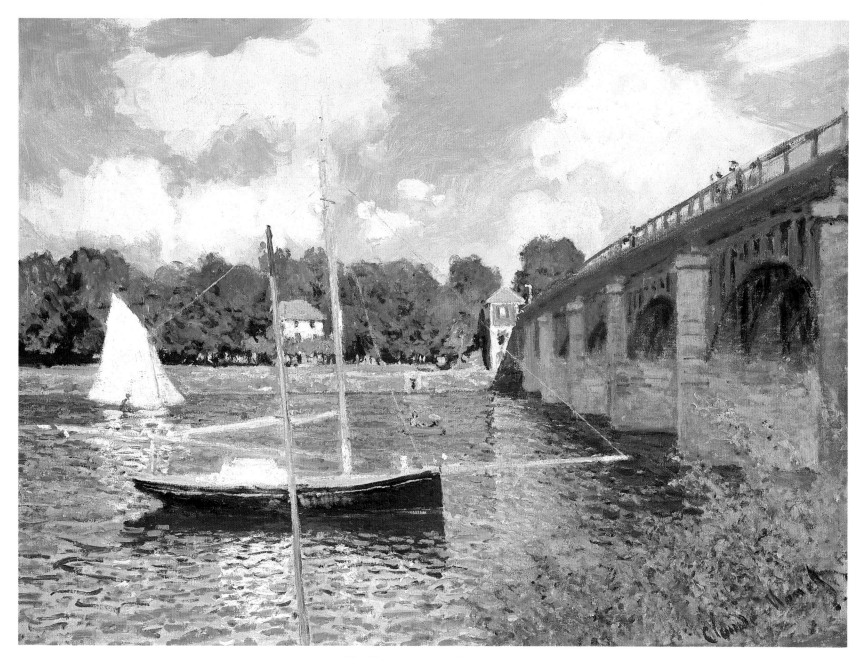

THE ROADBRIDGE AT ARGENTEUIL

1874

textures that makes this picture so pleasing: the firm body of the bridge against trees and rolling clouds, the hull of the boat riding black and shiny as a clarinet above the flickering light of the river.

Composition is a term with a funereal ring to it; the very mention of the word conjures up theories, formulas and inexplicable algebraic recipes, but to Monet it was simply a matter of clarity – a way of organizing the landscape. To achieve this he maintained a personal stock of tried and tested compositions, which he used over and again. The arrangement of 'The Roadbridge at Argenteuil', for example, follows exactly the same principle as the 1874 railbridge painting, the 'Petit Bras in Winter' and the 'Promenade along the Seine' series. Its mirror image appears in 'Sunday at Argenteuil' and 'The Roadbridge under Repair'. This particular composition first appears in his painting of 'Zaandam', painted in 1871 while he was away in Holland. During the troubled years of the Franco-Prussian war he had crossed over from England to Holland and travelled about the Dutch canals, returning with a series of limpid paintings, a storehouse of ideas and compositions that were in effect research for his paintings of the Seine. These were the basis of many of his later paintings, but while at Argenteuil he also attempted some more daring compositions. In 'The Bridge as a Single Pier' (right), Monet has cropped out just one section of the scene. Instead of showing the whole span of the bridge, he takes a fragment of it and uses it to divide the canvas into a powerful design, setting it squarely within the picture area with its two truncated arches reflected in the water, framing the factory chimney on one side and the silhouette of houseboat and buildings on the other. The disposition of the elements on the canvas is remarkably similar to that in Whistler's famous 'Old Battersea Bridge – Nocturne in Blue and Gold', painted at much the same time, and the link between the two paintings is in the Japanese prints that both painters collected. Monet had admired these prints since they first arrived in France – 'their refinement of taste has always pleased me' he said later – but what really intrigued him was their system of design 'which evokes presence by means of a shadow, the whole by means of a fragment'.

Through Japanese prints Monet discovered how to break the sanctity of a form, how to cut one small part out of the landscape and use it as the basis for a composition. Until this time the picture surface had been treated as a safety

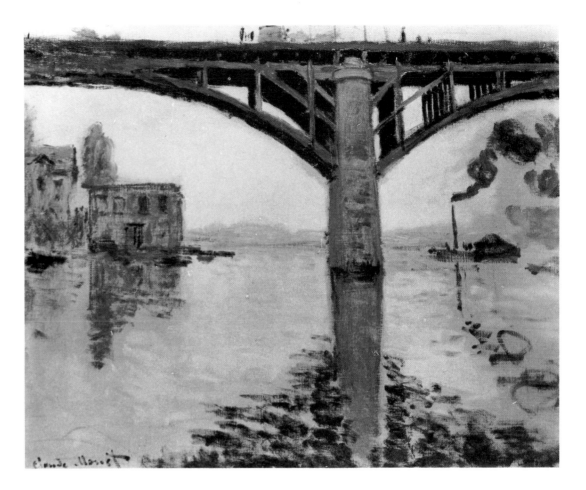

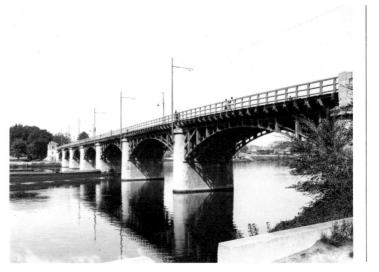

THE BRIDGE AS A SINGLE PIER

1874

THE ROADBRIDGE AT ARGENTEUIL

The bridge, with its cast-iron arches and stone piles, appears in many of Monet's paintings. This view shows almost exactly the same angle as his painting 'The Roadbridge at Argenteuil'.

deposit box, destined to hold everything of value in the landscape, but the Japanese proved that the most ingenious compositions could be built from apparently insignificant fragments of nature. This idea was reinforced still further by photography, for the camera often crops the subject unexpectedly: figures passing in the street are cut off by the frame of the picture, buildings are pruned at random while unnoticed details linger in the background. Even in the most carefully planned photograph there is an element of chance, but Monet had noticed that far from destroying the picture, this actually enriched its powers of description. The amputated parts remind us that the scene extends beyond the frame of the picture; that the painting is a window held up to nature, containing only a fraction of what is there. Monet didn't use a camera himself until some time later, but several of his friends were photographers.

Nadar, who had taken some of the earliest aerial pictures of Paris from a balloon, was often to be found at the Café Guerbois. Degas was an enthusiatic amateur photographer and used the camera to research the possibilities of his compositions: he regarded the new invention as a useful tool, but a poor substitute for painting. *'Faux art, faux peinture – photographie'*, he observed when pressed on the subject.

Study of the Japanese prints, and of the chance effects of photography, taught Monet how to strip his compositions to the bone. To nineteenth-century eyes these paintings, in which the identity of the individual parts were sacrificed to the overall design, were quite meaningless. Even Gustave Geffroy, one of Monet's first biographers, observed that if only the artist would speak in French rather than in Japanese more people would understand what he was saying. Monet, however, ignored these criticisms and tested the idea to its limits. 'Weeds by the Seine' (left) consists of nothing more than a tangle of undergrowth, a strip of horizon beyond and a blotchy sky above. Monet has described the entire space of the picture in the relative sizes of these few parts, defining the expanse of the river gliding past by the difference of scale between the rushes in the foreground and the tiny buildings behind them. Again, there is a strong family likeness between this painting and some of Whistler's Nocturnes, only its intention is rather less severe. To Monet, simplicity was not an intellectual ideal as it was to the American painter, but a means to an end. It offered him the chance to paint broad, open areas of colour, to study the atmospheric conditions of a landscape rather than its fussy details. In 'Sunset over Argenteuil' (page 92), for example, it is not the buildings, the boats or the rushes on the shore that have held Monet's attention but the evening light generated between them – the heavy, camphorated musk of cadmium orange and red laid over deep purple.

WEEDS BY THE SEINE

1874

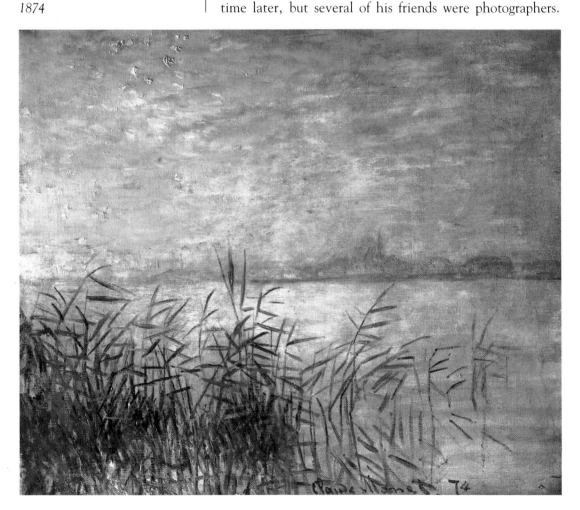

For Monet 1874 was a fertile year. Subject and technique were fused together into an increasingly coherent style, and the steady flow of paintings that he produced during the period reflects the satisfaction he felt in it. But it was also the year in which Impressionism was given its name. It was coined, as were so many such titles, during an exhibition. Bazille had been the first to suggest boycotting the Salon and putting on a group show; Monet now revived

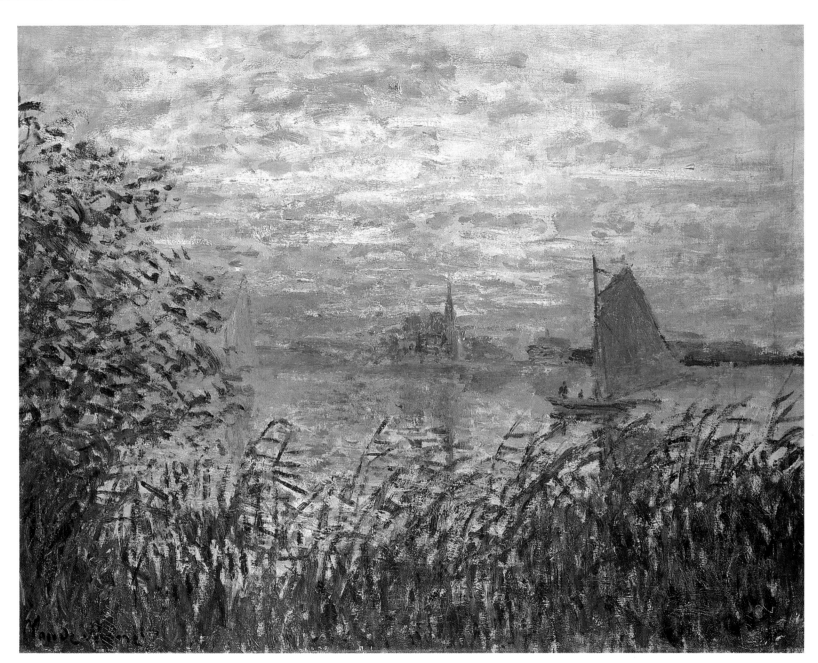

SUNSET OVER ARGENTEUIL

1874

the idea, encouraging his friends to join with him. Late in 1873 a society of artists was formed and among the first to sign into it were Monet, Renoir, Pissarro, Degas, Sisley and Berthe Morisot. Pissarro wanted it to be a co-operative with a strict code of regulations, like the Union of Professional Bakers that had recently started up in his home village of Pontoise. He showed them the terms that this body had drafted and suggested that they model theirs on similar lines. He recommended several additions and improvements of his own, but Renoir, who hated any sort of rule-making, objected to this excessive bureaucracy. Eventually, on 27 December, a charter was drawn up stating simply that each artist should pay an entrance subscription and then contribute one-tenth of his profits to a common fund. The exhibition opened on 15 April 1874 in Nadar's studio, which he loaned them without rent, on the Boulevard des Capucines. At first it had been suggested that they capitalize on this location and call themselves La Capucine, but fearing that this would label them as a 'new school' they settled for the less romantic title of 'The Anonymous Society of Painters, Engravers, Sculptors Etc'.

Degas wanted as many artists as possible to exhibit with them but, at the same time, he didn't want the show to take on too revolutionary a flavour. He was especially keen to recruit what he called 'hostages', painters that the public would tolerate but who were prepared to come in with the existing group. He invited the Italian artist De Nittis and

told him to send 'something important'. Tissot and Legros were also approached but, since they had recently moved over to England, both turned down the offer. Pissarro put forward Béliard, Guillaumin and Cézanne, but there was some difficulty getting the latter two accepted as some of the other members felt that their paintings could only incite an already hostile audience. Cals and Boudin sent pictures to the show, but for some reason Jongkind was not asked to take part. Others were conscripted from among the ranks of the artists' friends, and on the opening day the final list of participants included twenty-nine names. The painter most notable by his absence was Manet. He had notched up a success in the Salon in the previous year with a painting called 'Le Bon Bock'. Painted in a style somewhat reminiscent of Frans Hals, it showed the engraver Bellot, with a broad belly and face of white pastry, sitting back in the Café Guerbois comfortably grasping his pipe in one hand and a glass of beer in the other. The painting had wrung such praise from the critics that Manet was now wary of damaging his reputation by exhibiting alongside a group of rebel painters. He politely declined to join their society and encouraged Monet to abandon them also: 'Why don't you stay with me?' he asked, 'You can see very well that I'm on the right track'.

The exhibition was a disaster. The few members of the public who ventured up the staircase to see the show were undecided whether to laugh or take offence; some were amused by the paintings, others so enraged that it seemed they might tear them off the walls.

'Was art to be outraged like this?' asked the spectators in Zola's account of an exhibition such as this described in L'Oeuvre. 'One grave individual went away very angry, saying to his wife that he didn't like practical jokes. But another, a punctilious little man, having looked in the catalogue for the title of the work, in order to tell his daughter, read out the words, "In the Open Air", whereupon there came a formidable renewal of the clamour, hisses and shouts, and whatnot else besides. The title sped about; it was repeated, commented on. "In the Open Air! ah, yes, the open air…" The affair was becoming a scandal. The crowd still increased. People's faces grew red with congestion in the growing heat. Each had the stupidly gaping mouth of the ignoramus who judges painting, and between them they indulged all the asinine ideas, all the preposterous reflections, all the stupid, spiteful jeers that

Those artists who refused to submit their work to the Salon of 1874, held an exhibition in Nadar's Studio in the Boulevard des Capucines under the title 'The Anonymous Society of Painters, Engravers, Sculptors Etc'. The exhibition was a disaster and outraged both the critics and public alike. This cartoon was one of many to appear in the popular press, ridiculing the work of the 'Impressionists'.

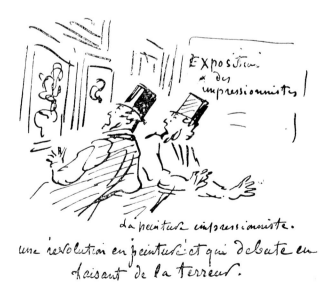

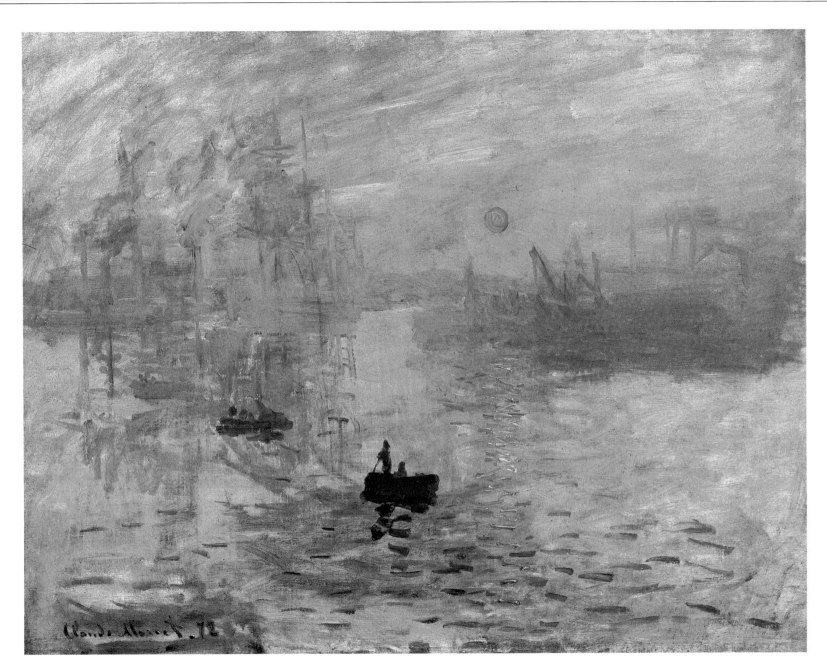

IMPRESSION, SUNRISE

1872

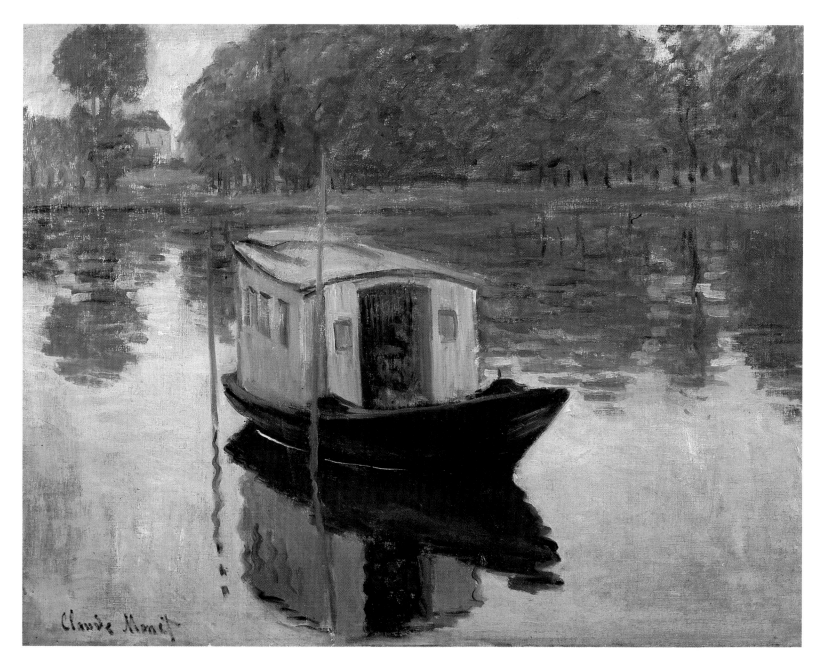

The Studio Boat at Argenteuil

1874

the sight of an original work can elicit from bourgeois imbecility.'

The pictures were referred to as 'daubs' and 'palette scrapings' and it wasn't long before a rumour confirmed that the artists didn't use brushes but loaded a revolver with their colours and fired them onto the canvas.

Monet had sent only five paintings and seven pastels to the exhibition. Among these was the painting he'd made in Le Havre of the sunrise over the Commercial Docks (page 94). He said later, recalling his reply on being asked how he wanted the picture entered in the catalogue: 'I couldn't very well call it a view of Le Havre so I said: "Put, Impression".' At once the critics pounced on the word and the works shown by the Anonymous Society of Painters, Engravers and Sculptors etc, became the first 'Exhibition of the Impressionists'.

It was the critic Louis Leroy who established this title in an article he wrote for the *Charivari* on 25 April 1874. In this he concocted an amusing, and entirely fictitious, conversation between himself and an aging academic painter whom he called M. Vincent:

> Oh it was a strenuous day when I ventured into the first exhibition on the Boulevard des Capucines in the company of M. Joseph Vincent, landscape painter, pupil of Bertin, recipient of medals and decorations under several governments! The rash man had come there without suspecting anything; he thought he would see the sort of painting one sees everywhere, good and bad, rather bad than good, but not hostile to good artistic manners, to devotion to form, and respect for the masters ...

As the old fellow tottered about the exhibition, Leroy described how his judgment was slowly eroded by the strange and bewildering pictures that confronted him.

> ... The poor man rambled on in this way quite peacefully, and nothing led me to anticipate the unfortunate accident which was to be the result of his visit to this hair-raising exhibition. He even sustained, without major injury, viewing the 'Fishing Boats Leaving the Harbour' by M. Claude Monet, perhaps because I tore him away from contemplation of this work before the small noxious figures in the foreground could produce their effect.
>
> Unfortunately, I was imprudent enough to leave him

too long in front of the 'Boulevard des Capucines' by the same painter.

> 'Ah-ha!' he sneered in Mephistophelian manner. 'Is that brilliant enough, now! There's impression, or I don't know what it means. only be so good as to tell me what those innumerable black lickings in the lower part of the picture represent?'
>
> 'Why, those are people walking along,' I replied.
>
> 'Then do I look like that when I'm walking along the Boulevard des Capucines? Blood and thunder! So you are making fun of me at last?'
>
> 'I assure you, M. Vincent ...'
>
> 'But those spots were obtained by the same method as that used to imitate marble: a bit here, a bit there, slapdash, any old way. It's unheard of, appalling! I'll get a stroke from it for sure.'
>
> ... I glanced at Bertin's pupil; his countenance had turned a deep red. A catastrophe seemed to me imminent, and it was reserved for M. Monet to contribute the last straw.
>
> 'Ah, there he is, there he is!' he cried, in front of No. 98. 'I recognize him, papa Vincent's favourite! What does that canvas depict? Look at the catalogue.'
>
> 'Impression, Sunrise.'
>
> 'Impression – I was sure of it. I was just telling myself that, since I was impressed, there had to be some impression in it ... and what freedom, what ease of workmanship! Wallpaper in its embryonic state was more finished than that seascape.'
>
> In vain I tried to revive his expiring reason ... but the horrible fascinated him ... finally the pitcher ran over. The classic head of *père* Vincent, assailed from too many sides, went completely to pieces. He paused before the municipal guard who watches over all these treasures and, taking him to be a portrait, began for my benefit a very emphatic criticism.
>
> 'Is he ugly enough?' he remarked, shrugging his shoulders. From the front, he has two eyes ... and a nose ... and a mouth! Impressionists wouldn't have thus sacrificed to detail. With what the painter has expended in the way of useless things, Monet would have done twenty municipal guards!'
>
> 'Keep moving, will you!' said the "portrait".
>
> 'You hear him – he even talks! The poor fool who daubed at him must have spent a lot of time at it!'

I F MONET WAS DISAPPOINTED by the outcome of the exhibition he didn't allow it to show in his work, and the paintings he made later that year reflected a world of

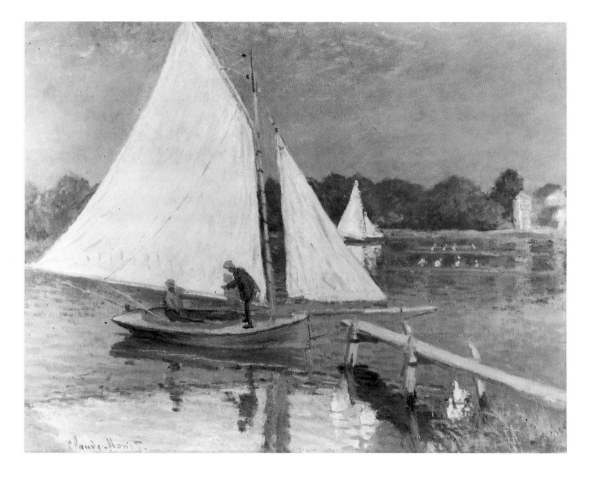

SAILBOATS AT ARGENTEUIL

1874

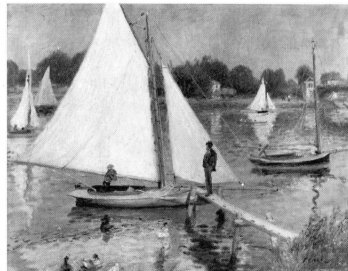

RENOIR:
SAILBOATS AT ARGENTEUIL

1874

increasing tranquillity. He had built himself a floating studio and in this he was able work in peace, rowing himself about the eddies and streams of the river in search of new motifs.

The inspiration for this boat had probably come from Daubigny who had owned one rather similar, known as 'Le Botin', which he had kept on the river Oise. The inside had been as neat as a gypsy caravan, with onions, fish and sides of smoked bacon hanging from the roof. Canvases, spirit lamps and bedding had lined the walls and in this little cabin Daubigny had lived and worked, sometimes for days on end. Monet's boat was similar in many ways, although it never seems to have been given a name. It was a curious looking craft with a striped awning and pale green cabin built over a shallow-draughted hull; its flat, sloping roof, high walls and square-cut windows gave it a strangely top-heavy appearance, as if it were a floating sedan chair.

In this ungainly vehicle Monet brought to its logical conclusion an idea that had been seeded in his mind many years before. On the hull of a boat he finally managed to bring studio and landscape together, floating his materials out into the open air. The boat offered him a range of new possibilities, but there were times also when he turned the tables and used it as his subject rather than his studio. In 'The Studio Boat at Argenteuil' (page 95) it lies at its moorings with the trees of the promenade stretched out behind, and in many of the paintings of the boat rental area the coachwork of its cabin can be seen jutting up above the hulls of the yachts.

It is possible that while designing and building the studio boat Monet had been helped by Gustave Caillebotte, a keen yachtsman who lived nearby. This tall and elegant young man had become a close friend of Monet, and being blessed with a good income as an engineer could afford to buy several of his pictures. There was a faint echo of Bazille in Caillebotte's personality and in many ways he came to fill this role in Monet's life. He was also an extremely capable artist in his own right; he had a good eye for colour and a natural love of life in the open air, and it was only a matter of time before he fell under the spell of Impressionism.

MONET HAD NOT BEEN working alone at Argenteuil. In 1872, during the first summer he was there, he had been joined by Sisley, his shy and gentle friend from student days. Renoir had stayed with him on several occasions and in 1874, following the first Impressionist Exhibition, they had once again worked together on the banks of the Seine. Here they revived their old, slightly competitive policy of painting identical compositions. Their two versions of 'Sailboats at Argenteuil' (page 97), painted within a few yards of each other, differ only in the fine details. Renoir's is slightly crowded; the horizon line of the far shore is high; the river fills two-thirds of the painting, with sailing boats and ducks idling on its surface. Monet's painting is more open; there is a broader belt of sky and the river is less busy. There is also a tiny variation in time: Monet has represented the scene about two minutes after Renoir; the figure on the jetty has jumped on board, the boat has slipped its moorings and moved out into the stream, falling back within the picture, and taking up fractionally less space on the canvas. It is interesting to notice that Monet has included only one yacht in the background of his picture but he has used it to hide the building on the far shore, whereas Renoir shows it clearly nestling among the trees and scatters its reflection on the water below. This little white-washed house, which can usually be seen in the background of Monet's paintings of the roadbridge, was a restaurant and café. It was well situated on the water's edge, although it doesn't seem to have been popular with the artists and there is no reference to any of them using it.

Another familiar figure to be seen on the river that summer was Manet. He was staying at the family home in Gennevilliers, where both his grandfather and his great-grandfather had been mayor in their time. He often joined Monet at Argenteuil and commemorated their days together with a painting of Monet at work on the studio boat, showing him sitting cross-legged on the foredeck, his brush poised before the canvas, while Camille sits in the doorway behind. The painting is rapid and sketchy, dashed down on the canvas in a single day. Around the firm capsule of the boat, the atmosphere flickers with blues, ochres and greens. It is quite evident that this painting has been worked in the open air. Despite his reservations, and the scathing remarks he had made on the subject, Manet had finally been tempted to work directly from nature. Watching Monet at work that summer of 1874, piecing his pictures together from small strokes of brilliant colour, had finally caught Manet's imagination: the influence reversed; the master

became the pupil and he announced Monet to be the 'Raphael of water'. Manet's paintings from this brief period come very close to Monet's; his brush darts and stabs at the canvas, creating light in a thousand touches of colour. He never allowed the new technique to smother his own, however, refusing to throw away his tube of black paint and still devising his pictures around the central focus of the figure, often cropping the subject into dramatic compositions.

What distinguished Argenteuil from the other towns that freckled the banks of the Seine was that it lay on one of the few stretches of the river that did not curve. From Epinay to the barrage at Bezons, it ran as straight as a Roman road. This made it ideal for racing boats, and in

POSTER FOR THE ARGENTEUIL REGATTA OF 1850

This poster, dated Sunday 25 August 1850, advertised the first regatta to be held at Argenteuil. Proudly comparing itself to the races at Le Havre, it boasted classes for sailing boats as well as sculls. The band of the National Guard accompanied the occasion with music and announced the start of each race with a fanfare. In the evening there was an open-air ball with illuminations and circus acts, and the promenade was lined with boats decked out with bunting. Regattas became a popular feature of the summer in Argenteuil and the colourful events were used by Monet as a subject for his paintings.

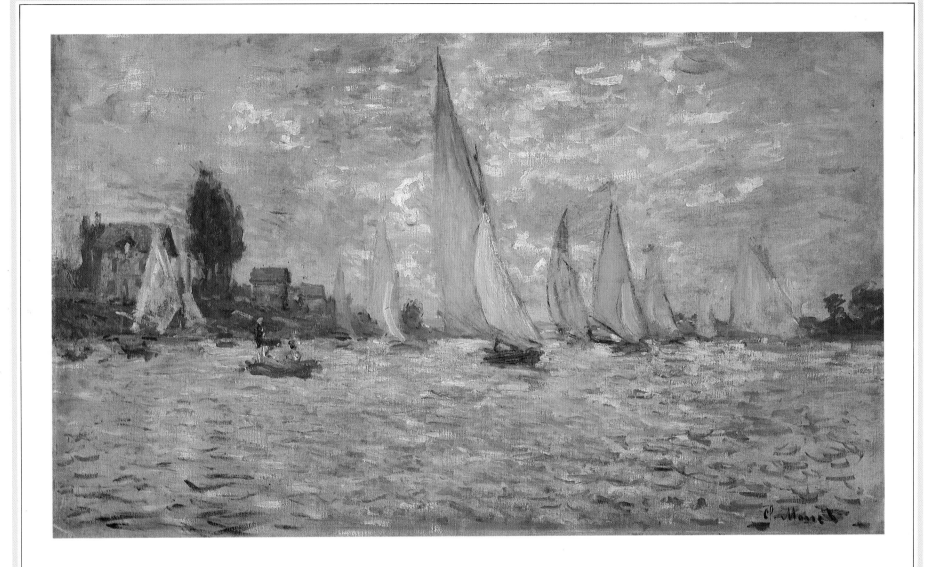

REGATTA AT ARGENTEUIL

1874

1850 Argenteuil had taken advantage of this topographical phenomenon by staging its first regatta, the poster proudly comparing the occasion to the famous races at Le Havre. Special trains from the Gare Saint-Lazare were laid on and an extra service from the diligence for those coming from outside Paris shuttled visitors from the station at Asnières. The site was so successful, and the regattas there so popular, that seventeen years later the Paris World's Fair held its boat races at Argenteuil. With this, the town's name became synonymous with yachting and regattas part of its everyday life:

Monet's painting of the races at Argenteuil (page 99) emphasizes how rapid his technique has become; he is able to watch a flotilla of boats speeding by and register the curve of their sails, the angle of their hulls and the light sparkling on their wakes in a handful of brushstrokes scattered down on the canvas. In holding a fleeting effect of light, Monet has also arrested a moment in time, suspending the boats on the water as they race towards the finishing line.

The locals were rather less captivated by the new sport. Boating seemed to bring out the worst in Parisians; it was healthy and carefree but it was also definitely time 'out of school'. The owner of one of the three wash-houses had complained that rowdy oarsmen had damaged his floating establishment, and demanded that they be forbidden to row within given distance of the roadbridge. Maupassant confessed that as a young man he had passed some wild days in Argenteuil:

> There were five of us, a small group of friends who are pillars of the community today. As none of us had any money, we set up an indescribable sort of club in a frightful pothouse at Argenteuil, renting a single dormitory bedroom where I spent what were the maddest nights of my life. We thought about nothing but having fun and rowing, for all of us with one exception regarded rowing as a religion.

Monet lived in Argenteuil for almost six years, longer than he had stayed in any one place since his childhood. During these years, however, he often went away on painting expeditions elsewhere. In 1872 he travelled down to Rouen, the old capital of Normandy, to see some paintings that he had on exhibition there. Napoleon had once said that Le Havre, Rouen and Paris were really one city with the Seine as its high street, and so it may seem inevitable that Monet,

who had worked in both the other districts of this 'city', should eventually find his way there. He had often been to Rouen before, but this was the first time he stayed long enough to paint in the city. Some of the pictures he made there in 1872 seem to anticipate those of the Petit Bras. His painting of a 'Ship at Anchor' (opposite), for example, with its heavy rigging and furled sails set against a sky of galvanized metal, has something of the same quality of loneliness he was to work into 'Pleasure Boats at Argenteuil'.

The personality of the river alters at Rouen: the banks become wider, the current slows down and the water-level is governed by the rise and fall of the tide. Until recently, the stone bridge at Rouen had been the final crossing point on the Seine before it flowed out towards the sea and the first that ships would encounter as they headed upstream. The city, as a result, had become the warden of the upper Seine. It was here that all seagoing traffic was stopped to be checked over by the customs officials. In addition to this, every captain had to prove that he had the correct river-charts before carrying on up the river towards Paris, and steamships were obliged to have their boilers inspected, to satisfy the port authorities that the peace of the Seine valley was not about to be shattered by a sudden unscheduled explosion.

Parts of Rouen had remained unchanged since medieval times. Alleyways trickled about the town with no more determination than a country stream, buildings leaned on each other for support and heavily gabled houses closed over the streets, their upper storeys hanging above the pavements like the carved sterns of wooden galleons. In the market square, site of the burning of Joan of Arc, the fish-wives sold herrings from Honfleur, their strident, argumentative voices advertising their wares and scattering the seagulls. Pascal had been born in Rouen, Henry V had built his palace there, Molière had visited the city as had Voltaire and, by the time Monet arrived, their memories had been preserved, with those of Rollo and William the Conqueror, in the names of the streets. The writer Flaubert had also been born in Rouen and was presently living some miles further downstream in a house that was regularly pointed out to tourists as they passed on the ferryboat to Le Havre. Of more immediate relevance to Monet, his brother Léon had moved to Rouen and had set up as a chemist in the city.

Monet made several further trips to Rouen and on one

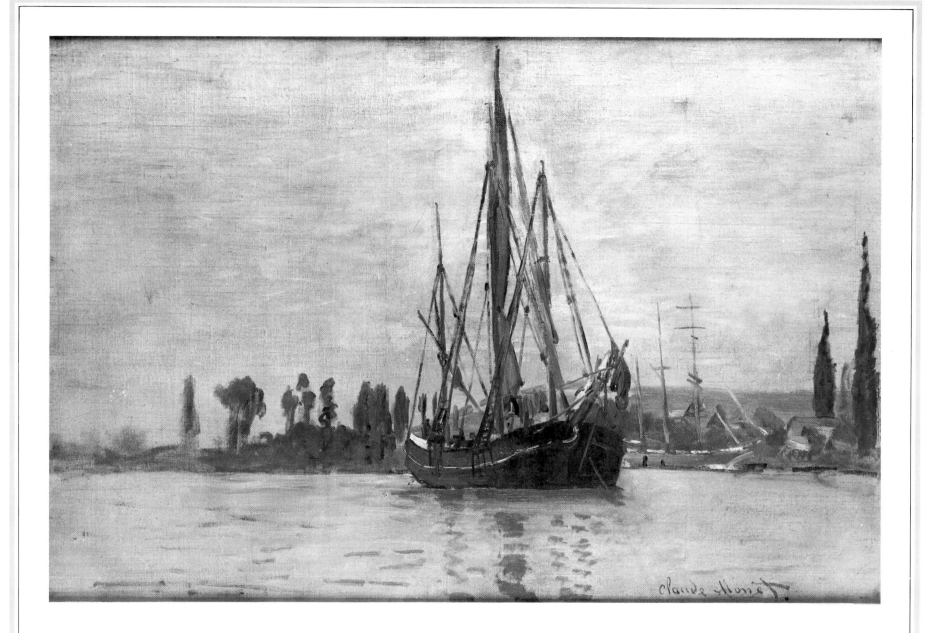

SHIP AT ANCHOR, ROUEN

1872

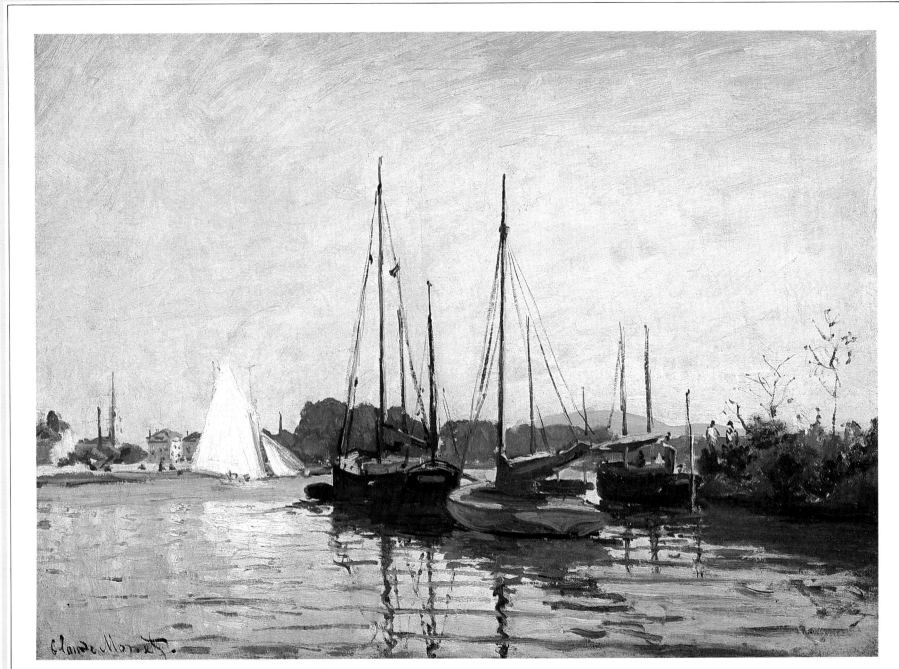

PLEASURE BOATS AT ARGENTEUIL

1872

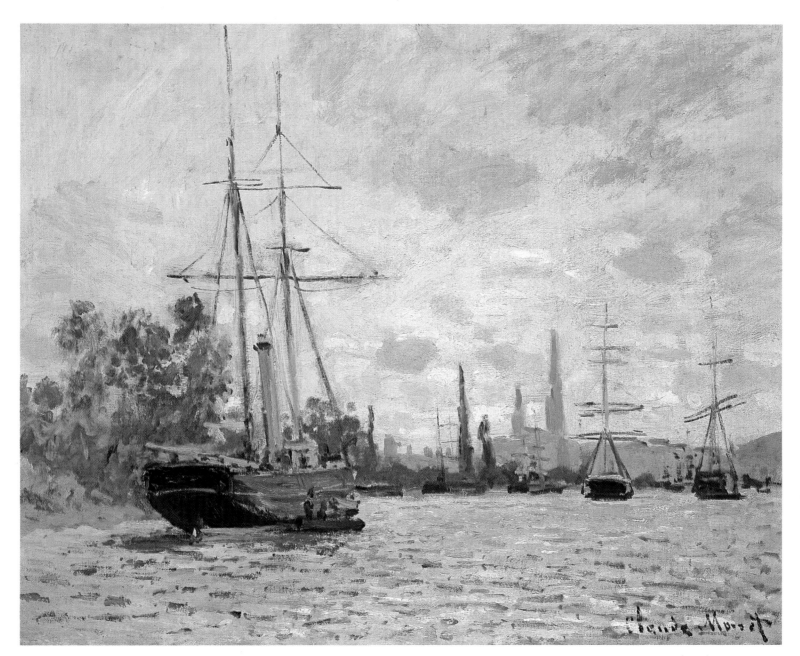

THE SEINE AT ROUEN

1873

occasion rowed the whole family down there on his floating studio. In 1873 he painted 'The Seine at Rouen' (page 103) from the deck of a boat on the river. Clouds muster above the distant spires, and a splendid steamship with a smoke-stack as high and thin as a cigar tube rides at anchor in the lee of the island: Monet rustles up the breeze on the river below in rapid brushstrokes dragged across the water.

Monet had many attractive traits of personality, but his attitude to financial matters invariably shows him in an unflattering light. As a young man he was constantly im-poverished and his letters to Bazille were soured by repeated demands for money. At Argenteuil, the situation was no different, and while he was living there he sent out endless distress signals to his friends in Paris. Without Bazille to turn to any longer, he tried touching anyone he thought might be worth a few francs, borrowing from Manet, Pissarro and many of his patrons. But this never seemed to solve the problem and in 1874, at the merciless hour of seven-thirty in the morning, he was finally thrown out of Mme Aubry-Villet's house and was forced to find lodgings elsewhere. It might be assumed from this, and other similar occasions, that Monet never managed to earn any money of his own, but this is not the case. In his first year in Argenteuil his income was around 12,000 francs, and over twice as much in the following year, at a time when the average wage of a working man was around 2000 francs a year. This was almost entirely due to the patronage of one man. In 1870, while he was staying in London, Monet had been intro-duced to a dealer called Durand-Ruel. This exiled French-man had recently opened a gallery in Bond Street and was on the lookout for new talent. He took a liking to Monet's pictures straight away and bought several, continuing to do so on his return to Paris after the war. Durand-Ruel was to be Monet's most faithful patron and it was to him that Monet would owe much of his later success and fame.

The first Impressionist exhibition had not improved Monet's reputation and a disastrous sale of paintings at the Hôtel Drouot in 1875 compounded the damage. Despite this, Monet still managed to find new collectors eager to buy his work. Caillebotte regularly bought his pictures, often paying for them in advance, De Bellio became an enthusiastic patron, and when Victor Chocquet was intro-duced to Monet in 1875 he was said to have cried out, with

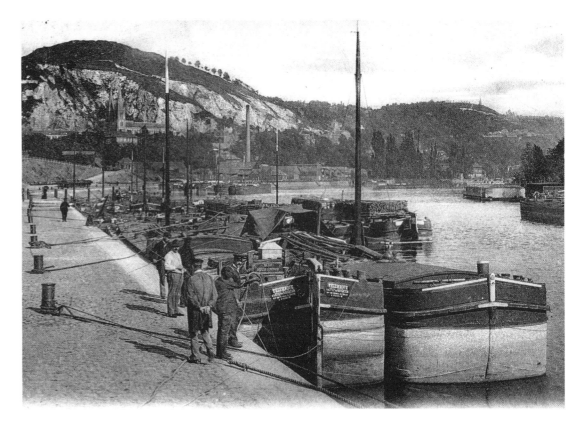

tears in his eyes: 'When I think of how I've lost a year, how I might have got to know your painting a year sooner. How could I have been deprived of such a pleasure!'

In addition to this, Camille came into some money of her own while they were at Argenteuil. At the time of the marriage her family had closed ranks against Monet, mis-trusting his motives, and had done their best to keep Camille's inheritance from him. She had been granted a small dowry of 500 francs at the time and the rest was locked away into a trust. In 1873 her father died, and it was only after this that she received the full sum of 12,000 francs. Even then there were difficulties, as Camille's mother tried to withhold payments and the money only reached them in instalments.

Nevertheless, with these resources behind him Monet need not have been burdened by any financial problems. He had a good income during his years at Argenteuil and yet he seemed incapable of living within it; whatever he earned he spent. Monet was a curious blend of stubbornness and sunny optimism; he looked upon the comfortable,

VIEW OF ROUEN

This famous medieval city had the distinction of being both the capital of Normandy and the final crossing-point on the Seine before the river flowed out to the sea. As a young man Monet had submitted paintings to an exhibition in Rouen and had visited the city to see them on view. While he was in Argenteuil, he rowed his entire family down to Rouen, so that he could work in the city for a while, and years later returned to paint the celebrated 'Rouen Cathedral' series.

middle-class life he led at Argenteuil as his birthright, and nothing would convince him that he should economize or keep control of the flow of his money. When Durand-Ruel suggested that it might take the strain off his budget if he were to drink wine made locally, rather than have it imported from the south, Monet was mortally offended. The remark was not intended to be sarcastic, however, as for centuries Argenteuil had been famous as a wine-producing district. Monet remained unimpressed by this local product, however, and possibly subscribed to Sauvan's view that 'the environs of Argenteuil produce a great quantity of wine, which is of indifferent quality, and sold at very low price, but it is nevertheless held in some estimation by the lower classes of the people of Paris'.

In 1875, Monet's handling of paint began to alter. He stopped using flat washes; the broad open areas of colour became smaller and were eventually reduced to tiny dots that seem to quiver on the canvas. In 'Boats on the Banks of the Seine at Gennevilliers' (page 6), water, trees and sky have been scribbled into the picture with the tip of the brush, the raw material of the canvas showing through between the strokes. Figures, buildings and boats emerge from the unfocused haze of paintwork and the colours dance together on the picture surface like the primitive, pulsating life-forms that can be seen under a laboratory microscope. Stippling the canvas with pinpricks of light, he dissolves the scene in a confusion of colour that defines the light, but scarcely contains the forms.

Petit-Gennevilliers, the nest of whitewashed houses that fills the foreground of this picture, was probably a less attractive place to live in than it may appear. During the rebuilding of Paris, Baron Haussmann had installed an elaborate maze of sewers under the foundations of the new city. Beneath each street there was a conduit as large as a railway tunnel that followed the line of the road, and the ground plan of these ambitious waterworks was therefore identical to that of Paris itself. Jean Valjean, the hero of Victor Hugo's Les Misérables, was able to make his way around the rabbit warren of these tunnels simply by imposing on them a mental picture of the streets above. The one drawback to this miracle of hygiene was that the entire contents of these sewers was pumped out into the Seine. Dead dogs floated on the water, plants were poisoned, and in

summer the smell was so appalling that the riverbanks became quite unapproachable. The only solution that the government could come up with was to use the effluent as fertilizer. Irrigation ditches were cut and the whole might of the Paris sewage system was redirected into the fields around Gennevilliers, to the dismay of the inhabitants who found themselves besieged by an evil black liquid that surrounded their homes and seeped into their gardens.

Monet left Argenteuil in 1877. This was no sudden whim; he had been restless for some time and in recent months had often been out of the town working elsewhere. In the hard winter of 1875 he had painted two spectacular views of the river under snow, flooding the canvas with a hard, crystalline light of blue and white in which the details of the frozen landscape seem to evaporate (page 106). In the summer he had worked on a series of paintings of his studio boat and after that he seemed to lose interest in the river, preferring the privacy of his garden. During 1876 he had stayed for part of the year in Paris, painting in the Parc Monceau and the Tuileries gardens.

Before leaving Argenteuil, Monet painted four final pictures of the promenade, returning to the theme that had caught his imagination when he first arrived in the town. Instead of standing on the towpath, however, he set up his easel in the little garden belonging to the bain chaud. The colour in these paintings is warm and pungent. In 'Argenteuil, the Banks in Flower' (page 107) a dense, inpenetrable screen of pigment fills the lower parts of the canvas. Monet slashes the surface of the paint with small, hooked strokes of the brush and the reds and yellows of roses burst like starshells in the shadows. The manor house, the factory chimneys and the trees of the Ile Marante are lost in a wall of colour and fall away without scale or reference, merging into the background. The paintings that Monet had made of the promenade in 1872 are calm and ordered, still in touch with the traditions of another age, whereas these latter versions are rich and drowsy, ungoverned by the past, with colour as heady as opium. In Monet's six years at Argenteuil his style had undergone an astonishing metamorphosis. The conventions of landscape painting were transformed into a personal language of paint and colour, orchestrations of light existing independently on the canvas.

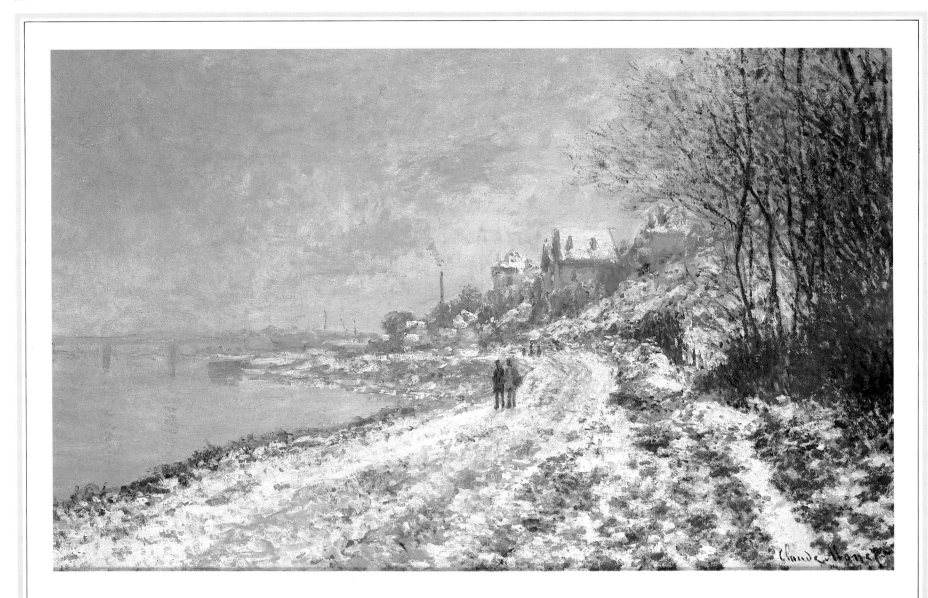

ARGENTEUIL IN WINTER

1875

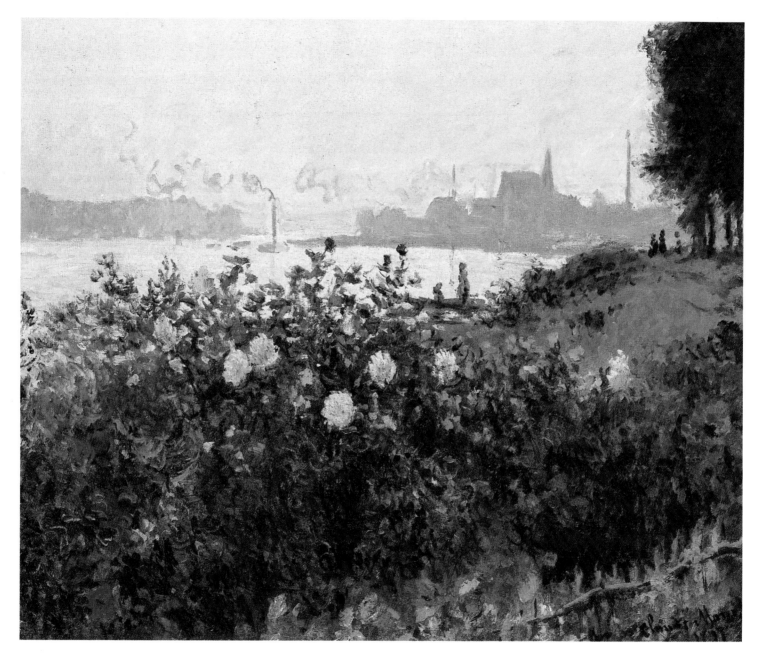

ARGENTEUIL, THE BANKS IN FLOWER

1877

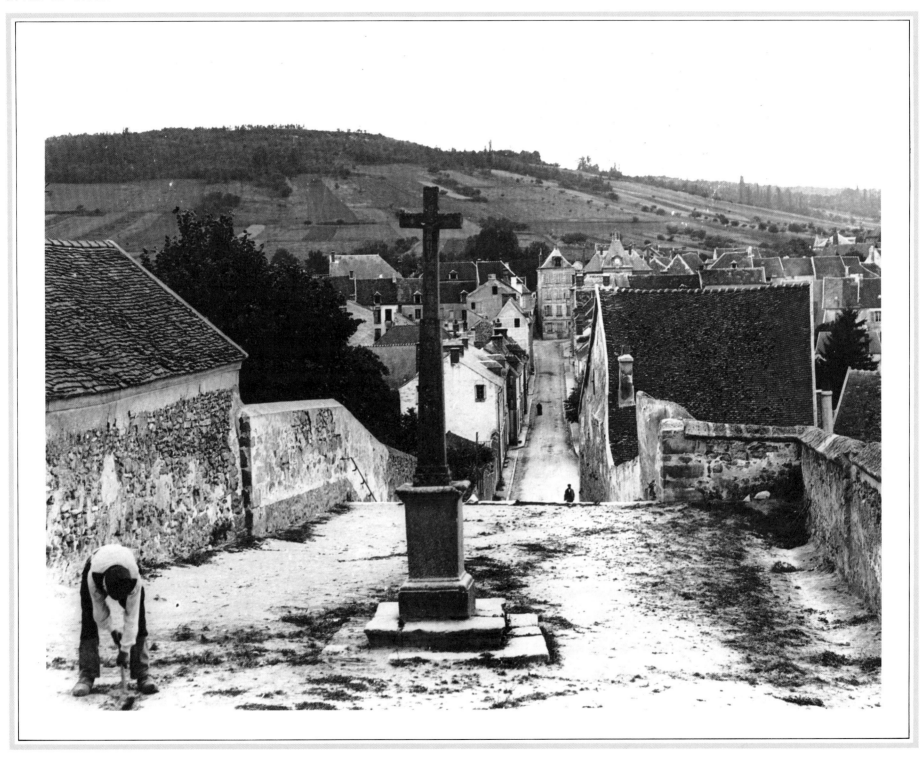

VETHEUIL

1878–1881

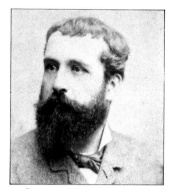

CLAUDE MONET, C. 1880

This photograph was taken from the door of a church, looking down over the tiled roofs of the town, which lies in a curve of the Seine valley and bedded between rolling chalk hills. Vétheuil was the most rural landscape that Monet had worked in for some years, quite different from the suburbs of Paris where he had pioneered Impressionism. Originally he had only intended to stay in the town for three months, but the scenery so fascinated him that he lived there for three years.

In 1880, WHILE MONET was living at Vétheuil, a journalist asked him if he could be permitted to see his studio. Without hesitation Monet crossed the room and throwing open the windows he pointed out at the landscape. 'Voilà,' he replied. The view was of a dusty road and a garden on the far side, bursting with sunflowers, geraniums and gladioli, that tumbled down the side of a hill into the Seine valley. Beyond this stretched the great expanse of the river, bordered by willows and warted with small islands, its course curving away between the rounded shoulders of chalk hills.

Monet moved to Vétheuil in 1878. He rented a house on the very edge of the village and here installed eight children, two mothers and a destitute businessman. At the time, he had been intending to stay no more than a few months before moving on. As it turned out, he was to live there with his large and complicated household for almost three years.

The story of this *ménage* had begun two years earlier when, in 1876, Monet had been invited to stay at the Château Rottembourg. This imposing country house lay to the south-east of Paris in the town of Montgeron. It belonged to one of his patrons, Ernest Hoschedé, a Belgian millionaire with a passion for modern paintings, who had submitted occasional pieces of criticism to the art journals and was often to be found at the Café Guerbois. He had been among the first to buy Impressionist pictures and his collection included works by Manet, Degas, Renoir and Sisley.

Hoschedé had inherited a large textile business from his father and a share in the successful '*Au Gagne Petit*' department store in the Avenue de l'Opéra. He and his wife Alice were lavish patrons, latter-day Medicis, who liked to entertain on a grand scale. Friends, celebrities and protégés would be invited to stay for as long as they chose, often arriving at the house on private trains that had been laid on specially from the Gare de Lyon. Manet, Sisley, Carolus-Duran and Baudry had been among the guests.

The setting at Montgeron was spectacular; manicured gardens spread out from the house, shaded by cedars. Avenues and arbours linked them together and beyond them stretched a swathe of parkland where turkeys strutted about in the long grass. There were fishing expeditions, shooting parties and games on the lawn to pass away the day, while a regiment of nannies was on hand to occupy the children in the meantime. Visiting artists were offered apartments of their own with studios immaculately fitted out: the Hoschedés would call in from time to time to see how work was progressing.

Monet stayed at the house for several months and during this time he became a close friend of the family. While he was with them he painted a portrait of Germaine Hoschedé, the youngest of the five children, and was commissioned to make four decorative panels for the house. The Hoschedés had a small fishing lodge on the Yerres, a tributary of the Seine, and here Monet was able to turn to his favourite

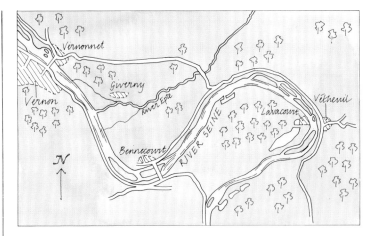

theme of painting light on water. Curiously, there is no evidence of Camille being at Montgeron with him.

In 1877 the whole fabric of this glittering world came crashing down when Hoschedé was unexpectedly declared bankrupt. There had been intimations of this collapse, slight tremors in the ground; only four years before he had been obliged to sell off some of his paintings, but no one at the time had appreciated quite how badly the situation was deteriorating. Unknown to his wife and family, for he had made a policy of never discussing financial matters with them, his resources had been dwindling for some time. The talent that he showed for collecting paintings unfortunately did not extend to his business affairs; his investments had been losing heavily and the board had eventually become impatient and demanded his resignation. With this, Hoschedé appears to have lost his head completely: he tried to commit suicide and when the attempt failed he bolted back to Belgium, leaving his family to fend for themselves. The great house, the furniture, and the collection of paintings that had been assembled over the years with such care and taste were all put up for auction; profits from the sale were immediately swallowed up by the creditors who were camped in the grounds. For Alice Hoschedé the catastrophe came as a bolt from the blue; one of the most feted hostesses of French society until a few weeks before, she now found herself with nothing she could call her own except five children and one maid who had refused to leave her. In desperation she returned to her family at Biarritz, a journey made all the more fraught when she went into labour prematurely and the train had to be stopped while she gave birth to her sixth child, Jean-Pierre.

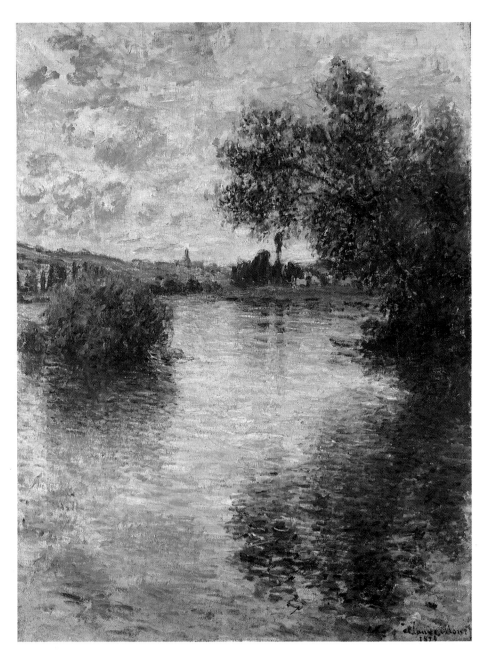

THE SEINE AT VÉTHEUIL

1879

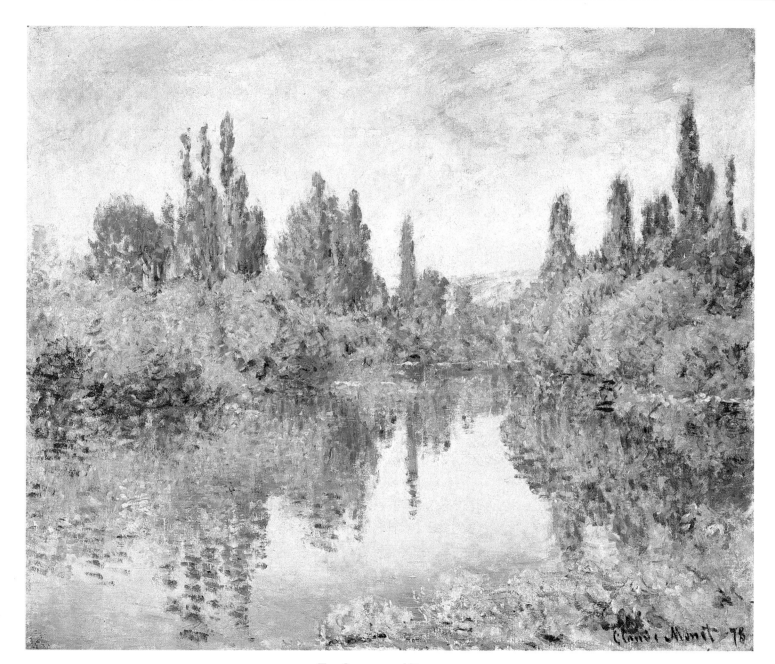

THE SEINE NEAR VÉTHEUIL

1878

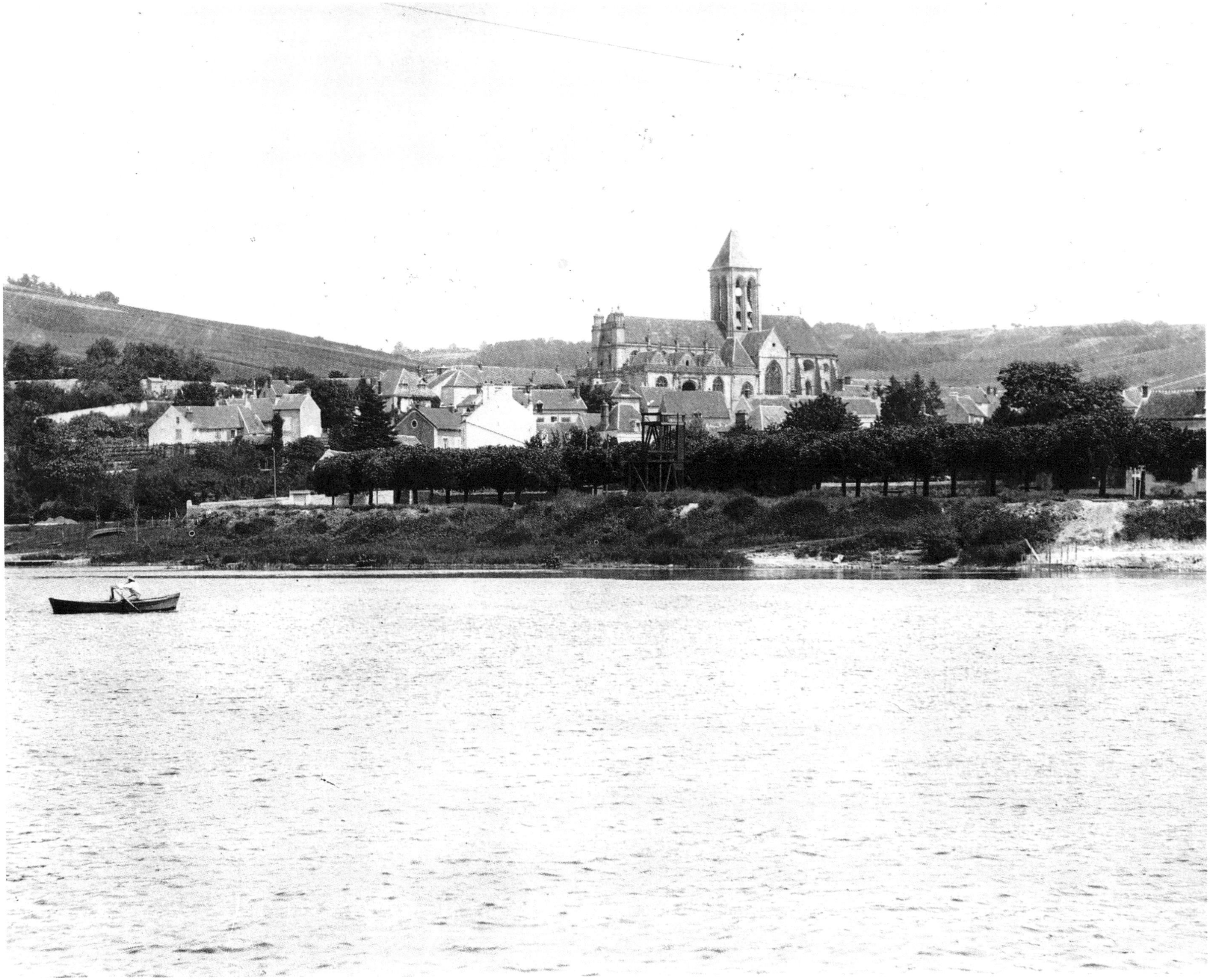

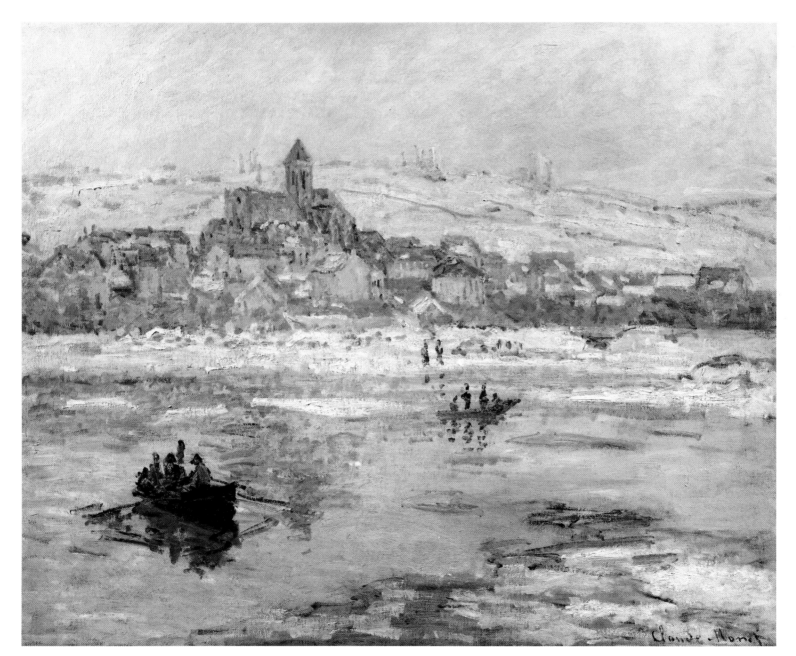

VÉTHEUIL IN WINTER

1879

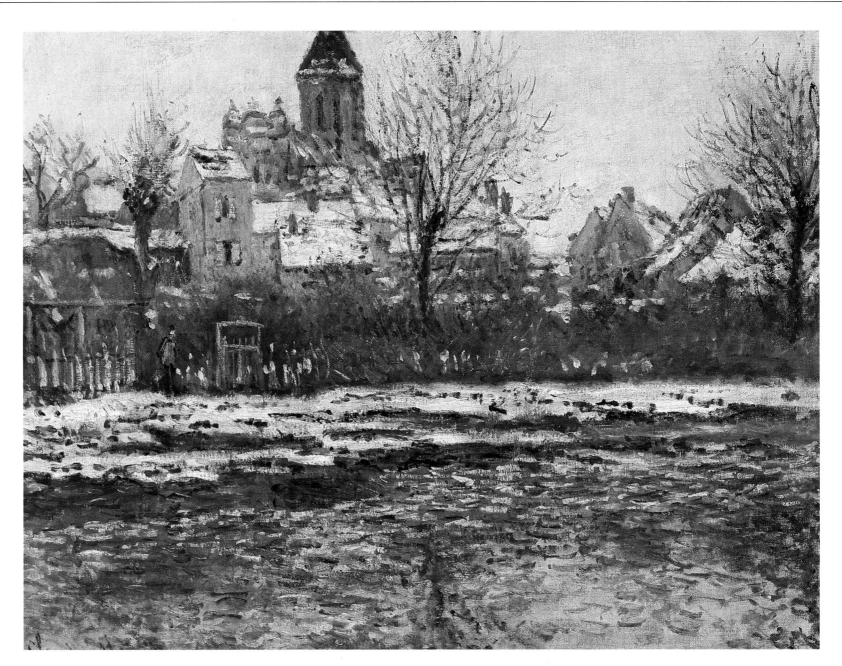

SNOW EFFECT AT VÉTHEUIL

1878-9

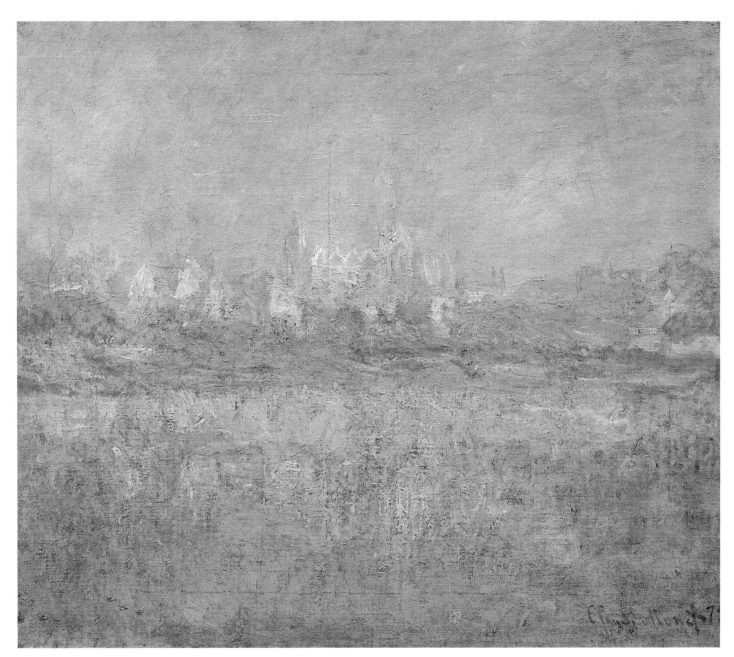

VÉTHEUIL IN FOG

1879

Given a small annuity from her family, Alice Hoschedé moved to Paris and rented an apartment in the north of the city. Here she would often run into the Monets, and their children played together in the Parc Monceau. By now Hoschedé had returned from Belgium and was making vague and generally futile efforts to rebuild his lost business empire. In the autumn of 1878 the two families decided to join forces and, pooling their meagre resources, they moved out to Vétheuil where they shared a house. Quite how they had arrived at this arrangement is not too clear. It could have been nothing more than convenience for all concerned but it is also possible that earlier at Montgeron, Monet had initiated some sort of affair with Alice Hoschedé. The reports on this subject are partisan, and consequently varied. The line that both families upheld at Vétheuil was that Alice Hoschedé had moved in with the Monets to nurse Camille, who had been ill since giving birth to her second son, Michel, in March of that year.

'Vétheuil is a sort of Sleepy Hollow', wrote one traveller on the Seine, 'prettily situated at the entrance to two charming valleys. It consists practically of a single street, paved with sets, with two narrow footpaths, and gutters of running water. A short, narrow, undulating passageway runs at right angles to the main street, at the top of which, on a small plateau, reached by a flight of steps, is the old church, the principal feature of interest in the place.'

Above the town there rose a steep escarpment that followed the line of the river towards La Roche Guyon, crumbling in places to expose high chalk cliffs. A ragged coat of vegetation covered its back. The views from these heights were famous and one local guidebook, translated for English travellers, warmly recommended the pathways in the valley to ramblers, naturalists and other 'amateurs of footing'.

'I've pitched my tent in a ravishing landscape on the banks of the Seine,' Monet told Murer shortly after his arrival. In those days Vétheuil was completely rural; the local community was provincial and the rhythm of its life had remained unchanged for centuries. The one dash of exoticism in the town was added by the tobacconist, who was reported to be able to speak a few words of English. Vétheuil was not easy to reach; the train only went as far as Mantes and from there the journey had to be completed on board *père* Papavoine's coach, a single-horsed, unsprung contraption that rattled between the two towns when the weather permitted. Although he had never worked in Vétheuil before, Monet would have known of this little town, with its brown stone buildings and blunt church steeple, for some time. He would have seen it as he rowed downstream on his way to Rouen, and it may be no coincidence that the town was set on the river only a few miles from Bennecourt.

Monet's interest in the Seine, which seemed to have been waning in his last days at Argenteuil, had returned to him once more. Early in 1878, while he was still in Paris, he had painted on the island of La Grande Jatte, viewing the river through a screen of spring leaves and embroidering the surface of the canvas with stitches of brilliant green. When he arrived at Vétheuil he immediately began to explore the possibilities of the river. On board the studio boat, which he kept moored below the house, Monet rowed through the backwaters formed by the islands in the river, between banks heavy with undergrowth and summer foliage.

'It is delightful to paddle among the sinuous waterways,' recalled one such oarsman at Vétheuil, 'and to follow the windings of the gentle current as it curves among the many eyots and under overhanging branches and masses of trembling foliage through which the sunshine struggles, illuminating the whole with an endless range of shades of tender green; here and there, streaks of bright light shoot across the water, and in the warm beams dragonflies play, and now and again a kingfisher darts across, his bright plumage lighting up in the gleam like the flash of an emerald.'

Monet's first paintings of Vétheuil, made early in the autumn of 1878, show the river thick and overgrown and still as a dew-pond (page 111). These are peaceful and secluded pictures, with no human presence to disturb them, but as winter approached he turned his attention to the town, centering his pictures on the church. Parts of this building dated back to the thirteen century and its stonework was so soft and worn that timber piers had recently been added to shore up the nave. The stump of the church steeple, with the clam-shells of the buildings clinging to its base, became one of Monet's favourite subjects at Vétheuil; his chosen motif, so to speak.

Sometimes working from the deck of his boat, on other occasions viewing it from one of the many islands in the stream, he returned to the subject over and again, painting it in every season and change of weather. In 'Vétheuil in Winter' (page 113) it stands out firmly against the frozen hillside, riding above the rooftops of the town and separated from the water below by a band of thickly painted snow. In 'Snow Effect at Vétheuil' (page 114) Monet frames the church more closely, clipping off the tip of the steeple and concentrating on the horizontal strata of the scene. The colour, even in this subdued world, is deep and sensuous: touches of ultramarine accent the areas of grey and copper green. Slashing strokes of pure white are interrupted by shadows as dark as treacle.

Monet's handling of the paint is particularly clear in these winter scenes. The accepted practice dictated that a painting should be worked 'from dark to light', but Monet has clearly dispensed with this technique altogether. Instead, he laid in his pictures with a mid-tone, a blush of atmospheric colour somewhere in between light and shade, and developed the picture from there. In its early stages the painting must have been simply an association of colours, with little form or definition. As it progressed, Monet clarified the structure of the landscape, analyzing the colour more precisely and increasing the understanding of its form as he did so. The extremities of the picture, the highlights and deep shadows, were added last, literally written onto the surface of the canvas, and with these finishing touches Monet explained the finer details of the scene.

This formidable technique can be seen clearly in the rendering of the church in 'Snow Effect at Vétheuil'. The bulk of the building has been laid into the painting in a warm, putty grey and the defining details of the roof, facade and lantern windows are scribbled over the picture surface in hasty strokes of blue and white, almost as a postscript. So much of the painting relies on implication. Avoiding any stress on the outline of the hedge on the riverbank, Monet simply allows the tree trunks and the lower parts of the houses behind to tail off; the viewer is invited to discover the bushes which have caused this effect. In 'Vétheuil in Fog' (page 115) Monet carried this principle a stage further, orchestrating the canvas with a sequence of dazzling colours and leaving it to the imagination to discover the ephemeral image of mist melting from the river in the morning sunshine.

As summer approached Monet continued to work on this theme. Like an animal put out to pasture, he seemed tethered to the steeple of Vétheuil church and worked all around its fulcrum, viewing it from every side and angle. His brush races across the canvas, noting down the clouds billowing through the sky, the poppies, the trees and long grass tossing in the breeze. At times he sets the town squarely in the picture, his brush dicing up its reflection into tough little blocks of colour, while at others he is more coy and hides its face behind a fan of bushes.

Paintings such as these encourage us to believe that the two families led an idyllic life in Vétheuil, but this was anything but the truth. Even in the depths of the countryside they were dogged by financial troubles. They often had difficulty affording food, and the local laundresses had refused to clean their sheets until they had been paid. At times there was scarcely enough money to buy clothes; on one occasion Monet was forced to barter a portrait for a pair of shoes for the children, while Alice and Camille could never visit Paris together as they only had one good dress between them.

The first winter in Vétheuil had been cold, the next was to be worse, with roads snowbound and the river frozen over completely. Camille had been growing weaker by the day and did not survive to face the onset of this terrible freeze. At 10.30 on the morning of 5 September 1879 she died, slowly and painfully. Since their first summer together in Fontainebleau, thirteen years before, she had lived with Monet through all the difficult days of his career. At the time of her death she was just thirty-two. Monet was stunned by the loss.

As the winter hardened the roads around Vétheuil became impassable. For several weeks the town was cut off from the outer world and the price of food and fuel began to escalate. For some days Monet remained indoors painting still lifes but then, taking his easel out into the bitter cold, he set to work on the devastated countryside around his house. Here was a strange, boreal world of ice and sullen light. Lead-lined skies were reflected in the water, colours waned and guttered in the short-lived day and the horizon stained the snow with the livid reds and oranges of the

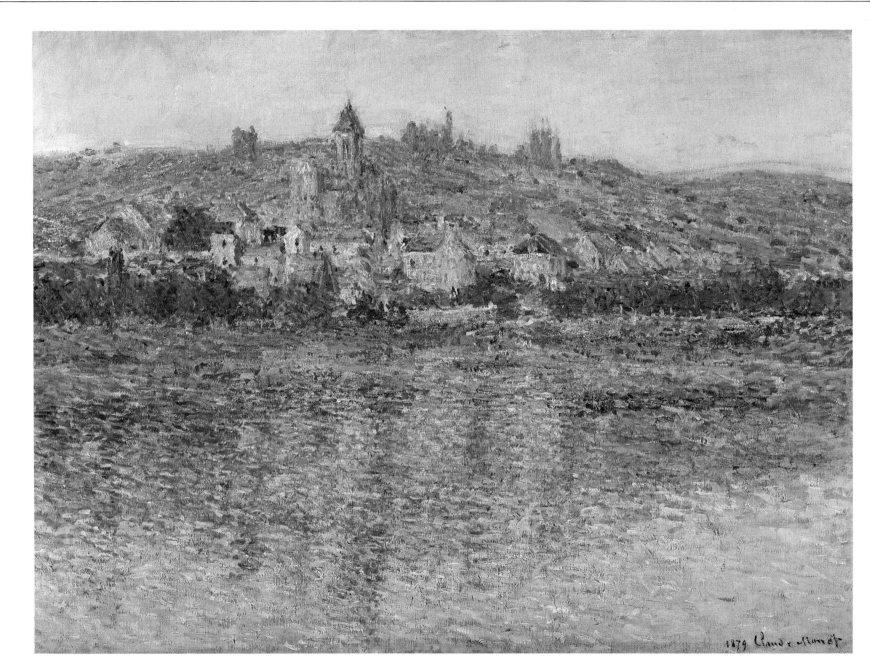

VÉTHEUIL IN SUMMER

1879

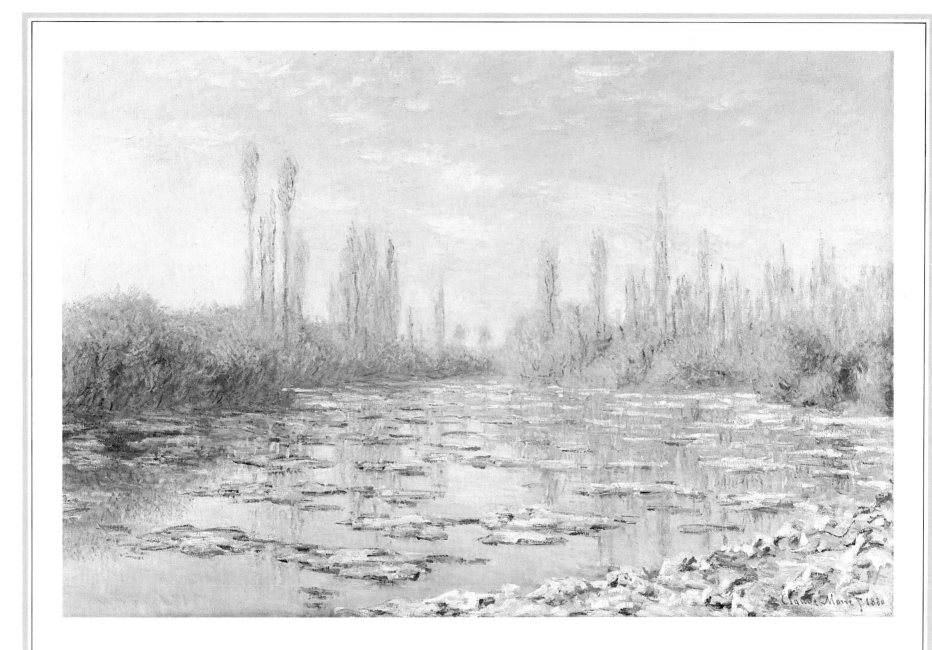

ICE-FLOES

1880

setting sun. At the end of December the weather broke and a thaw set in. A few days later Alice wrote to her husband describing the awe-inspiring sight of the river breaking up:

> At five in the morning, I was woken up by a frightful noise, like the rumbling of thunder … on top of this frightening noise came cries from Lavacourt; very quickly I was at the windows and despite considerable obscurity, saw white masses hurling about; this time it was the debacle, the real thing.

By morning the commotion was over, peace settled over the river once more, and ice-floes floated silently on the water like the frozen pads of enormous waterlilies. That winter, in a burst of energy, Monet produced twenty-six pictures of this hostile landscape, often stripping the composition down to the bare necessities of sky and water, separated from each other by a mere ribbon of wasted land.

Even Monet's strongest supporters were disturbed by these new paintings. De Bellio and Théodore Duret felt he had gone too far in his search for visual simplicity. Durand-Ruel urged him to give his canvases more finish but Monet, stubborn and headstrong as ever, ignored the advice and eventually quarrelled with his patron so badly that he took his pictures to another dealer, Georges Petit. In 1879 he had exhibited with some success in the third Impressionist exhibition, and in the same year Duret had written an article which laid out the principles of Monet's painting. Despite this, opposition was growing on every side. Zola, once the champion of the Impressionists, was now actively working against them. Writing in a Russian magazine, he had accused Monet of lacking the true 'passion' of a great landscape painter and later resumed the attack: 'Monet has given in too much to his facility for production. Too many informal drafts have left his studio in difficult hours, and that is not good; it pushes an artist on the slope of unworthy and cheap creation. If one is too easily contented, if one sells sketches that are hardly dry, one loses the taste for works based on long and thoughful preparation.'

Petit suggested that it might restore confidence if Monet were to exhibit in the Salon once more. The year before, Renoir had done very well for himself with a large group portrait of Mme Charpentier, wife of the publisher Georges Charpentier, and her children. The success of this picture had immediately led to further commissions and opened doors for him not only in the world of art, but in society as well. Monet was inclined to agree with Petit and at once put three paintings into production. Only two of these were for the Salon; the other he felt was 'too much to my liking to send, it would be refused'. Monet's experiences with the Salon had made him cynical; he took it for granted that any picture to his own taste would not be to the jury's, and he was convinced that he 'ought instead to do something more discreet, more bourgeois' for them.

Equally, he was under no illusions as to what his friends would make of his decision to exhibit at the Salon. 'It is a crude role that I am about to play,' he told Duret, 'not to mention that I shall be treated as a traitor by the whole group, but I believe it is in my interest to play this part.' As it happened, his predictions were right. Pissarro was furious at the submission and Degas treated it as such an act of betrayal that for some time he refused to speak to Monet at all.

In the event, only one of the three paintings that he sent to the 1880 Salon was accepted, and this was hung so high in the gallery that few people noticed it as they passed. This painting (page 122), with its silvery light, represents the view of the river that Monet could see from the end of his own garden. Surprisingly, however, it had not been painted directly from nature but had been put together from various paintings made there in the previous year. This may seem rather ironic in the light of his response to Emile Taboureux, a few weeks later, that the countryside was his only studio, but Monet was in the process of creating a legend about himself. It was the principle of painting in the open air that he upheld and it was this that he stressed to Taboureux, insisting as he did so that he was still, first and foremost, an Impressionist.

The whitewashed houses in the background of this painting were part of the village of Lavacourt. This was nothing more than a row of cottages and barns strung out along the line of the far shore, directly opposite Vétheuil. Flights of stone steps led up to homes on first-floor level, chickens clucked about the doorways and hobbled cows grazed on the bank. The river looped around Lavacourt so sharply that the village was practically set on an island and its only link with the outer world was by a ferry, whose landing stage can be seen on the righthand side of the canvas. Normandy was one of the wealthiest agricultural regions of France at this time, but villages such as Lavacourt, stranded alone on the banks of the Seine, were among its poorest inhabitants. It is no exaggeration that when a yacht belonging to an American millionaire moored alongside one such village a few miles further downstream, the money these visitors spent in one day inflated the local economy for several years to come.

In 1880 Monet broke with the Impressionists once more, and instead of exhibiting with the group he put on a one-man show at *La Vie Moderne*, Charpentier's publishing house. All that year he had been working on the river and his new paintings were saturated with sunlight and summer scents. A shoreline rampant with wildflowers fills the foreground of 'Banks of the Seine at Vétheuil' (page 123), beads of yellow and white dance on the picture surface and pollen rises from the crust of its colour. Standing on the towpath at Lavacourt, Monet painted the church steeple of Vétheuil rising from the quivering moat of the river (page 125). This is a painting of effortless virtuosity; Monet's brush flitters about the canvas like the wings of a butterfly, touching in details, defining and enriching the light and darting in the shadows cast below.

This effect of light is generated largely in the shadows. Monet had observed that colours in nature shift and alter in sunlight, passing through an intricate sequence of transitions. At midday the steeple of Vétheuil church is a warm orange, the colour of newly baked bread, whereas the shadows cast by the eaves and window ledges are a deep blue. As the stonework moves from shadow to light it is transformed from a cool tone of cobalt blue to a blush of pale ochre; in between these two extremities are further subtle variations of colour, delicate, fluttering interchanges that define the exact quality of the daylight.

In the past many artists had treated shadows as a negative part of the painting, describing them uniformly as a dark brown or black tone. Monet now proved that it was only through a meticulous analysis of the shadow that he could recreate the image of sunlight in his paintings; it was the complex association of colours in the darkness that precipitated light onto his canvases.

'I have often followed Claude Monet in his search for impressions', wrote Maupassant in excitement after watching this miraculous technique. 'He was no longer a painter, in truth, but a hunter ... Before his subject, the artist lay in wait for the sun and the shadows, capturing in a few brush-strokes the ray that fell or the cloud that passed ...'

Many of the colour sequences that we see in nature are in fact created within the eye; they are a necessary distortion. Light has a physical effect on the human eye, burning the sensitive surface of the retina with high-pitched colours. Trees in brilliant sunshine, for example, flood our sight with a range of intense yellow-greens. The eye at once defends itself against this invasion by attempting to neutralize the colour. It creates a filter, flooding the retina with the complementary colour; in this case a screen of red. The two mixed together succeed in reducing the brilliance of the green to an appreciable level. At the same time, the surrounding area is tinted with the same red and changes colour: the shadows, instead of being a green-blue, become slightly purple, as does the blue of the sky.

By recording these intricate colour systems, Monet was able to deceive the viewer into receiving a sensation of light from his canvases, as if the eyes were indeed altering the colours of the shadows to compensate for the impact of sunshine. Watching Monet painting at Etretat, Maupassant was overwhelmed by the effect this created:

> I have seen him thus seize a glittering shower of light ... and fix it in a flood of yellow tones which, strangely, rendered the surprising and fugitive effect of that unseizable and dazzling brilliance.

THE EXHIBITION at *La Vie Moderne* was the largest single collection of Monet's pictures to have come on show to date, but it did little to sway the critical opinion of Impressionism:

'They are all forerunners,' Zola complained. 'The man of genius has not yet arisen. We can see what they intend, and find them right, but we seek in vain the masterpiece that is to lay down the formula ... they remain inferior to what they undertake, they stammer without being able to find words.'

To complicate matters still further, life at Vétheuil was becoming increasingly difficult. Hoschedé's business affairs were doing no better than before and his creditors had now tracked him down in the country. One arrived on the doorstep, demanding to be allowed inside. He was ushered into the front room but as soon as he was left alone he tried to break the furniture, and before he could be stopped had smashed a vase over the piano. Hoschedé was not even there at the time: he was only at Vétheuil now when it suited him and preferred to live in Paris.

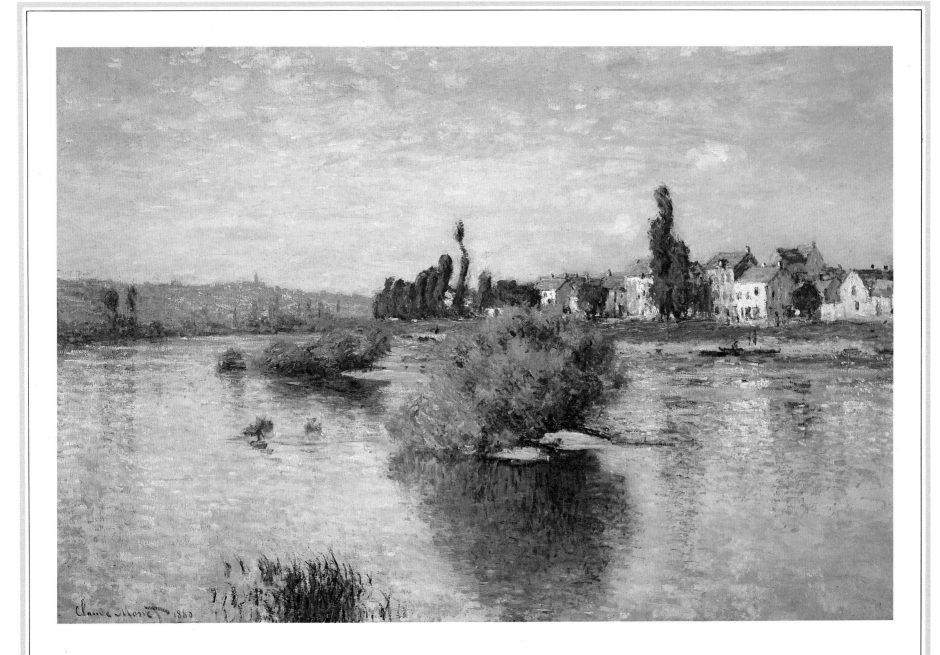

THE SEINE AT LAVACOURT

1880

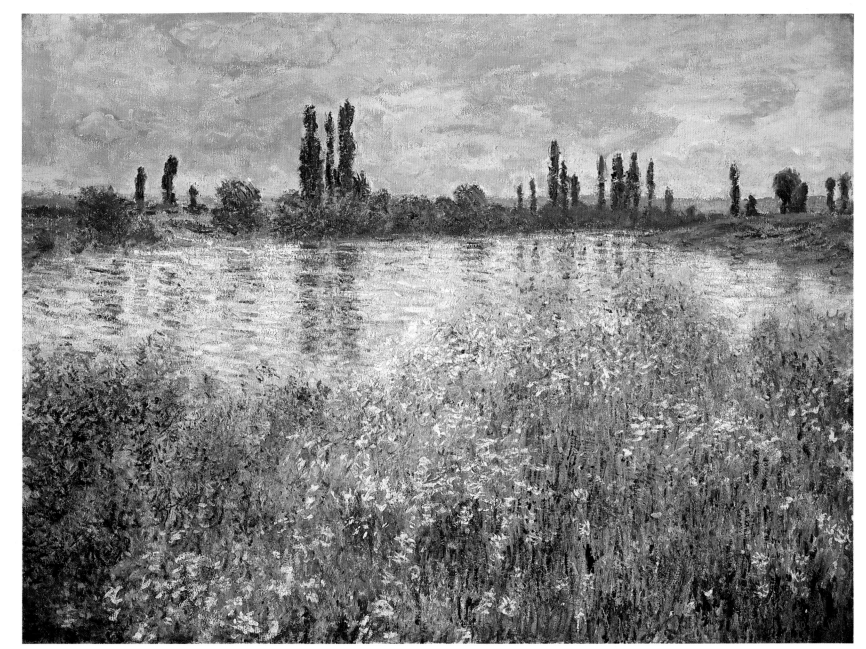

Banks of the Seine at Vétheuil

1880

Late in the summer of 1880 Monet spent a few days in the little resort of Les Petites Dalles with his brother Léon. The following year he returned to the Normandy coast and painted the cliffs around Fécamp and Grainval. Hoschedé took the opportunity to pester his wife Alice to leave the country and join him in the city but she prevaricated, unwilling to go back to a husband who had already deserted her and yet fearful of the consequences should she refuse.

Alice Hoschedé was a remarkable woman: calm, good humoured and slightly spiritual by inclination. Her only defect, according to her mother-in-law, was that her voice was a little too loud. She was devoted to the children and looked upon the two motherless boys, Jean and Michel, as her own. Monet didn't want her to leave; he simply couldn't do without her, and since the death of Camille he had come to rely on her judgement completely. The rivalry between the two men became intense, and feeling ran so high that eventually Hoschedé would only come to Vétheuil if Monet was out of the way. It reached such a point that when Hoschedé wanted to attend his son's communion in the village, Monet had to take himself off to the coast for a few days.

In the autumn of 1881 this confrontation came to a head when the lease on the house at Vétheuil ran out. Monet was hoping to move to Poissy where there was a better school for the children. He asked Alice to go with him and eventually, after some misgivings and a crossfire of letters, she agreed.

THE MOVE TO POISSY was made partly on the recommendation of Zola, who had recently bought a house at Médan, a few miles downstream. The town was not as attractive as Monet had hoped, and after Vétheuil it must have seemed very surburban. The bridge at Poissy was rated as one of the finest on the river, but apart from that the town had very little to recommend it; the streets were the worst paved in the Seine valley and one guide book at the time went so far as to warn that the Rue de Paris was 'a terror to cyclists'.

Poissy took its name from the ancient word Poissiacum, meaning a place for fishing and that, it seems, was the town's one true attraction. In early days the fishing had belonged to a powerful guild but by the nineteenth century it had become a universal sport on the river:

'The dwellers of the Seine Valley are great fishermen,' one traveller observed, 'not so much for the sport or the quarry it may provide, nor for sociability, since the fisherman's art is the least sociable of sports, as, it would seem, for the purpose of meditation. There is good fishing in the Seine, as all who partake thereof well know. From the Paris bridges and quays down to Rouen are many famous fishing grounds. Here it is that you see the true fisherman in all his glory. He sits beneath his big hat, or under an umbrella if the sun shines strongly, in a low-backed chair in a punt, and patiently holds his rod from early morning to night.'

An English visitor in Poissy noted that for all their dedication, these fishermen weren't as hardy as those in his own country: 'When he lays down his line for a time the French fisherman begins to think of eating and drinking. None of your ordinary picnic lunches either, of cold ham and hard-boiled eggs; but most likely a cold fowl, washed down with good wine.'

This pleasant and thought-provoking occupation was not the preserve of the men in Poissy either: 'We came across two nice old ladies in a beautiful mahogany-built boat and white kid gloves, attended by a faithful servitor, presumably to put the bait on and to take off any little victim of their piscatorial skill; but the sport was not sufficiently exciting to keep him awake. A little farther on there were two priests engaged in the same arduous pursuit; one was reading aloud while the other was charged to watch if by any chance a float should bob down.'

Monet hated Poissy. After three years in the open countryside he felt he was stagnating in this surburban backwater. As in all such moments of indecision, he returned to Normandy. In 1882 he moved the whole family up to Pourville for the summer and when the lease on the house at Poissy expired he began to search for a new home. This time he didn't ask for anyone's advice; he knew exactly what he was looking for. It had to be a house large enough to take the whole brood of his family, somewhere in the Norman countryside and, above all, it had to be on the banks of the Seine.

With this clear objective in mind Monet began methodically to search the district he now knew so well around Vétheuil and Bennecourt. Travelling by rail, he scoured the Seine valley and it was in this way that on a spring morning in 1883, he stepped off the train at a little station called Giverny.

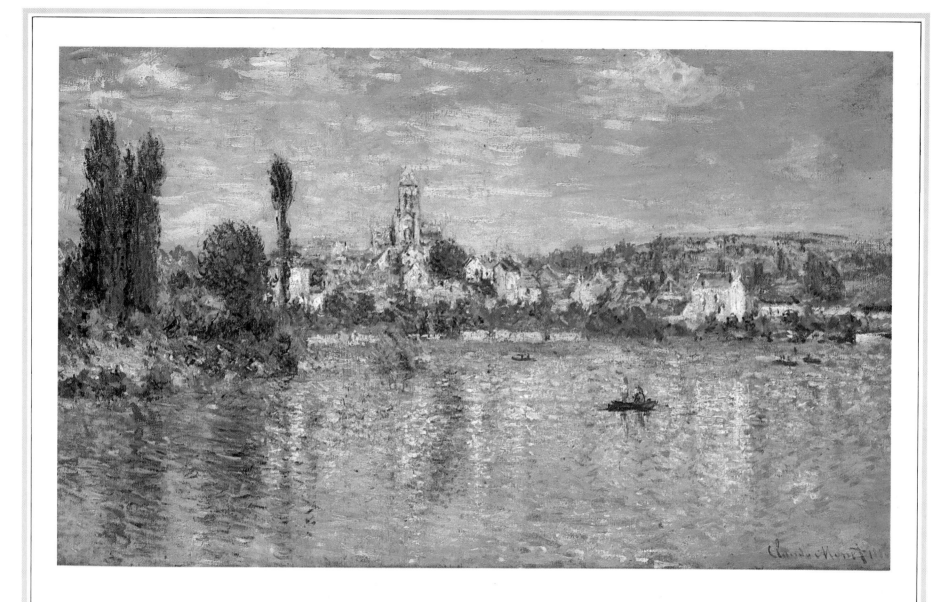

VÉTHEUIL IN SUMMER

1880

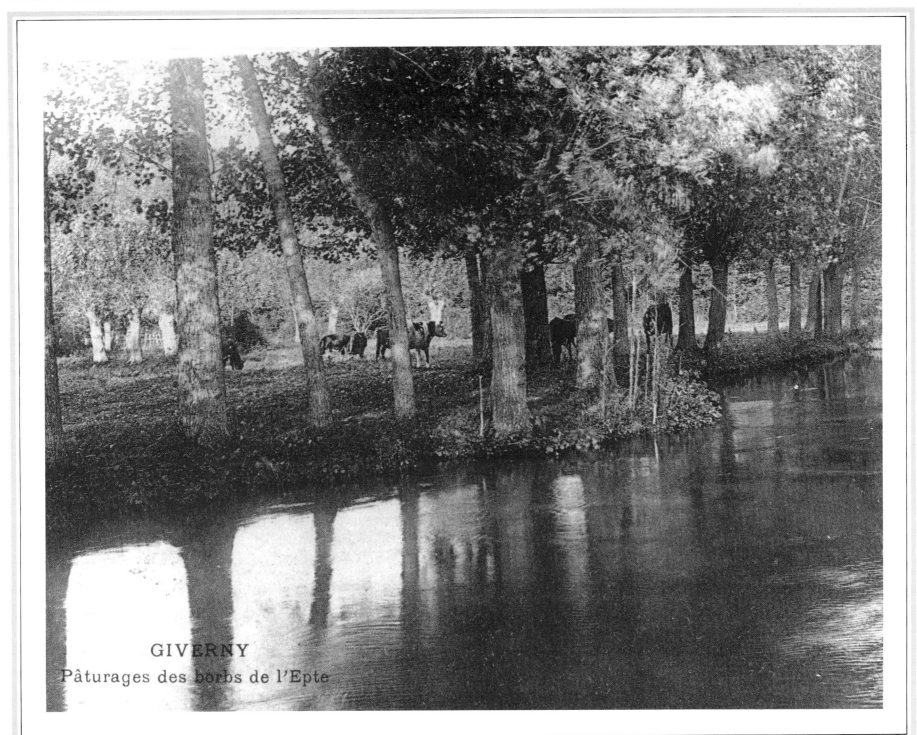

GIVERNY
Pâturages des borbs de l'Epte

GIVERNY

1883–1926

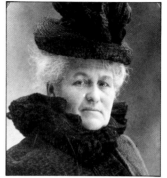

ALICE HOSCHEDÉ

THE BANKS OF THE EPTE

This stream was a small tributary of the Seine that flowed through the fields below Monet's house at Giverny. The only historical importance of the Epte was that for many years it had marked the official boundary of Normandy. Monet frequently painted along its banks, although it was difficult to negotiate by boat as the water was shallow in places and the boat's hull had to be dragged over rocks.

MONET LIVED AT GIVERNY for exactly half of his life. The Maison du Pressoir, the house he rented in the old part of the village, was to be his home, his studio and the central theme of his work for over forty years. It was here that he would see his children grow up, here that the great cycles of waterlily paintings would be made, and from here that his many painting expeditions abroad would be launched.

The Maison du Pressoir was a long, narrow building, faced with rose pink plaster, on the lower slopes of the village. Standing at the end of a row of private houses, it took its name from the cider press that had once operated nearby. None of the wood-panelled rooms were large or particularly elegant but they suited Monet's needs at the time and, what was more important, there were enough of them to absorb all the members of his family. The garden was laid out formally, with an orchard, gravel paths and flowerbeds contained within clipped hedges, the whole area boxed in by a high stone wall. Beyond the garden gate there was a flour-white road, the narrow gauge track of the Gisors railway and a little stream of water called the Ru. Cutting through the meadows to the east of the village was the river Epte, once the boundary of the old Duchy of Normandy, and this in turn flowed into the Seine in the fields below the house.

Monet arrived at Giverny, in April 1883, with an avalanche of debts behind him. He'd run up credit all over Poissy and only managed to escape the town after Durand-Ruel had stepped in and settled the worst of his outstanding bills. Alice and the family travelled out with him on the train; his boats were towed down the river behind a barge to be moored on the riverbank below the house. As soon as he'd moved in, Monet stacked his pictures and painting equipment in the coach house that joined to one end of the building. Later, when polished boards had been laid over the hard earth floor, a window cut into the wall and a staircase added to give access from inside the house, this was to be his studio; the First Studio as it was called.

Monet had been in Giverny no more than a few hours when the sad news reached him that Manet had died. He immediately returned to Paris and, at Eugène Manet's request, acted as one of the pallbearers at the funeral. To Monet, the death of Manet marked the end of an era, and the move into Giverny the beginning of another. Hoschedé had all but given up hoping for his wife to return to him; over the years his attempts to see his children were to become weaker and eventually faded away altogether. Equally, Camille's name was very rarely mentioned at Giverny and her memory lived on only in the paintings on the studio walls. Although there was still no formal arrangement between himself and Alice, Monet now looked upon the household at Giverny as a single, unified family and he treated all the children as if they were his own. In the eyes of the visitors to the house they appeared to be related anyway; they didn't look dissimilar and they often wore identical clothes.

One of the first motifs that Monet discovered on the river was the church at Vernon (below right). High-roofed and solid as a fortress keep, it towered above the town, poised between the outspread arms of its flying buttresses. Working from the deck of his boat Monet painted three versions of the church during that first summer of 1883, separating image and reflection with the firm horizontal of the shoreline. There is an element of nostalgia about these paintings, for in them Monet appears to be trying to reconstruct the theme that had so preoccupied him during his years at Vétheuil. The determined analysis of light, the flickering water and the grid-like structure of the design are all instantly reminiscent of those earlier paintings.

Many of the buildings that gathered around the church at Vernon dated back to medieval times and their half-timbered frames were as crooked and twisted as the stumps of a grapevine, with every gable carved into an evil-looking gargoyle. The fragments of ruined castle, left stranded in the town when its influence receded, reminded passing visitors that Vernon had once been an important border fortress and guardian of the Seine. Blanche of Castile had spent her honeymoon in the castle and Saint Louis had once commented on the quality of the local watercress, but apart from this the town had little claim to fame. There was the weekly market, the bridge was still the only crossing on the river between Mantes and Les Andelys, and a contemporary historian had recommended the town to his readers as he had noticed that many of the residents lived to be over a hundred and diagnosed that the air around these parts must be particularly invigorating.

In 1894, eleven years after his first painting expedition to Vernon, Monet moored his boat on the riverbank opposite the town once more. By this time his observation of the scene had undergone a subtle transformation (opposite). It was not the light falling on the church that now interested him so much as the atmospheric effect that lay between himself and the town, filtering and modifying the colour of the light. He described how he saw it:

Thus having stopped one day at Vernon, I found the silhouette of the church so strange that I undertook to render it. It was early summer and the weather was still a little crisp. Cool foggy mornings were followed by sudden bursts of sunshine whose rays, warm as they were, succeeded only slowly in dissolving the mists

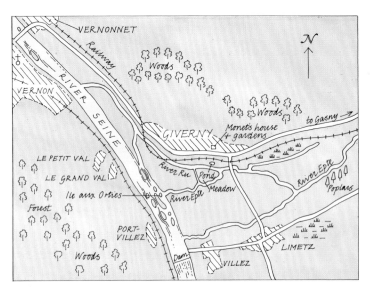

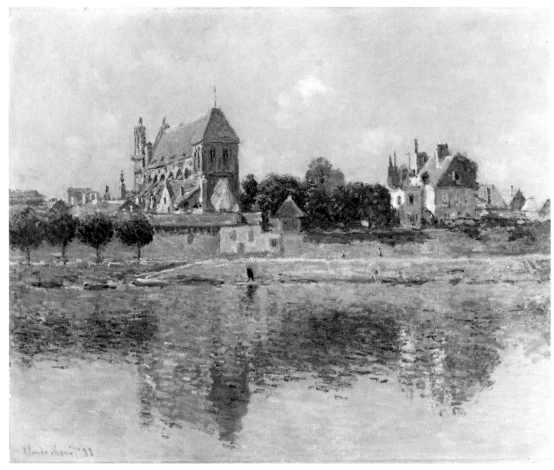

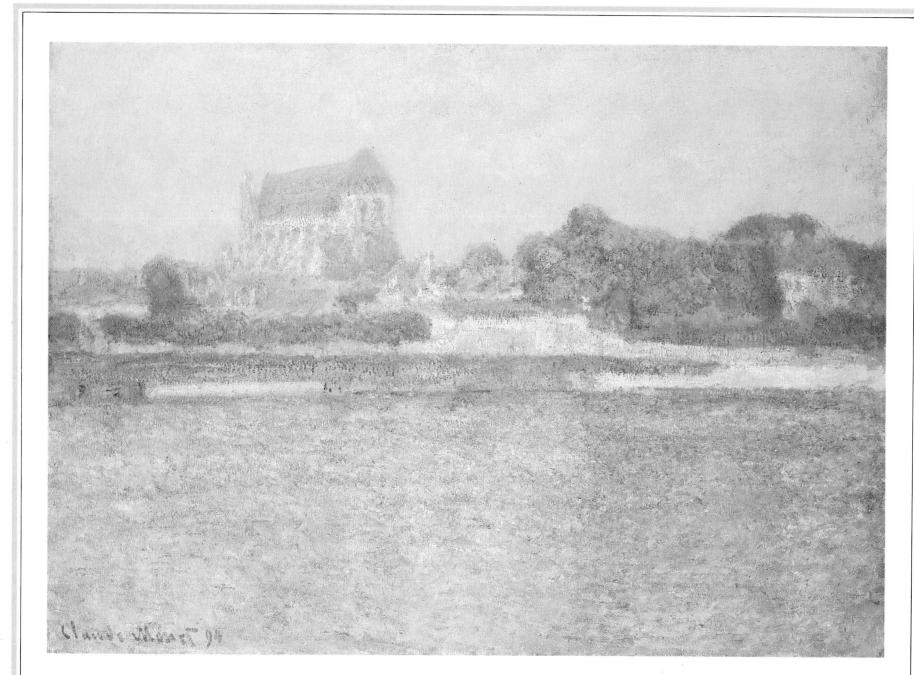

VERNON CHURCH

1894

clinging to all the rough surfaces of the building and which put an ideally vaporous envelope around the stone that time had made golden.

In these ghostly images of Vernon church, Monet painted light, atmosphere and landscape mirrored in water – a sequence of transformation that he had been perfecting for the past twenty years. A few weeks later he developed this idea still further: renting a hotel room in Rouen, he started work on a series of paintings of the cathedral. The river was not part of this new motif, but despite this, the paintings are linked intimately to those of the Seine and could never have existed without them. The vital lesson Monet had learned and absorbed over the years was that water has no colour of its own but steals it from the surrounding atmosphere. The colours that he saw on the river, and which he mixed on his palette, were the colours of daylight reflecting off the surface of the water. When he came to paint the facade of the great cathedral, Monet approached it in exactly the same way. He used the rough grey face of the stonework as a mirror, reflecting the presiding quality of light. In this series of paintings, the knowledge that he had pioneered and researched on the surface of the river Seine was lifted from the water and transferred to the facade of the building. What Monet painted was not the cathedral, but the light bouncing off the cathedral.

ONE OF MONET's first tasks when he moved to Giverny had been to build a boathouse on the Ile aux Orties – the Island of Nettles. He had discovered that it was unsafe to leave the boats out in the open; the village boys had found them tethered to the riverbank and cut the moorings, leaving them to drift away to the barrage downstream. Monet's flotilla had grown over the years; as well as the studio-boat he now had two sculls with varnished mahogany hulls and a 'norvègienne', a sleek rowing skiff with a high prow.

During the years at Giverny, these boats were to give rise to a series of ingenious compositions. 'The Boat' (page 132) shows the norvègienne tethered to the shore beneath a fringe of foliage. Viewed from above in the manner of a Japanese print, a solid wall of bottle green water fills the picture, pushing the little hull into the upper corner of the canvas and offering no horizon. The composition is top-heavy, but there is nothing unusual about this. Most of Monet's paintings are designed this way; instead of placing the solid substance of the land beneath an open expanse of sky, Monet had always preferred to have it in the upper part of the canvas, with its image mirrored in the water below. The paintings of the churches at Vernon and Vétheuil, for example, all have the solid body of the buildings riding above the fluid surface of the river.

Monet carried the idea a stage further in 'Boating on the Epte' (page 133). Here the splinter-sharp scull, rowed by Blanche and Suzanne Hoschedé, rests above the densely woven carpet of the river, the warm oranges of its polished woodwork singing out from the dark paintwork. In this picture we sense that, although he has claimed the boat to be his subject, Monet's real preoccupation is with the water, the rich and complex braid of colour below the hull.

'I have taken up things impossible to do,' he wrote, 'water with grass undulating at the bottom. It is wonderful to see but one can go crazy trying to do this thing.'

The picture has very few active elements to it, but Monet has balanced each in turn as carefully as the delicate limbs of a mobile. The blade of the boat slices through the upper margin of the painting, parallel to the riverbank. The thin line of one oar reaches down the canvas to the far corner, linking the top and bottom of the frame. Monet has taken one section of the boat and used it to divide up the picture surface, cutting through the shadowed water with the fine golden filament of its hull.

'They pass so quickly, these two women, and we are on the other bank,' wrote René Gimpel, who became the owner of this picture. 'They pass like a dream, or like desire that cannot be satisfied. All of us, in adolescence, have been in the country on such a sunlit day … and always we saw her whom we lacked on the opposite bank, unattainable and lovely.'

Like the Japanese artists he so admired, Monet discovered his composition in a single part of a boat and ruthlessly cut the rest out of the picture. 'The Blue Barque' (page 136) is framed around the stern of the norvègienne. The two girls are set against a ground of iris blue, heightened with liquid shadows, and the picture focuses on the blossom of colour generated in summer dresses, straw hats and reflected sunlight, the glow of warm tones breaking through a crust of lilac paint.

Monet's love of boating was infectious and in time the

THE WATERLILY POND AT GIVERNY

This was Monet's own creation. Working with a handful of gardeners he transformed a patch of marshy land below the house into the famous lily pond. Irises, agapanthus and bamboo were planted along the banks, and a wooden bridge was built over the water, which in turn supported climbing wisteria and soon became a mass of foliage.

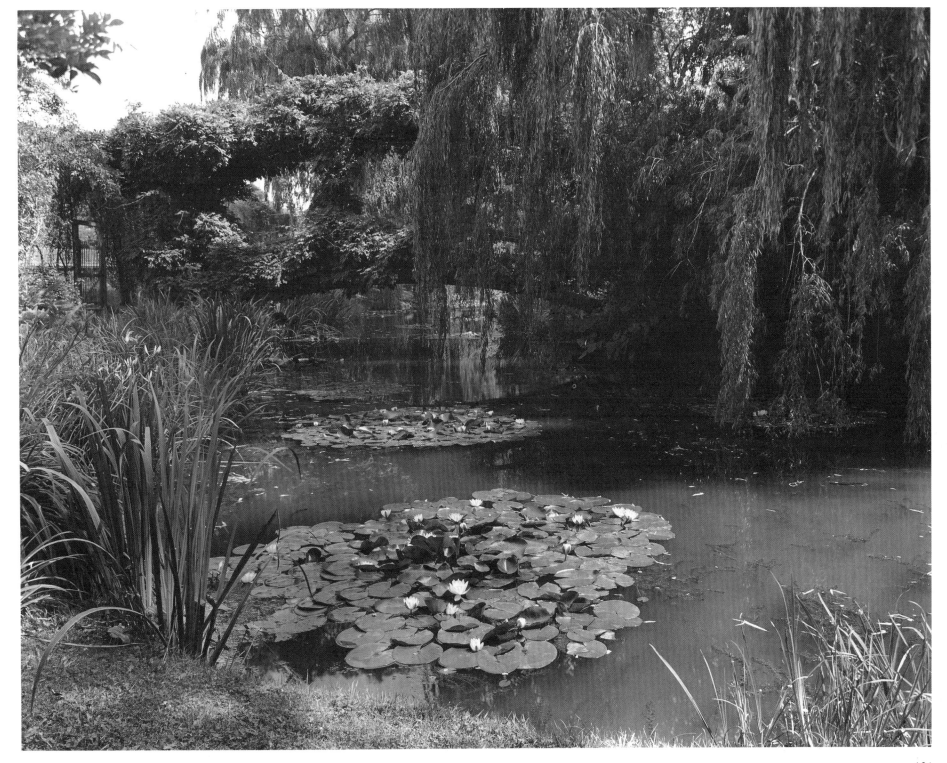

whole family caught it. The girls were practically brought up on the water and paintings such as 'The *Norvègienne*' (page 137) speak of peaceful childhood hours on the river. Jean Monet and his friend Deconchy were to become legendary oarsmen, winning prizes at the September regattas up and down the Seine, and were often referred to as the 'kings of the river'. Jacques Hoschedé also developed a keen interest in boats and was eventually to become a shipbuilder in Norway.

During the course of his career, Monet had confronted the problem of how to paint what he saw as faithfully and as accurately as possible. At Sainte-Adresse he had stood by an open window on the first floor to give himself a clear view of the terrace below; later at Bennecourt, he had learned to grasp at the changing light by adopting a rapid, sketchlike technique; finally at Argenteuil he had built himself a boat to take him out into the open theatre of the landscape. At Giverny Monet now reversed the principle: instead of trying to take the studio out to the river, he brought the river into his studio. He had managed to buy the strip of land that ran alongside the Ru, on the far side of his garden, and this he transformed into a water garden. It proved to be quite an undertaking. In 1893 he applied for permission to build an inlet and sluice gates, but it was only with the greatest difficulty that he persuaded the authorities to agree to the proposal. Aquatic plants and elegant water-lilies were planted in the water and, inspired by a Japanese print, a graceful bridge was built at one end. In time the pond was enlarged and improved, a trellis was added to the bridge and climbing wisteria encrusted the framework, transforming the arch into a tunnel of scented foliage, as described by a visitor to the garden:

> You enter the aquatic garden over a hog-backed bridge covered with wisteria. In June the fragrance is so heavy that it is like going through a pipe of vanilla. The clusters, white and mauve, a light mauve that one would say was painted in watercolour, fall like fanciful grapes in the watery greenery of the creepers. The passing breeze harvests the aroma.

Monet had been introduced to gardening by Caillebotte and so it was perhaps fitting that he should be one of the first to visit Giverny. He sailed up from Argenteuil on his yacht, the '*Casse-Museau*', and stayed for a few days moored alongside the lock. When he heard of Caillebotte's

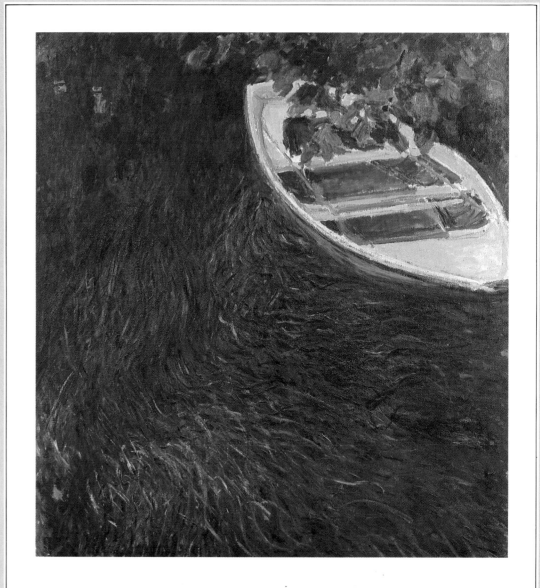

THE BOAT

1887

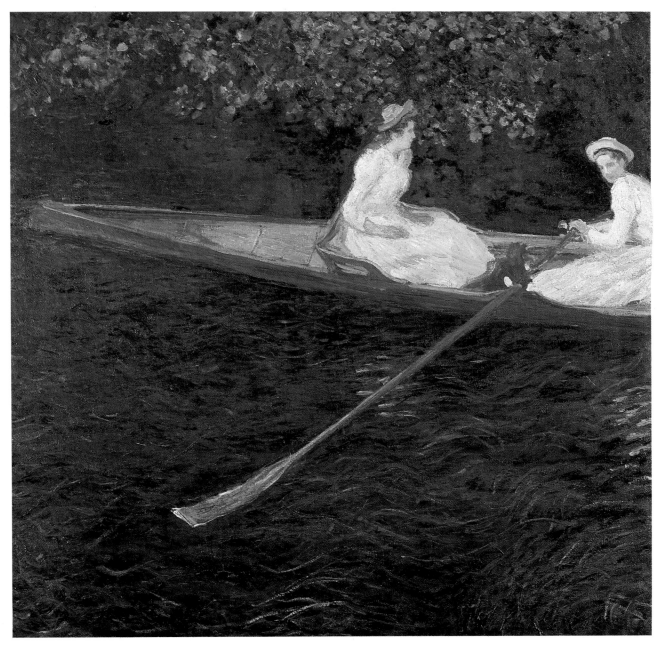

BOATING ON THE EPTE

1890

arrival, Monet sent a note to his friend and neighbour, Octave Mirbeau, suggesting that they both come over to see him. The poet at once replied in flamboyant style: 'I'm very glad that you're bringing Caillebotte. We'll talk gardening, as you say, because as for art and literature, it's all humbug. There's nothing but the earth. As for me I've reached the point of finding a lump of soil marvellous, and I spend whole hours contemplating it.'

The gardens at Giverny were really a great machine, designed specifically for Monet's painting. The two were quite inseparable in his mind; he planted the flowers to suit his pictures and created the paintings in direct response to the flowers. By now Monet had torn out the old garden with its orchards and hedges and devised a completely new layout in its place. The flowerbeds were cunningly planned to renew themselves with the passing of each season, the banks of flowers orchestrated to bloom from early spring until the first frosts of winter. Monet carefully arranged each growth, each harmony and sequence of colour, touring the garden, inspecting, watching over the plants and checking their progress. This painterly conception of flowers often led to heated discussions with his head gardener, Breuil, who considered it to be a form of horticultural anarchy and pleaded for the more restrained arrangements of a formal garden. Nevertheless, the results were spectacular, as every visitor to the gardens confirmed.

'As soon as you push the little entrance gate on the main street of Giverny,' recalled Gustave Geffroy, 'you think, in almost all seasons, that you are entering paradise.'

The peasant farmers of Giverny saw the water gardens not as a paradise, however, but as a serious health risk. They were convinced that the 'foreign' plants that Monet had introduced into his garden would poison the water and kill their cattle. The locals didn't particularly like Monet; they found him aloof and remote and they couldn't place him. The stream of influential visitors who made their way to his house over the years suggested that he was some sort of celebrity and yet he was often to be seen about the village dressed like a labourer in blue smock, felt hat and sabots. Added to this, the Monet household was a scandal; as far as the villagers could see, the artist was living in the Maison du Pressoir with a mistress and eight illegitimate, and curiously clothed, children. Some years later, when Jean Monet married Blanche Hoschedé, this only succeeded in confusing matters still further.

134

When Monet moved to Giverny it was an unknown village on the slopes of the Seine valley, but this peaceful anonymity did not last for long. The American painters Deconchy and Theodore Robinson were first to discover the village. Willard Metcalf, an American student at the Académie Julian, arrived by chance and stayed for a few days at the café-bistro owned by Mme Baudry. He was so entranced by the place that he returned, bringing some of his friends; they spoke of it back in Paris and within a matter of years Giverny had become an artists' colony. The café-bistro was promoted to become the Hôtel Baudry and became an agency for artists' materials made by Foinet, studios were built in the back garden, and maple syrup, Boston beans and English tea were introduced to the larder.

Among this group of artists was the American-born painter John Singer Sargent. One of his particular memories of a stay at Giverny was Monet's attempt to dissuade him from using black paint. Sargent replied that he couldn't do without it, as small additions of black were essential for modelling the structure of a form: what he meant by this was that the delicate half tones that he saw in nature could only be created with colours tinted with black paint. Black is not a neutral pigment, it actually behaves like a very dark blue; mixed with yellow or red it produces the most luminous tones of green and purple and Sargent needed these colours to describe the planes between light and shade. There is a long tradition of using black paint in this way which can ultimately be traced back, through Manet and Sargent's own teacher CarolusDuran, to Goya and Velàzquez. As Monet did not try to carve solid forms from the surface of the canvas, and in fact tended to dissolve them, he had been able to do without the services of black. He achieved the equivalent effect with a patchwork of colour, building the picture from a mass of small touches of paint that collectively mould his forms and suggest the subtle variations of light playing across the surface.

Monet had not only dispensed with black paint; he also tried to use white as little as possible as it tended to weaken the impact of his colours, lending them a chalky appearance. Instead, he created the contrasts of light and shade in his paintings from the natural tones of the pigments. Every colour, as it comes from the tube, has its own tone: Prussian blue, for example, is exceptionally dark, whereas any yellow is comparatively pale. Monet turned this to his

The Garden at Giverny

Monet lived at the Maison du Pressoir for forty-three years – exactly half his life. During this time, the gardens came to play an increasingly important role in his work. When he first arrived, they were a formal arrangement of gravel paths and flowerbeds enclosed within a stone wall. Within a few years Monet had torn out this traditional system and replaced it with a confusion of colour as rich and varied as one of his own paintings.

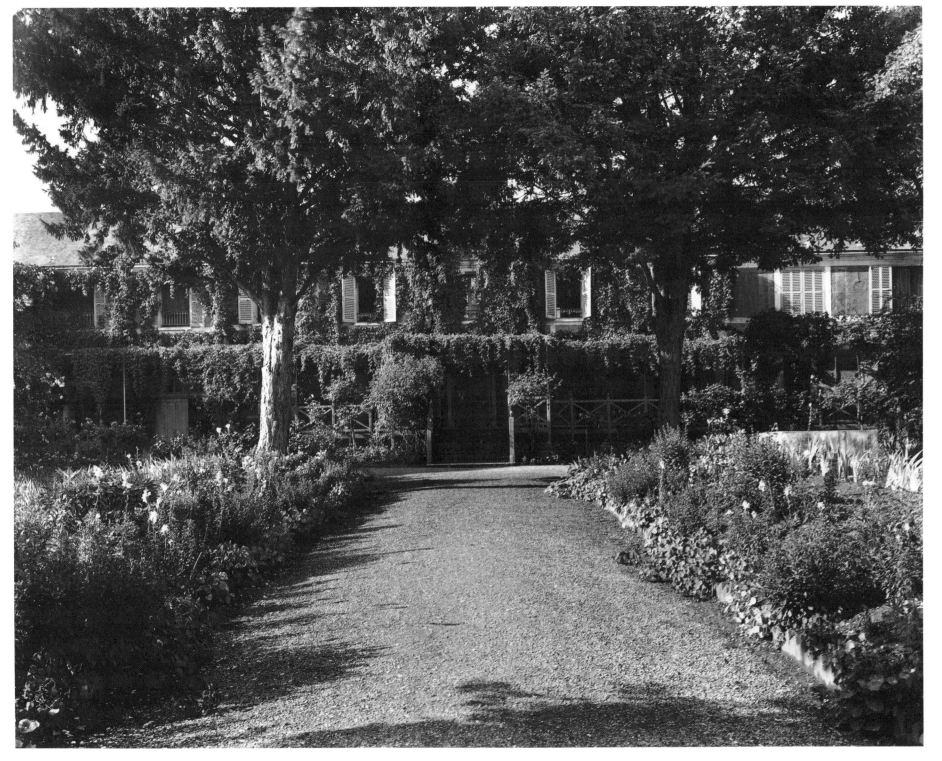

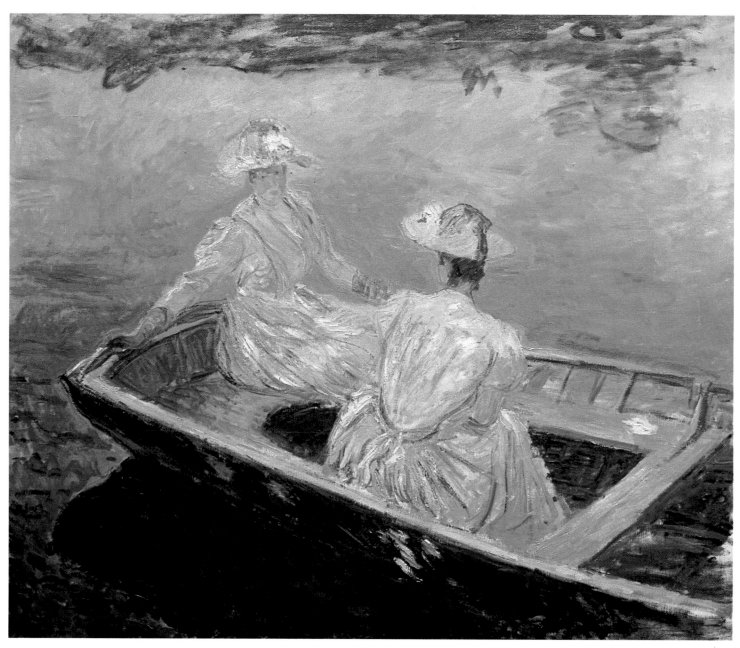

THE BLUE BARQUE

1887

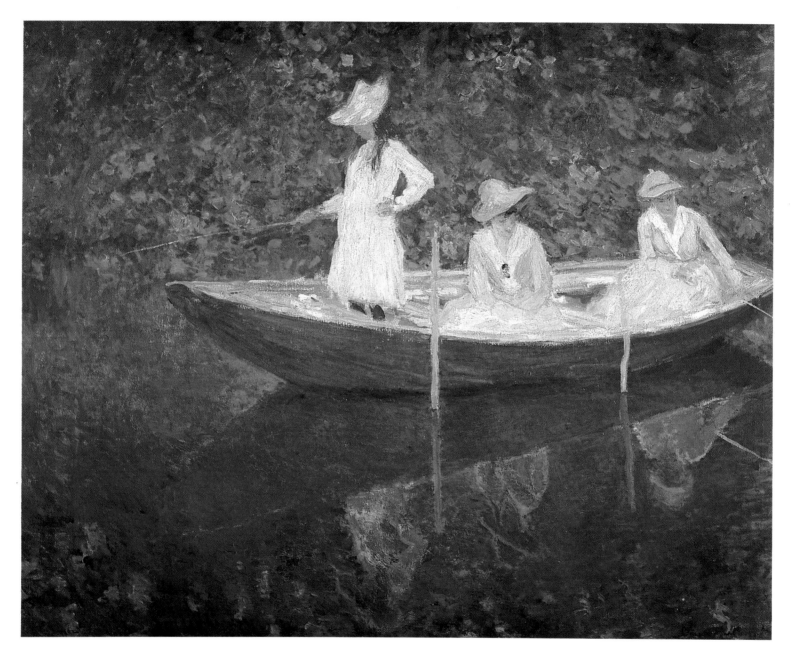

THE NORVÈGIENNE

1887

advantage; in the shadows of his paintings he used the deep ranges of colour such as ultramarine, viridian and alizarin crimson; whereas in the lit parts, where the sun is striking, he turned to mixtures of cerulean blue, cadmium red and yellow, all of which are naturally high-keyed pigments. As far as possible he matched his paint to the effect of light, without relying on additions of white. In doing so he kept his pigments at their full concentration, and it is this that accounts for their gemlike intensity on the canvas. At the same time it must be understood that while this was a vital principle in Monet's painting, it couldn't always be achieved in practice. Inevitably, white was needed to describe clouds, summer dresses, the sails of ships and the crisp linen of tablecloths. Coupled to this, Monet would often add small quantities of white to fatten the consistency of his paint, and some of the bleached tones due to the effect of sunlight could not be created at all without the aid of white. Nevertheless, wherever possible Monet would try to retain the natural intensity of the saturated colours on his palette, mixing them together as necessary, but diminishing their strength as little as possible.

THE SUCCESS THAT Monet had been expecting almost daily for the last thirty years finally arrived. He exhibited at Georges Petit's gallery in 1885 and then again in the following year. These two shows were greeted with some enthusiasm but the real breakthrough came when Monet and Rodin held an exhibition together in 1889, the year of the Universal Exhibition in Paris which once again filled the city to the brim with foreign visitors. Monet put up a hundred and forty-five pictures, spanning the whole of his career, and Mirbeau wrote a glowing introduction to the catalogue. The exhibition was an unqualified triumph and Monet's prices immediately began to escalate. That same year he sold a single canvas to Theo Van Gogh for 10,350 francs, and within two years his annual income had topped 100,000 francs. With this new-found wealth he paid off some of his debts and, what was closer to his heart, he was able to buy the freehold on the Maison du Pressoir.

Success didn't make Monet any easier to deal with, however; far from mellowing he became, if possible, more demanding. He pushed his prices as high as they would go and continued to play off one dealer against another. He had quarrelled violently with Durand-Ruel over the sale of paintings to the United States. American collectors had proved to be less pedantic in their taste for pictures than their European counterparts and as a result Durand-Ruel had been intending to ship a fair proportion of his stock over to his New York branch. Monet was incensed by this; selling paintings over there was not the point; it wasn't in America that he wanted to be discovered. Paris was still the battleground and it was there that his pictures must remain.

Durand-Ruel – 'Monsieur Durand' as Monet called him – was never ruffled by these storms. He was almost saintly in his devotion to Impressionism: over the years he had patiently and consistently bought paintings, paid bills and advanced money to the artists, often pushing himself to the brink of bankruptcy in doing so. He weathered the squalls of Monet's bad temper, never allowing it to interfere with his long-standing friendship with the artist.

Although Monet often proved difficult and volatile over money matters, there was also a strong streak of loyalty in him. With his improved status he was determined to win official recognition not only for himself but for those who had helped and inspired him over the years. In 1889 he visited the Universal Exhibition with Sargent. Seeing the Manets on exhibition and fearing that many of them might shortly be lost to the country, they decided to launch an appeal to buy the 'Olympia' for the Louvre. Monet badgered friends, dealers and collectors for the asking price of 20,000 francs. Most of them subscribed willingly although one notable exception was Zola, who felt that the Louvre should not be forced to accept a painting under pressure. Antonin Proust also raised an objection; writing in *Le Figaro* he suggested that the fund was simply a way of providing a pension for Manet's widow. Monet was disgusted by this damp cynicism, coming from one who had been a pallbearer at the artist's funeral, and told him so in no uncertain terms. Proust was flustered by the sharpness of this reply; he at once took offence and challenged Monet to a duel. Fortunately for all concerned, their seconds managed to defuse the situation and talked the two protagonists back to their senses.

In the end Monet had his way; he raised the money and the 'Olympia' was eventually purchased from Manet's widow. It hung in the Luxembourg palace until 1907 when at the insistence of Georges Clemenceau, then the Prime Minister of France, it was finally moved into the Louvre.

LIFE AT GIVERNY was dominated by the routine of Monet's painting. Claire Joyes, who has made a detailed study of this aspect of his career, records that he was up every morning at five and would throw open the bedroom window to check the weather. Downstairs, he began the day by stoking himself up on an enormous cooked breakfast of eggs, sausages and scalding hot tea, a habit he had picked up on his travels abroad. Sometimes one of the children would be allowed to join him in this ritual and help as his painting equipment was loaded into a wheelbarrow and trundled down the garden to wherever Monet was working at the time. He would then work uninterrupted for the rest of the morning until, promptly at eleven, he returned for lunch and the rest of the family was summoned indoors with two rings on the bell. After lunch he would take a glass of plum brandy in the studio and then, followed by a procession of gardeners, he toured the pond, inspecting the plants, discussing new plans and issuing orders for the day. He would also spend hours walking in the countryside, searching for new motifs, absorbed in the light and the shifting sequence of colours he found around the river. Dinner was early, as soon as the daylight failed, and he was always in bed by nine-thirty.

Monet's moods, which could change as quickly as the autumn sky, were governed by his work. When the weather was fine and his paintings were coming along to his satisfaction, he was cheerful and good humoured. An air of tranquillity would settle over the household and the days would pass in the measured rhythm of his working routine. He would even take time off to play with the children and join them on picnics and expeditions up the river, but if anything disturbed his strict timetable he could fly into a rage and become quite unmanageable. If it was raining he might refuse to get out of bed altogether and would lie upstairs sulking under the covers. On these days even Alice couldn't draw him out of his black depression; the whole household was instructed not to make a sound and they all moved about on tiptoe, hoping for the weather to change.

It was on one of Monet's many walks in the country that he discovered the row of poplar trees. They lay on a bend of the Epte near the village of Limetz. Poplars were not planted along the rivers for shade or decoration in those days; they were an important industry. The short lower limbs were regularly pruned and bundled up to be sold to the bakers, who used them in in their ovens; the wood burned at a particularly high temperature and this was needed to put the hard crust onto the loaves. In time the rest of the tree would be cut down and auctioned off to cabinet makers.

Monet used the line of poplars as the basis for a series of paintings. He pulled the studio boat up over the shallow water where the Epte joined the Seine and moored it in position. This worm's-eye view of the river offered him a range of compositions: directly opposite the boat the tree trunks, the riverbank and the reflections formed a powerful grid structure that divided his canvas at right angles; whereas looking down river, the trees zig-zagged across the picture surface as they snaked away into the distance. Throughout the summer and autumn of 1891 Monet worked on this motif. He had a painting ready for every change in light or weather and kept them stacked in sequence along the hull of his boat. If he observed a new effect that had not previously revealed itself to him, he would send one of the children scampering across the fields to fetch him a fresh canvas. Gradually, as the series developed, the time lapse between canvases grew shorter until, like the rapid sequence of frames in a cinefilm, the paintings became a sucession of stills that animated the daylight.

All his life Monet had been driven by a relentless perfectionism that forced him to scrape and repaint, never satisfied with what he had done. Only rarely did a picture live up his his expectations and many would be destroyed or painted over before he was finished. Clemenceau, Gustave Geffroy and Durand-Ruel all tried in turn to cure him of this destructive self-criticism, but it was impossible. They saw what he had achieved in a painting; Monet could think only of what he might have achieved.

Before starting work on a series of paintings, whether of haystacks, a row of poplar trees or the facade of Rouen cathedral, Monet would study the subject for days on end, checking that it was going to measure up to his exacting requirements. The first of these was that the motif had to be chameleon, changing colour with the light and reflecting every mood of weather. At the same time it was vital that, in physical terms, it was quite unchangeable. It must not move or alter its shape over the days, so that Monet could return to it as often as he liked and only have to concentrate on the variations of colour he found. If his motif began to change, Monet would do his best to prevent it; when an oak tree at Fresselines came into bud, after he had been working on it all winter, he employed forty workmen to tear off the leaves.

Like the surface of the Seine, the subjects of Monet's series had to be an unmoving mirror of light; they must change colour but not shape. Looked at in this way, it is easy to see that Rouen was ideal: the haystacks should have been, but the local farmer, disturbed that Monet was somehow profiting from his labour, began to pull them down. Monet had the same problem with the poplars; no sooner had he started work on them than he discovered that they were due to be felled and sold. He tried to persuade the mayor of Limetz to postpone the auction for a few weeks, but he was assured that this was out of the question.

> The only thing I could do was to attend the bidding myself, not a pleasant prospect for, as I was saying to myself, 'They're going to make you pay plenty for your caprice, old man!' Then I had the idea of going up to a wood dealer who wanted the lumber. I asked him how high a price he expected to pay, promising to make up the difference if the bid went over the amount, on condition that he would buy the trees for me and leave them standing for a few more months. And that's what happened, not without some sacrifice to my wallet.

When the locals heard of this eccentric behaviour they assumed that Monet had more money than he needed and they set about finding ways of lightening this burden, one of them even attempting to make a charge to the painter for walking through his field.

The series of poplars was completed by the end of the year and this time Monet offered them directly to Durand-Ruel. Shortly before the exhibition opened, on 29 February 1892, Octave Mirbeau wrote Monet a letter in which he described the wonder and admiration he'd felt on first seeing the paintings:

> It is an absolutely magnificent work, this series, a work in which you renew yourself, through craft and feeling, and in which you reach the absolute beauty of great decoration. There I felt complete joy, an emotion that I can't express, and so deep that I would like to have kissed you. The beauty of those lines, the newness of those lines and their grandeur, and the immensity of the sky and the thrill of it all … you hear me, my dear Monet, never, never has any artist expressed such things, and it is again a revelation of a new Monet …

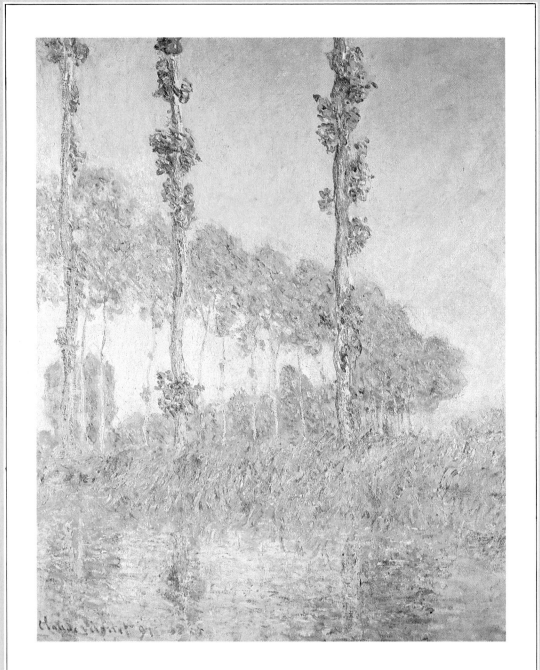

POPLARS

1891

In 1892 THEODORE BUTLER, a member of the colony of American painters, asked if he could marry Suzanne Hoschedé. Monet was disturbed; he didn't like losing his pictures to the USA and was even less keen to see one of his children going to live there. He made inquiries and finally, after discovering that Theodore's family had distinguished themselves in the American War of Independence, he agreed. The wedding date was fixed, but at the last moment there was a delay. There was an air of tension about the house; Suzanne was on the verge of tears and Alice was 'less friendly than was her wont'. It wasn't long before the cause was discovered; Monet wanted to be the one to lead Suzanne to the altar, but this entailed making himself her legal father. Hoschedé had died the year before, so there was nothing to prevent Monet from marrying Alice. On 16 July 1892, at a quiet wedding service to which Mirbeau and Durand-Ruel were invited, Alice finally became Monet's wife. Four days later there was a second, much greater, wedding at which Monet gave Suzanne away.

The Maison du Pressoir was to witness many such occasions. There is a photograph at Giverny of the reception after Marthe's marriage; the women are dressed in white and the men in frockcoats, with the exception of Monet. He sits on the steps of the house, larger than life in his felt hat and baggy jacket, his face tanned from years in the open air, dominating the picture like some earth-god.

Monet was a natural patriarch; he literally ruled over the household at Giverny. When Germaine Hoschedé wanted to marry Pierre Sisley, he refused to allow it. The young man was an inventor and therefore, in Monet's mind, not a suitable husband for one of his step-daughters. It made no difference that this was the son of one of his closest friends, or that he himself had married without a penny to his name. Disregarding her pleadings, he packed Germaine off to stay with friends in the south until she got over her infatuation. The ploy worked and six months later she was married to Albert Salerou, a promising young lawyer who was later to distinguish himself as a politician. After the wedding the whole party sat down to a six-course lunch: *hors d'oeuvres* followed by turbot in Hollandaise or prawn sauce; roast venison and turkey; lardons fried in marrowbone; crayfish; *pâté de foie gras*; salad; praline and ices; the menu for this feast was written on a card printed with a photograph of the bridge over the lily pond.

Monet had always taken the subject of food very seriously. As a young man he had despised the rigid formality of bourgeois life, but he had never fully escaped its influence and mealtimes at Giverny were an important ceremony at which the whole family was on parade. Monet insisted on punctuality: lunch and dinner were heralded by two rings on the outside bell; Monet would then take his place in the primrose yellow dining room, checking his watch and coughing impatiently if anyone was late. Whether or not there were guests present, Monet presided over the table, carving the meat, tossing the salads and grinding fresh pepper. The estate was practically self-supporting; turkeys and chickens were kept in a compound alongside the house and fish were caught in the streams. Monet had refused to allow vegetables to be grown with his flowers and so a second garden had been bought next door; the contents of this were ferried to the kitchens by a complement of maids. There was a sucession of cooks at Giverny, but the most famous of them was Marguerite. She came to be so precious to Monet that when she asked to get married he at once employed her husband, Paul, as his butler rather than risk losing her. Art historians have discovered significant phases in Monet's late work, but it has been said that he himself divided his days at Giverny into life before and after the reign of Marguerite.

Monet had been christened Oscar and as an artist had chosen to use his second name, Claude, but everyone at Giverny, from the servants to Alice and the children, knew him simply as Monet. The man, the artist and the legend were becoming united in the one name.

'Monet is perhaps seen at his best,' wrote one English visitor, 'and certainly in his most genial mood, when, cigar in full blast, he strolls around his *"propertie"* at Giverny, discussing the mysteries of propagation, grafts and colour schemes with his small army of blue-nosed, saboted gardeners. He is now fifty-six years of age, in the fullness of his powers, active and dauntless as ever. Each line of his sturdy figure and determined features, and the glint of his keen blue eyes, betoken the grit within. He is one of those men who would succeed in any line of life, and despite all – strong man, strong painter.'

By now Monet was a celebrity. Statesmen, writers and artists all wanted to be part of the fable and made their way to Giverny to see him. His fame was such that there was

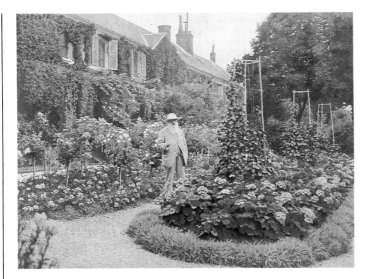

MONET IN HIS GARDEN AT GIVERNY, c.1923

nothing that he painted that went unnoticed; every picture was recorded from its infancy. In 1897 Maurice Guillemot, a journalist for the *Revue Illustrée,* stayed for a few days and left this vivid description of Monet at work on a new series:

At daybreak, in August, three-thirty a.m.

His torso padded with a white woollen sweater, his feet shod in heavy hunting boots with thick soles impervious to dew, his head covered in a brown felt hat picturesquely dented, the brim down for protection from the sun, a cigarette in the mouth – a gleaming point of fire in the thickness of the large beard – he opens the gate, descends the steps, follows the path in the middle of his garden where the flowers stretch and awaken in the sunrise, crosses the road, deserted at this hour, passes between the barriers on the track of the little Gisors railroad, goes around the pond, marbled with waterlilies, steps over the stream that ripples between the willows, enters the meadows all misty with fog and reaches the river. There he unties a skiff moored among the reeds along the shore and, with a few strokes of the oars, reaches the large anchored rowing boat that serves as his studio. The peasant, a gardener's assistant, who goes with him, unwraps the packages – as he calls the stretched canvases tied in pairs and numbered – and the artist sets to work.

There are fourteen canvases begun at the same time; practically a complete range of studies, representing one single motif, which change with the hour, the sun and the clouds.

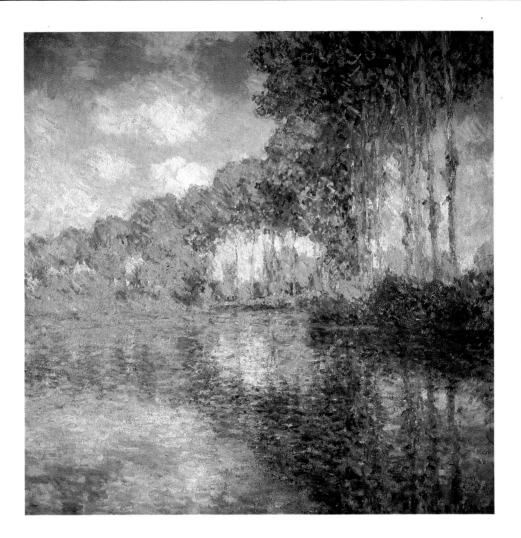

POPLARS ON THE EPTE

1891

The Seine at Giverny: Morning Mist

1897

It is at this point where the Epte merges with the Seine, amid small islands shaded by tall trees, some branches of the river forming what appear as peaceful and secluded lakes under the foliage, the mirrors of water reflecting the greenery, this is where Claude Monet has been working since last summer.

The series of paintings referred to here, which took two years to complete, was titled 'Morning on the Seine' (page 143). It went on exhibition at the Georges Petit gallery in 1898 and a week later Gustave Geffroy wrote his review:

> He looked at that spectacle in the morning mist, at sunrise, during the bright hours and the grey ones, at the golden hours of sunset. He became enamoured of the nuances of that great passage of brightness, he followed them in the depths of the sky and water, he expressed them by the bluish darkenings and greenish and golden awakenings of the foliage. It is these landscapes that are here assembled, these dark forms, these distant ghosts, these mysterious evocations, these transparent mirrors.

ALL HIS LIFE MONET had travelled by either train or boat, but in 1901 he bought himself a car, a Panhard-Levassor. Tall and square as a four-poster bed, this machine was always referred to at Giverny as the '937 YZ', after the number painted on its beehive radiator. Monet never attempted to operate it himself but employed Sylvain, a chauffeur who played the French horn in his spare time, to drive him about the countryside. The 937 YZ quickly became Monet's favourite means of transport and as soon as it arrived he had himself driven over to Vétheuil to work on a new series of paintings of the church.

Alice was particularly taken with the new car. When Suzanne died in 1899, Alice had been quite inconsolable, visiting the cemetery each morning and locking herself away in a private cell of solitude. The arrival of the 937 YZ proved to be a great distraction and she developed quite a taste for speed. She arranged automobile trips to Rouen or up to the coast, and visits to friends. In 1904 she and Monet travelled in the car down to Spain, to see the Velàzquezs in the Prado.

The whole family became motoring enthusiasts and never missed the the hillclimbing contests at Gaillon or a glimpse of the annual 'fireball races' passing through the district on their way from Madrid to Paris. In time more cars arrived at Giverny; Jean-Pierre owned a Hotchkiss and

Michel, who later designed and patented a little motorized quadricycle, had a Bonnet-Zedel. Picnics and family outings became major expeditions, with a convoy of cars heading out of Giverny and thundering away through the lanes of Normandy; Monet was in the vanguard directing operations, a cigarette clamped between his lips.

MONET'S ONLY OBJECTION to cars was that as they passed through Giverny their hard rubber wheels boiled up a cloud of dust that settled on his garden. To prevent them from damaging his lilies, he paid to have the stretch of road near his house laid with tarmac. Around the turn of the century his interest had begun to focus on his waterlily pond. By that time all he required of a subject was an imperturbable mirror of light, and nothing fitted the bill as well as the surface of unruffled water. In many ways the waterlily pond was to become a substitute for the Seine, a specimen of the river brought into the laboratory of his studio-garden. As soon as he'd started work on the new motif he wondered why it had taken so long for him to discover it:

> 'It took me some time to understand my waterlilies ... I had planted them without thinking of painting them. A landscape doesn't get under your skin in one day. And then all of a sudden I had the revelation of how enchanting my pond was. I took up my palette. Since then I've hardly had any other subject.'

At first he had painted the whole scene with the willows in the background and the Japanese bridge rising above the islands of lilies. But gradually, as his concentration grew, he dispensed with the land and closed in on the undisturbed sheet of water. The paintings were stripped of all direct subject matter and became studies of light and reflection; 'upside-down paintings' as one critic called them.

From the very beginning it seems that Monet was thinking in terms of a great series of these pictures, an unbroken sequence of images that would link and flow into each other: 'Imagine a circular room,' he told Maurice Guillemot in 1898, 'whose wall beneath the support plinth would be entirely occupied by a horizon of water spotted with vegetation, partitions of transparency made by turns green and mauve, the peace and quiet of the still water reflecting flowering expanses; the tones are vague, delightfully varied, of a dreamlike subtlety.'

When Alice died in 1911 Monet lost all interest in life.

His painting and his garden were ignored and he sank into a well of grief. For months he mourned, sitting alone in the studio-salon, scarcely bothering to eat and passing away the time thumbing through old letters and articles. Eventually he stirred himself to work again and made some amendments to his 'Venice' series but the results held no charm for him: 'More than ever today, I realize how artificial is the undeserved fame I have won,' he told Durand-Ruel. 'I keep hoping to do better, but age and sorrow have drained my strength.'

It was Clemenceau who revived the creative force in Monet. He needled and pestered the artist, goading him back into action: 'Think of the old Rembrandt in the Louvre,' he reminded him, 'hollowed, ravaged, under the towel that hides his bald skull. He clings to his palette,

resolved to hold fast until the end through terrible trials. That is the example.'

Slowly the dormant idea of the great decorations awoke once more in Monet's mind. In 1912 the project became more sharply defined when Rodin bequeathed his entire collection to the nation. This sowed the seed of a new possibility in Monet's imagination; he began to wonder whether he might do the same. That summer it was diagnosed that cataracts were forming over his eyes and that, although not dangerous at present, they would gradually destroy his sight. With the threat of this blindness, the waterlily project now assumed a desperate urgency in his mind. Designs were drawn up for a huge new studio to house the pictures as they were produced. What Monet was planning was not just a series of paintings but a massive

MONET IN HIS STUDIO

Sunlight on water was the true subject of Monet's work, and in his last years he painted little else. To house the series of waterlily paintings he had an enormous new studio built beside his house, where he could work in peace. Here, his eyesight beginning to fail from old age, he created the great cycle of paintings recording the reflections on the water among the lilies from morning to dusk. This was to be the final project of his life; the paintings were left in his studio at the time of his death and became his bequest to the nation.

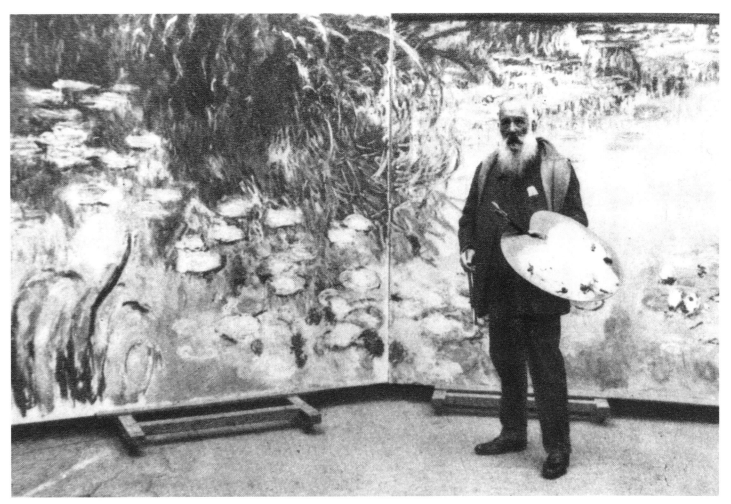

145

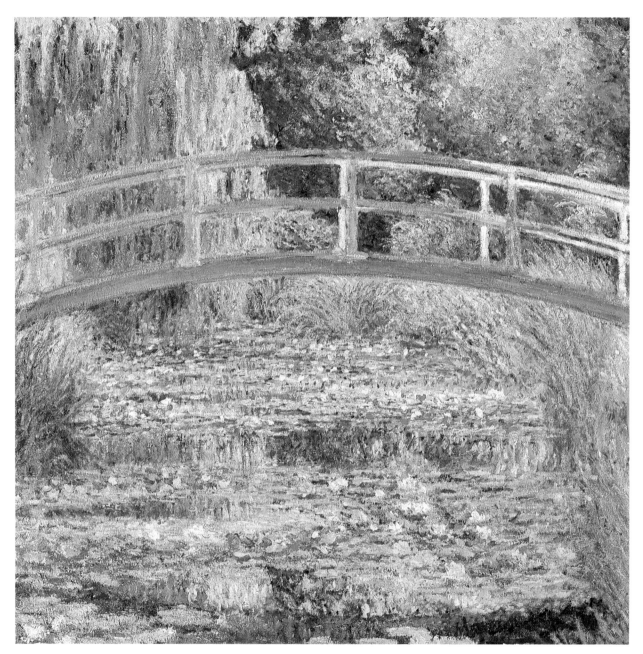

THE LILY POND AND BRIDGE

1899

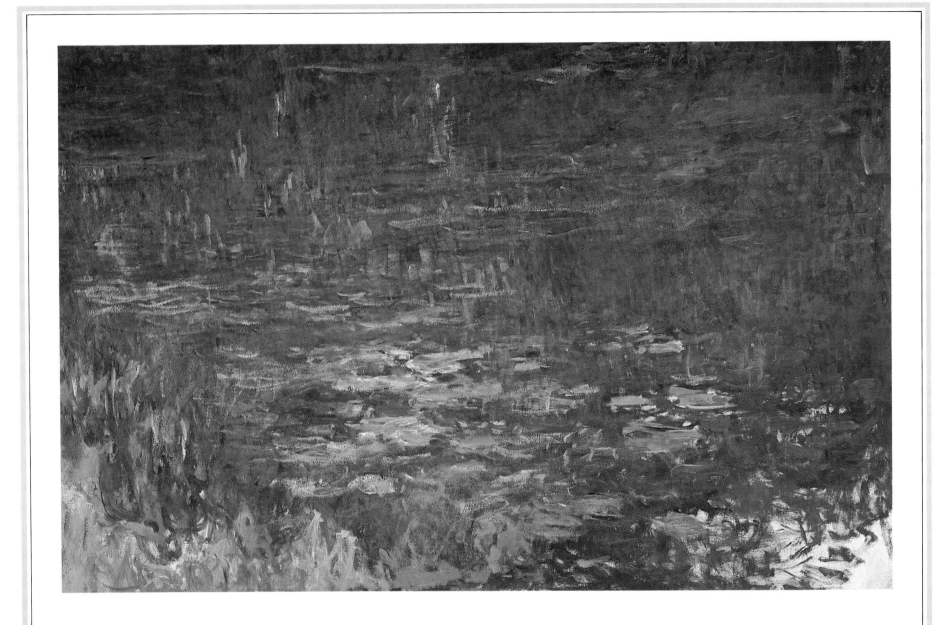

WATERLILIES: SUNSET

1918-26

testament to the ideal of his work. As early as 1909 he had conceived the waterlily cycle as a gentle, almost mystical retreat for eye and mind:

> ... it would have produced the illusion of an endless whole, of a wave with no horizon and no shore; nerves exhausted by work would have relaxed there, following the restful example of those stagnant waters, and to any-one who would have lived in it that room would have offered a refuge of peaceful meditation in the middle of a flowering aquarium.

The pilgrimages to Giverny were to continue for the rest of Monet's life. Ministers and museum curators came to pay their respects and to see the strange, inverted images of reflected light that now filled the studios. Japanese collec-tors arrived to buy Monet's pictures and brought him exotic bulbs for his garden. In 1922 the opera singer Marguerite Namara insisted on singing to the master, and a piano was wheeled into the studio to accompany her performance.

Monet endured the praise and esteem with stoical good will. From time to time he would leave the sanctuary of his garden to visit aquaintances in the neigbourhood, often dropping in on Bonnard, who was living in Vernonnet. As a young man Bonnard had been unable to appreciate Monet's pictures, but he gradually came to respect him to the point of reverence and awaited the arrival of the 937 YZ with nervous anticipation. It has been said that when he came to show Monet his pictures the slightest grunt of approval from the older artist was worth more to him than any quantity of official criticism. But what Monet enjoyed more than anything was when one of his friends from the distant past visited Giverny. Then he would sit on the balcony, his chair carefully positioned so that he could watch the light working across the garden, and talk of Manet and Bazille, the battles with the Salon, the Café Guerbois and the days at the Ferme Saint-Siméon.

In 1914, on the eve of the Great War, Jean Monet fell ill and returned with his wife Blanche to live at the Maison du Pressoir. In a matter of days he became delirious and even-tually died on 10 February at the age of forty-seven. Follow-ing his death, Blanche gave up her own career as a painter to become Monet's housekeeper, agent and companion. Throughout the war they lived at Giverny in near solitude, walking in the gardens, playing backgammon, sometimes bickering with each other, frequently cackling with laughter over some private joke, but always together.

Monet didn't want to leave the house but scanned the papers each day for news of the fighting. He could hear the guns firing in the distance and was appalled by the unend-ing stream of casualties that passed by his gates. In his new studio he worked on the waterlily paintings, the bequest of sunlight on water that in his mind was already taking the form of a memorial to the war. At first he'd had trouble procuring the materials but Clemenceau, once again hold-ing the office of Prime Minister, settled this problem. He brought Etienne Clemental, the Minister of Commerce, to Giverny. Clemental at once appreciated the importance of this work and, brushing aside the red tape, he comman-deered trains to bring huge canvases down from Paris, arranged for coal to warm the studio and quantities of oil paint to be prepared for the undertaking.

In 1918 Monet wrote to Clemenceau saying that he would like to give two pictures to the nation and wanted them to be signed and dated in the Prime Minister's presence on Armistice day. When this meeting occurred, Monet showed the statesman his new paintings and, in the strictest secrecy, they agreed that not two but the whole cycle of paintings would eventually form the bequest.

Monet worked on the project relentlessly. His eyes were weakening and he found it almost impossible to gauge the colours he was working onto the canvas. When he stood back from the painting he could see well enough, but up close the colours faded and seemed to lose their intensity. He was forced to mix the paint by instinct, relying on sixty years of experience to pitch the subtle tones correctly, unable to see the effect until he'd laid in the colours and distanced himself from the picture. As his eyes dimmed he found himself mechanically re-enacting the process of creation that he'd been engaged on daily all his life: orches-trating the sequences of light, measuring and controlling colours that existed more in his memory than his eye.

'Monet tried to seize the light and throw it on his can-vases' wrote Clemenceau, as he watched the huge series of paintings unfolding over the years. 'It was a madman's idea. A moment came when what he was doing was no longer painting; he had left painting behind. It was a kind of escape ... He should have lived another ten years: then we would no longer have understood anything of what he was doing; there might not have been anything on his canvases.'

The site for the waterlilies cycle caused endless problems. At first it was hoped that they would hang in the Hôtel

Biron, where Rodin's bequest is now held, but this could not be agreed. For a while it looked as though the whole idea was going to founder, but eventually a new location was found: the Orangerie in the Tuileries gardens, just a short distance from the Paris Salon. After prolonged arguments and debates, it was finally agreed that this was where the waterlilies could be put on view.

In these last years, Monet's moods oscillated between determination and despair; at times he was fired with a prodigious energy and work progressed by leaps and bounds, while on other occasions he was paralysed by self-doubt and threatened to throw away the whole idea. Paintings were destroyed, discarded or started over again. Monet would not be outlived by anything that didn't measure up to his exacting standards, to be seized on and sold by the dealers after his death. All the while Clemenceau watched over the project, constantly encouraging and chiding the old painter: 'I love you because you are you and because you taught me how to understand light,' he told him in 1922. 'You have thereby made me bigger. I only feel sorry for not being able to give it back to you. Paint, paint always until the canvas bursts from it. My eyes need your colour and my heart is happy with you.'

By 1923 the condition of Monet's eyes had become so bad that an operation was necessary. At first, when the bandages were removed, his sight appeared to be improved and he noticed that the colours in his most recent pictures were well off-key and would have to be reworked. Later, however, new problems arose; colours didn't remain constant, but appeared to change and alter. The surgeon who had originally pronounced the operation to be a success was puzzled by these after-effects. He still held that Monet's eyes were good enough for a 'quiet bourgeois' but accepted that the artist required more of them. A further operation was attempted, but again the outcome was only moderate. In 1924 an occulist was recommended who had helped Maurice Denis when he went blind; with new Zeiss lenses, Monet regained his sight well enough to continue work.

Early in 1925, work stopped once again. In a sudden fit of depression Monet announced that he was going to abandon the waterlily pictures and offered to give his private collection of paintings to the nation in compensation. Clemenceau was furious and at once fired off a letter to Blanche; he always used her as the go-between in these disputes:

'My dear friend
I have received a shocking letter from Monet, and I won't stand for it. By this same post he will get my answer, which you will probably find very harsh, but which is absolutely sincere.
If he does not alter his decision I will never see him again.'

Between the two of them, Blanche and Clemenceau persuaded Monet to go back to work. During the summer of 1926, in a tremendous burst of energy, he brought the cycle to its present state. By then Clemenceau had begun to understand that the paintings were to be Monet's final task in life and would never leave Giverny while he was alive.

In the autumn of 1926 Monet appeared to be tired and began to weaken. His enthusiasm for work had smouldered down to a cinder. Clemenceau saw him in October and noticed how frail the artist had become. After that he visited the house regularly and on 5 December was at the bedside, with Blanche and Michel, when Monet died.

'Two weeks before his death, I had lunch with him at the table', he recalled later. 'He had talked to me about his garden, had told me that he had just received a whole shipment of bulbs, Japanese lilies, his favourite flower, and that he was expecting any day two or three boxes of seeds, very expensive but which, once they had bloomed, would produce magnificent colours. "You'll see all this in the spring" he told me. "I won't be here any more." But one felt that secretly he didn't believe it at all ...'

AT HIS OWN REQUEST Monet's funeral service was a small private affair with only close friends and relatives invited. He was buried, alongside Suzanne, Jean, Ernest Hoschedé and Alice, in the little cemetery at Giverny on the slopes of the valley overlooking the Seine. In his will he left the great cycle of waterlilies to the nation. His instructions were that they were only to be opened to the public after his death.

Many writers and critics have attempted to express Monet's strange mixture of talent, stubbornness, good humour and determination; his preoccupation with his work, his love of life and the almost indescribable vision of his paintings. But it was perhaps Cézanne who contained it best when, after a visit to Giverny, he observed: 'Monet is only an eye – but, my God, what an eye.'

LIST OF ILLUSTRATIONS

70 CLAUDE MONET: The Seine at Bougival (*La Seine à Bougival, le Soir*), 1870, 60 x 70.3 cm (23⅔ x 27⅔ in). Smith College Museum of Art, Northampton, Massachusetts.

71 CLAUDE MONET: The Bridge at Bougival (*Le Pont de Bougival*), 1870, 63 x 91 cm (25¾ x 36⅜ in). The Currier Gallery of Art, Manchester, New Hampshire. Mabel Putney Folsom Fund.

72 MOLLER: Regatta at Argenteuil (*Les Régates d'Automne à Argenteuil*), engraving after Renouard. Photograph Bibliothèque Nationale, Paris.

73 Félix Nadar, self-portrait. Photograph Bibliothèque Nationale, Paris.

74 Courbet's Card as a Member of the Commune. Photograph Jean-Loup Charmet, Paris.

75 CLAUDE MONET: Roadbridge under Repair (*Argenteuil, le Pont en Reparation*), 1872, 60 x 80 cm (23⅔ x 31½ in). Collection of the late Lord Butler of Saffron Walden. Photograph Fitzwilliam Museum, Cambridge.

76 CLAUDE MONET: The Wooden Bridge at Argenteuil (*Le Pont de Bois à Argenteuil*), 1872, 54 x 73 cm (21¼ x 28¾ in). Private Collection. Photograph by courtesy of Christie's, London.

77 CLAUDE MONET: Sunday at Argenteuil (*Le Bassin d'Argenteuil*), 1872, 60 x 80.5 cm (23⅔ x 32 in). Musée d'Orsay, Paris. Photograph © Musées Nationaux – Paris.

79 CLAUDE MONET: Argenteuil, Late Afternoon (*Argenteuil, Fin d'Apres-Midi*), 1872, 60.3 x 80.5 cm (23¾ x 32 in). Private Collection. Photograph Bridgeman/Giraudon, Paris.

80 Factory by the River at Argenteuil. Photograph Roger-Viollet, Paris.

81 CLAUDE MONET: Promenade along the Seine (*Les Bords de la Seine, Argenteuil*), 1872, 55 x 73.6 cm (21⅔ x 29 in). Private Collection: courtesy Ellen Melas Kyriazi.

82 CLAUDE MONET: Men Unloading Coal (*Les Déchargeurs de Charbon*), 1872, 55 x 66 cm (21⅔ x 26 in). Private Collection. Photograph Durand-Ruel, Paris.

83 CLAUDE MONET: The Petit-Bras in Spring (*Le Petit-Bras d'Argenteuil*), 1872, 53 x 73 cm (20⅞ x 28¾ in). Reproduced by courtesy of the Trustees, The National Gallery, London.

85 CLAUDE MONET: The Seine at Argenteuil, Autumn (*Effet d'Automne à Argenteuil*), 1873, 56 x 75 cm (22 x 29.5 in). Courtauld Institute Galleries, London (Courtauld Collection).

86 The Railway Bridge at Argenteuil. Photograph Roger-Viollet, Paris.

87 CLAUDE MONET: The Railway Bridge at Argenteuil (*Le Pont du Chemin de Fer, Argenteuil*), 1873, 60 x 99 cm (23⅔ x 40 in). Private Collection. Photograph courtesy of Sotheby's, London.

88 CLAUDE MONET: The Railway Bridge (*Le Pont de Fer, Argenteuil*), 1874, 54 x 73 cm (21¼ x 28¾ in). John G. Johnson Collection, Philadelphia. Photograph courtesy of the Philadelphia Museum of Art.

89 CLAUDE MONET: The Roadbridge at Argenteuil (*Le Pont Routier, Argenteuil*), 1874, 60 x 80 cm (23⅔ x 31½ in). National Gallery of Art, Washington, D.C. Collection of Mr. and Mrs. Paul Mellon, 1983.

90 CLAUDE MONET: The Bridge as a Single Pier (*Le Pont Routier d'Argenteuil*), 1874, 50 x 65 cm (19⅔ x 25⅝ in). Present location unknown. Photograph courtesy of Professor Paul H. Tucker.

90 The Roadbridge at Argenteuil. Photograph Roger-Viollet, Paris.

91 CLAUDE MONET: Weeds by the Seine (*La Seine près d'Argenteuil*), 1874, 55 x 66 cm (21⅔ x 26 in). Photograph © Durand-Ruel, Paris.

92 CLAUDE MONET: Sunset over Argenteuil (Marine View, Sunset/*Coucher de Soleil sur la Seine*), 1874, 49.5 x 65 cm (19½ x 25½ in). Philadelphia Museum of Art: Purchased The W.P. Wilstach Collection.

93 The First Impressionist Exhibition, 1874, caricature by Cham. Photograph Jean-Loup Charmet, Paris.

94 CLAUDE MONET: Impression, Sunrise (*Impression, Soleil Levant*), 1872, 48 x 63 cm (19 x 24⅞ in). Musée Marmottan, Paris. Photograph

Bridgeman Art Library, London.

95 CLAUDE MONET: The Studio Boat at Argenteuil (*Le Bateau Atelier*), 1874, 50 x 64 cm (19⅔ x 25⅛ in). Rijksmuseum Kröller-Müller, Otterlo, The Netherlands.

97 CLAUDE MONET: Sailboats at Argenteuil (*Canotiers à Argenteuil*), 1874, 60 x 81 cm (23⅔ x 32 in). Private Collection. Photograph Giraudon, Paris.

97 PIERRE-AUGUSTE RENOIR: Sailboats at Argenteuil, 1874. Collection, Portland Art Museum, Portland, Oregon. Bequest of Winslow B. Ayer.

98 Poster for the Argenteuil Regatta of 1850.

99 CLAUDE MONET: Regatta at Argenteuil (*Les Barques, Régates à Argenteuil*), 1874, 60 x 100 cm (23⅔ x 39⅓ in). Musée d'Orsay, Paris. Photograph Bulloz, Paris.

101 CLAUDE MONET: Ship at Anchor, Rouen (*Chasse-Marée à l'Ancre, Rouen*), 1872, 48 x 75 cm (19 x 29.5 in). Musée d'Orsay, Paris. Photograph © Musées Nationaux, Paris.

102 CLAUDE MONET: Pleasure Boats at Argenteuil (*Bateaux de Plaisance*), 1872, 47 x 65 cm (18½ x 25½ in). Musée d'Orsay, Paris. Photograph Bulloz, Paris.

103 CLAUDE MONET: The Seine at Rouen (*La Seine à Rouen*), 1873, 50 x 65 cm (19⅔ x 25½ in). Staatliche Kunsthalle, Karlsruhe.

104 View of Rouen.

106 CLAUDE MONET: Argenteuil in Winter (*Le Chemin d'Epinay, Effet de Neige*), 1875, 61 x 100 cm (24 x 39⅓ in). Private Collection. Photograph courtesy of Sotheby's, London.

107 CLAUDE MONET: Argenteuil, the Banks in Flower (*Argenteuil, la Berge en Fleurs*), 1877, 54 x 65 cm (21¼ x 25⅝ in). Private Collection.

108 Street in Vétheuil. Photograph Roger-Viollet, Paris.

109 Claude Monet, circa 1880. Photograph Jean-Loup Charmet, Paris.

110 CLAUDE MONET: The Seine at Vétheuil (*La Seine à Vétheuil*), 1879, 81 x 60 cm (31⅞ x 23⅔ in). Musée des Beaux-Arts, Rouen. Photograph Bulloz, Paris.

111 CLAUDE MONET: The Seine near Vétheuil (*Le Matin dans les Iles, Environs de Vétheuil*), 1878, 54.5 x 65 cm (21½ x 25½ in). Private Collection. Photograph courtesy of Sotheby's, London.

112 The Seine at Vétheuil. Photograph Roger-Viollet, Paris.

113 CLAUDE MONET: Vétheuil in Winter (*Vétheuil l'Hiver*), 1879, 69 x 90 cm (27 x 35½ in). © The Frick Collection, New York.

114 CLAUDE MONET: Snow Effect at Vétheuil (*Eglise de Vétheuil sous la Neige*), 1878-9, 52 x 71 cm (20½ x 28 in). Musée d'Orsay, Paris. Photograph © Musées Nationaux – Paris.

INDEX

Page references to illustrations are underlined. All painting titles are italicized.

Acknowledgements
The author wishes to particularly acknowledge the researches of: John Rewald, in his *History of Impressionism*; Paul H. Tucker's *Monet at Argenteuil*; Robert Gordon and Andrew Forge's formidable monograph, *Monet*; Daniel Wildenstein's documentation of the artist's life; and Claire Joyes' intimate study of Monet's late years in *Life at Giverny*.